Joanne Fedler is the author of the international bestseller, *Secret Mothers' Business*, and other titles including *When Hungry, Eat* and *The Reunion*. She is a former law lecturer and women's rights activist. She teaches creative writing and takes women on writing adventures in exotic destinations. (www.joannefedler.com)

Graeme Friedman is the author of two non-fiction books, various short stories, and a novel, *The Fossil Artist* (shortlisted for a 2011 Commonwealth Writers' Prize). He has practised as a clinical psychologist for over 25 years, specialising in relationship issues in his work with individuals and couples. (www.graemefriedman.com)

IT DOESN'T HAVE TO BE

so hard

The Secrets to Finding and Keeping Intimacy

Joanne Fedler & Graeme Friedman

EBURY
PRESS

An Ebury Press book
Published by Random House Australia Pty Ltd
Level 3, 100 Pacific Highway, North Sydney NSW 2060
www.randomhouse.com.au

First published by Ebury Press in 2012

Addresses for companies within the Random House Group can be found at
www.randomhouse.com.au/offices

National Library of Australia
Cataloguing-in-Publication entry

Fedler, Joanne.
It doesn't have to be so hard : secrets to finding & keeping intimacy / Joanne Fedler
and Graeme Friedman.

ISBN 978 174275 490 1 (pbk.)

Interpersonal relations.
Man-woman relationships.
Courtship.
Intimacy (Psychology)

Other Authors/Contributors:
Friedman, Graeme.

306.7

Author photograph by Richard Weinstein
Internal design and typesetting by Midland Typesetters, Australia

Printed in Australia by Griffin Press, an accredited ISO AS/NZS 14001:2004
Environmental Management System printer

Random House Australia uses papers that are natural, renewable and recyclable
products and made from wood grown in sustainable forests. The logging and
manufacturing processes are expected to conform to the environmental regulations
of the country of origin.

For Zed and Tracey

The minute I heard my first love story I started looking for you,
not knowing how blind that was.
Lovers don't finally meet somewhere.
They're in each other all along.

Rumi (Persian poet and mystic, 1207–73)

Contents

Prologue

THE BEST STORY YOU EVER heard was probably a love story. Two people had never been so crazy about each other. But stuff got in the way — evilness and tragic circumstances and whatnot. You thought they were going to lose each other, but in the end they made it. Or maybe they didn't and how sad was that?

Somewhere inside you, in that tangle of fairy lights called the imagination, that story still flickers. *A glass slipper. A hidden love letter. A vial of poison.*

Long after the book was closed or the words said, that story burrowed into you and made a home in your dreams.

Stories help us make meaning of our lives. In the mythologist Joseph Campbell's words, 'it's the trail back to yourself.' Stories are lanterns, lighting our way so we can cross the bridge into our own experience. In tales, we watch as people grapple with overwhelming questions, make big decisions and reach for each other, clumsily, but in every way we recognise as human. Stories trigger our right brains, fire our fantasies, and pull us into the narrative. *What will he do? Will she make the right decision? Will he tell her he loves her?*

Stories bring us into our own empathy and creativity, two of the treasure-houses of self-knowledge. Through stories we learn the shape of our hearts.

Love isn't an idea, it's a story that happens when people meet.

The Sorry State of Love

THEY WEREN'T LOOKING TO HOOK up when they met. Daniel, a rising star in the digital world, was still stinging after Olga swept in and out of his life like a flash flood, returning to Holland with her kinky moves (he never knew women could do *that* sort of thing with their mouths). Stephanie, an arts administrator, was single for the first time in her twenties, having finally ended her relationship with Nathan, which, let's be honest, wasn't going anywhere. The fact that she'd never orgasmed with him wasn't the *only* reason; his not knowing this was another (it's not like she couldn't climax, okay? She'd had great orgasms with Alistair who went to study at UCLA and would be back but wasn't yet). But Nathan's hay fever exasperated her more than involuntary sneezing ought to, flashing red against any long-term commitment.

Steph and Daniel were each doing their respective grocery shopping one hot Sunday evening, when stocks of fresh fruit and vegies were plundered low by end-of-weekend shoppers. Steph was examining the few remaining bananas, looking for the least bruised, when Daniel sidled up next to her. He took one look at her in her sun dress and made the kind of inappropriate joke bruised bananas inspire. She laughed. They ended up ditching their shopping and going for fish and chips. And later that night, Steph had a long-overdue orgasm on Daniel's couch.

Daniel took her partying at the hippest clubs and kayaking in Thailand. Steph dressed him up and took him to movie premieres and art exhibitions. Jesus, he was funny. She laughed more in those first three months than in . . . maybe her whole life. He said it was a Jewish thing – in the tradition of Lenny Bruce and Woody Allen. She'd never dated a Jewish guy before but all her friends said Jewish boys made the best husbands. He teased that she was the brains of the outfit. She made him think and use big words, stretching him beyond syllables. She was drawn to his charm, the boyhood in him still raw and tactile. Her poise, remoteness in her eyes, and sweet-tasting skin, drove him wild. After twenty months, they were married in a civil ceremony on the beach, with Mike and Jenny, Steph's Protestant parents, wincing in every wedding photo. Daniel said it was just as well both his folks were dead but if you put your ear to the ground you could hear them spinning in their graves. It made Steph laugh like hell.

Fast-forward fifteen years. Daniel's forty-eight, Steph's forty-three. They have an architect-designed, family-friendly home and a not-so-family-friendly mortgage. They also have two kids: Justin, who's thirteen and dyslectic, and nine-year-old Georgia, who's pudgy despite her busy schedule of swimming, gymnastics and tap-dancing. After juggling the flaming torches of motherhood and career and burning herself out, Steph quit her job to be a full-time mother. Daniel, now CEO of his own digital marketing agency, occasionally gets home in time to have dinner with the family and tries to make up for it by doing most of the run-around to and from sports and friends on weekends. Things had been fine – for a while. Steph enjoyed being a stay-at-home mum. But now that the kids don't need her so much anymore, Steph's poise is slipping and Daniel's jokes have gone stale. These days, everything he does irritates her. And he knows it. She's restless. She wants more from life, and wonders if that includes Daniel. He's working himself ragged, and wants more sex. She thinks about going back to work, getting a new wardrobe, doing something for herself for godsakes. He cringes when he sees the contempt in her eyes. Noisy arguments trip over the words 'trial separation'. She hasn't dared tell her parents – they got over the fact that he is Jewish, and now they think he's one of those 'nice Jews with a good head for business – just look at the life he's given Steph and the kids. Daniel doesn't think about what his folks would say, but there'd be guilt. Buckets of it, for marrying a *shiksa*, a 'gentile woman'.

Steph and Daniel are up Shit Creek. Unless they do something about it, they'll either end up an elderly couple muttering over the break-fast table, 'You ruined my life, you bastard . . . I mean, please pass the butter, dear,' or trading insults in a divorce court.

Sadly, they're not alone. Divorce statistics expose us as a generation with marriage ADD, consumers who give up on relationships as if they're dispensable commodities, and then impatiently shop around for new models. Long-term love is either a freakish lottery win or an extreme endurance sport for the masochists among us. What's clear is that finding love isn't the same as keeping it. The people we are when love is new change into unrecognisable strangers when love is worn. 'Who are you, again?' we ask of ourselves and each other, bristling with distaste and incongruence, as if we've been robbed, not only of our happiness, but of our identities too. What happens between 'I do' and 'fuck you'? Why is love such a bitch to hold onto? What are we doing to stuff it up for ourselves? Are there any secrets to making it any easier? Does it really have to be so hard?

Who pissed on love?

Bloated with unrealistic expectations and a sense of entitlement (the two cancers of intimacy), we were taught that every girl is a princess-in-the-making even if she starts out as a domestic worker, and that to find her prince she only has to be hot – not good or kind or smart, or even *breathing*. (Does it ever worry you that Snow White's prince fell in love with her as she lay pale and lifeless in a coffin – the absence of any vital signs apparently not a turn-off in the slightest?) And guys will always get the girl as long as they can handle a customised weapon and the occasional dragon. The cultural hype around beauty and romance has done the same hatchet job on our love lives as the media's done to body image, setting the bar so high that nothing short of knee-shivering, heart-screeching attraction to someone is good enough. We want designer relationships. Royal weddings. Soul mates. You know, like the celebrities have. We're too special to 'settle'. And we don't have to do anything. Love, like home delivery, will come to us.

The glamour magazines, Hollywood movies and TV 'reality' shows (our modern day fairytale equivalents) are all traders in this delusion, peddling the vibe that love is an inheritance which, when plonked in our laps, will fulfil our every need and make us happy. Without 'it', we're doomed to a life of microwavable TV meals and loneliness – *not* the happy ending we had in mind (even with a super-duper-extra-strength vibrator or a blow-up doll with real hair and lifelike features). Those of us still waiting for love might wonder about filing a Missing Persons report – because unless they've gone off into outer space or been swallowed by the Bermuda Triangle, someone forgot to make us a soul mate. We're *this* close to giving up because all men are dickheads or women bitches (or some version of this story). Seriously, what other conclusion can we draw?

Those of us who have found 'the one' aren't much better off after we have made our vows, cut the cake, bought the house and had the kids. As Steph and Daniel's sorry story shows, there's nothing neatly happy about the ever after; today's soul mate is tomorrow's pain-in-the-arse who leaves dirty dishes on the counter or drinks from a bottle and then puts it back in the fridge (c'mon, how gross is that?). The fairytales never have post-wedding sequels where the prince turns back into a frog and the heroine becomes a pumpkin. Or his royal highness has an affair with the chambermaid and the princess puts on twenty kilos eating imperial chocolate mousse in a fit of existential depression. Nothing in the ideal-ised ending intimates that we could very well end up with someone who never listens or always nags; never/always wants sex; doesn't pull his or her weight around the house; carries too much weight in all the wrong places; doesn't spend time with the kids and doesn't appreciate anything we do. If love were an investment, we'd demand our money back, cancel our subscription and invest in shares in Bitter And Twisted Inc.

Bloody hell, no wonder we're in trouble. These nonsense notions of love are poisoned apples – captivating on the outside, vile in the flesh. They make us superficial and jealous, and pollute our understanding of what real intimacy is, the kind we have when we grow up. The kind Rainer Maria Rilke, the German writer, was thinking of when he wrote, 'For one human being to love another, is perhaps the most difficult task of all, the epitome, the ultimate test. It is that striving for which all other striving is merely preparation.' No kidding, Rilke.

Keeping intimacy going in a monogamous, long-term relationship isn't for wusses – much easier to get a cat, which at least cleans itself and craps in a litter box instead of on you. But we are here to tell you that this is no time to give up on love. You can have both cat litter *and* candlelight. We're at the threshold of an exhilarating renaissance in human relationships. The world we're in is changing – the emerging confluence of neuroscience, quantum physics, psychology, democracy and spirituality means we have a chance to reconceptualise intimacy. Marriage and monogamy (love's conventional straightjackets) have been churned up and spat out of the tumble-dryer of social evolution. Women in western cultures are shrugging off the 'biology is destiny' curse. More men are happy SNAGS (Sensitive New Age Guys), eager to share the nurturing *and* the breadwinning. Gay and lesbian couples are marrying and having kids. Sexuality in all its forms and varieties is more understood and celebrated. Celibacy, monogamy, cohabitation, marriage, divorce, merged families – all are expressions of choice on love's playing field. Intimacy in its dazzling parade of forms is coming in from the cold. As a human species, we're finally grown-up enough to work out how we think *about* intimacy and to think our way *towards* intimacy.

No matter what love has done to you in the past, with change comes hope. Love has a big future. With all that's wrong in the world today, never before in history has there been such potential for people to experience it as true equals.

Our Love Stories

IT SEEMED LIKE A GOOD idea. Two friends writing a book together. What could go wrong? Our friendship (begun over twenty years ago in a writers' group) and the snugness of our families have given us heaps of time to talk – and argue, given that the chasm between our world views is pretty ginormous. Graeme's grounded in rational Western psychological theory and Jo's all over Eastern spiritual practice. Out of respect, Jo doesn't roll her eyes whenever Graeme uses psycho-analytic jargon and he tries to do the same whenever she suggests a 'ritual'.

We've also come to our own marriages from opposite direc-tions, Jo thinking she'd never commit to a long-term monogamous relationship, Graeme thinking he'd never manage without one. In fact, Jo believes monogamy is completely counter-intuitive and that, beyond the whole social expectation and convention of procreating to continue the species, there's nothing natural or intuitive about pledging yourself to another person in emotional bondage, with the professed intention of remaining there indefinitely. Not that she wants to love-bash or be the Grinch who stole Valentine's Day, but, like, where's the fun in having sex with the same person *for the rest of your life*? She wonders whether monogamy is even good for us, like bran or spinach. For all we know, it may in fact be unhealthy to repress the desire to shag different people – the sublimation probably clogs us up like cholesterol. She'd like to know why an open relation-ship isn't on the agenda, for example? And whether commitment can ever be . . . you know, fun?

If Jo's the prosecutor in the case of The People vs Monogamy, Graeme's defence counsel. He believes that fantasies of sex with others is natural, but crossing the line into reality is a symptom of a relationship in deep trouble, and can only tear further at the fabric of intimacy. Still, we're *not* promoting monogamous intimacy as a morally better choice. Nor are we favouring it because it's the most popular choice around. It's simply what we've opted for in our own relationships and so it's the one we know.

Between us, there aren't many relationship issues we haven't come across. Jo's work as a domestic violence counsellor in the nineties shook her faith in healthy intimacy. She spent tough years trying to help people escape dangerous relationships, and then watched helplessly as they went straight back into them to endure another round of violence. It wasn't hard to feel like The World's Most Epically Failed Counsellor. Graeme has been a psychotherapist for thirty years. Bolstered with plenty of tissues in his office, he spends his days helping men, women and couples (gay and straight) through insight-oriented therapy. He's seen human beings at their best, their worst, and in the deepest pain. He's worked with trauma survivors, has assessed murderers on death row, counselled victims of torture, and given expert evidence for freedom fighters in political show trials. And he's seen the power of people's internal resources – to mourn, overcome shame and hatred, love, and grow their capacities for intimacy.

But as with anything, it's our own journeys – from our first love relationships with parents and siblings to our current ones with partners and children – that have taught us the most.

Jo's story

When I was ten, my cartoonist father painted a Superman poster for me, with the words 'Superman Loves Joanne' emblazoned across the sky, setting the bar on my romantic aspirations. By the time I became a radical women's rights advocate in my twenties, any dreams of a tall brooding lover sweeping me off my feet (you know, like Heathcliff did to Cathy, but without the psychotic head-bashing) had pretty much died a grisly death. It was obvious that marriage was for unintelligent girls who had no ambition to travel or write books. I was never going to be 'given away' or called Mrs Someone Else's Surname. I figured

I'd mother a few kids, fathered by different lovers that came and went, preferably on a rotation basis, like a sushi train, so I wouldn't get bored. I couldn't imagine negotiating this in the context of a marriage, which is top-heavy with expectations of things like fidelity, for example.

I had to grow up pretty quickly in my household – my older sister was deaf and so I started to talk early (nine months, they tell me) and became her interpreter. I learned to turn inwards when I felt needy, and became impatient and intolerant with anything resembling help-lessness and dependence. Naturally I shaped myself to be someone who would never be dependent on a man. So I flitted between men, always with one foot out the door. By day, I was a feminist warrior in thigh-high black leather boots, but by night – and only in private – I'd confess in self-indulgent tragic poetry my longing to find my one true love.

In my late twenties, after I'd had enough of this turnstile approach to relationships, I befriended the smart, funny guy whose office was next to mine in the law department where I taught. We became really good mates – he made me laugh – but I never thought about him romanti-cally. What? He was shorter than me.

But one night, after a couple of drinks, he told me that I was The One. You know, that he wanted to spend the rest of his life with. I was *furious* that he'd risk such a great friendship because he clearly just wanted to shag me (which was nice to know). But my rage aside, it was the most gutsy thing I'd ever seen any guy do, including the tall ones. So I said, 'Okay, but I want a baby next year.' And after I'd revived him, he said he'd have to think about it because he wasn't sure he wanted kids. It only took a few days before he came back and said, 'Let's do it.' We had our daughter a year later and our son a few years after that, all this time procreating out of wedlock much to the barely concealed hysteria of our various parents.

Eight years later, we got married surrounded by a few friends, barefoot in a park. Don't ask me why I did it. I'm still not sure. I understand why people run from it and why it scares people shitless. Maybe I did it because it seemed such a ridiculous thing to do. And I can always get a divorce, right?

Graeme's story

While Jo had a poster of Superman on her wall, as a teenager I had a poster of Super-shrink: Sigmund Freud's profile defined by the image of a reclining naked woman, with the caption 'What's On a Man's Mind'. I had a lot on my mind, and hooking up with girls was only part of it. While my parents loved and cared for me, I grew up absorbing the tensions of their loveless union, witness to my mother's resignation and my father's trigger-happy temper. I was a sensitive child, vigilant to the needs and moods of others. And then, when I was eight, my father died. I joined my sister and brother in a code of silence: if we never mentioned Dad, we wouldn't have to feel the pain of losing him. That combination of factors will pretty much make a shrink of most people.

It also turned me, in my late teens and twenties, into a serial monog-amist, girlfriend-hopping in leaps of one or more years, managing the honeymoon period with varying degrees of connection but withdraw-ing in the face of intimacy's deeper challenges. I looked like a rock from the outside and felt like a twig on the inside, guilt-laden and anxiety-ridden. I would fall into a kind of stasis in my relationships, paralysed by the paradoxical fears of too much closeness and of too much distance. *Feel things too intensely*, went my unconscious script, *and someone dies.*

But while my unconscious mind had me trapped, it also showed me the way out: become a clinical psychologist – 'to help people', I told myself. In truth, of course, I was looking to help myself, dipping my toe in the waters of Eastern spirituality, trying meditation, reading Jung. I was as lost and disconnected as ever. If there were universal truths out there, I wasn't hearing them. And then I found my way into psycho-therapy and the world of psychoanalysis. The therapeutic relationship gave me what I was looking for: the sense of being understood and a place to shed tears, to let out anger, and to think. I got to mourn my losses and began to know myself. Gradually and somewhat imperfectly, I learned to love (and, incidentally, to begin to really engage with my work as a psychotherapist). And only then was I able to make a choice to be with the woman who would become my wife, someone with whom I could carry on this learning and to whose embrace I have been able to find my way back when old demons have raised their heads. Twenty years and three great kids on, we've found much to struggle with, and much love to be grateful for.

Rubbing each other up the right way

Given her advocacy past, Jo's vision for this book is to inspire an intimacy revolution, to motivate people to save love as if it were a rainforest or an endangered whale. Graeme modestly hopes to encourage people to think about their relationships in a different way, but wonders how many will carry the lessons of these pages beyond the 'honeymoon' period that accompanies the reading of them. Yeah, yeah, Jo agrees, but then maybe, like in the story of the hundredth monkey, one could encourage three, and three might inspire ten – you know, go viral. That's a bit too 'evangelical' for Graeme's sensibilities, but even he concedes that because each couple makes up the human collective, there could be some domino effect.

But frankly, as we set out we had no idea whether we'd pull this off or just piss each other off. Our writing styles, beliefs and practices clash. Jo's impulsive, Graeme, considered. Jo likes to dive in and let things unfold organically, while Graeme prefers charts, tables of contents and spreadsheets. Jo meditates and believes in God, which Graeme thinks is a generic term for a non-prescription drug. Jo's convinced therapy is a 'crutch' where people rehash old wounds and become more attached to their victim-stories – which, were it true, would put Graeme out of business. See what we're saying? From the starting line, it looked as if our friendship could be doomed.

෬

So why did two people who can't even agree on a favourite soup choose to co-write a book about intimacy? It would've been simpler to do it alone, right? There'd be no-one to argue with, send you tetchy text messages, delete your favourite lines or threaten to call it quits if you leave *that* paragraph in. Sole authorship would be easy, comfortable. Well, that's exactly why. We figure a book about intimacy – negotiating difference while keeping close to each other – demands precisely these prickly conditions. Our process would mirror the content. We'd pick holes in each other's assumptions. Knock back cherished beliefs. Diss each other's pretentions and call each other on our blind spots. We knew along the way we'd have a few fights and be forced to find creative ways to resolve them. Either that or refund Random House our advance.

But what exactly is intimacy? You know, the thing this book's about? Is it cuddling? Smooching? Warm, fuzzy adoration? Low voices? Kindness? No nastiness? Heaps of *yes dears* and *as you wish, my darlings*? No way, Jo shuddered. And Graeme *agreed*. Here, then, was something we settled on upfront: intimacy encompasses conflict. Think about it: most of us can't even sustain internal serenity for any length of time (ever felt unsure? Torn? Ambivalent?), so what are the chances of enduring peace between two differently shaped folk? Harmony is lovely – in music, and even as a girl's name, but it's founded on our childhood craving for safety and the illusion that we can banish the unknown. In fact, a bit of fighting (not so much that we feel unsafe) keeps us on a slow sizzle with each other. Squashing differences between us puts eroticism on a starvation diet. Where's the edge? A fraction of friction to fuel the fire? Without passion, intimacy's sputtering for oxygen. If we want to be unconditionally worshipped, we should get a dog. Jo confesses that if she were married to a sycophant, she'd be driven to acts of exasperation involving a rolling pin or some other heavy household object. Graeme's not into rolling pins, but he's also not into pushovers. So while living with a woman who has her own dreams and desires can be exasperating, it's also exhilarating.

So roll out the red carpet for conflict. It's inevitable, and in appropriate doses and well-handled, even *desirable* and we'll show you why. See, we define ourselves and our relationships by bumping up against each other, gently but sometimes a little roughly too. Intimacy is a multi-tasking act where we have to hold on to who we are (our own differentiated and boundaried selves) while *at the same time* remain connected to our partner (by giving of ourselves, being open to what they bring, listening and sharing). Our challenge is to sustain a system fraught with volatility, to gracefully handle some door-slamming, and a couple of *you're-a-pig* here and an *I-hate-your-guts* there and transform that energy into exciting arguments and fantastic sex. So really, how we *think* about and *manage* the bumps can work out to be the difference between 'Talk dirty to me' and 'Talk to my lawyer'.

The blind men and the elephant

> *There are three sides to every story: mine, yours and the truth.*
> — Joe Massino, mobster

There's an ancient story of a group of blind men who were touching an elephant and were each asked, 'What is it?' The one who touched its trunk said it was a snake; the one who could feel its leg said it was a tree trunk; the one holding onto its ear claimed it was a fan; the one grasping its tail said it was a rope.

So imagine that being in a relationship is like touching an elephant while blindfolded. Where we each stand is going to limit what we feel. Neither of us can get our arms around the whole thing all at once. What we're saying in this book is that there are different ways of handling and standing back in your relationship that can help sustain intimacy in the long-term. So even when all we can feel is the scraggly tail where it all stinks like crap, we can still imaginatively hold the whole elephant of our partnership in our head.

There is no secret or formula to intimacy. This isn't one of those paint-by-numbers books. Intimacy is freeform and each of us moves into it with our own bodies, rhythms and energy, like a dance. So it makes no difference whether you prefer the salsa, the samba, the foxtrot, dirty dancing, the cha-cha or ballroom — as long as you keep moving, together. We're hoping this book will offer you a different way of thinking about love which can lead to a new way of being.

And even though we all like a finish line, intimacy, unlike a tub of ice-cream or your favourite TV series, is never-ending. There's no empty container or season finale. It's an ongoing (lifelong) practice of figuring out who you are as you get to know someone else, because there is *always* more to learn.

∽

So what about Steph and Daniel? Are we just going to leave them at each other's throats? Will they find a way back to each other? And what about us, Jo and Graeme? Will our friendship make it to publication? We're counting on you sticking around as we check in on Steph and Daniel during the course of the book, and introduce you to other couples and singles; some looking desperately for love, some flailing about in it, some doing the hard work, and some going, 'Ah fuck it, this is just too hard.' All the themes, conflicts and psychodynamics that follow are based on real people, relationships and conversations, but the characters are entirely fictional and any resemblance to any person is completely coincidental. Except for the Epilogue, which is about us. But if you do happen to recognise bits of yourself in the unfolding dramas, that's what you might call an opportunity, a lantern to light your way across the bridge into your own relationship.

PART I

When Strangers Meet

I.

Falling

THE ROAD TO INTIMACY BEGINS anywhere, anytime. There you are, going about your business when suddenly, in a world full of strangers, someone you've never met appears. And that's it. You're falling. And your love story begins.

Erin and Mitch

The bar is crowded. Erin shifts uncomfortably. Her pants are too tight. *I should've stayed home,* she thinks. *There's a re-run of* Sex and the City. *And the last of the Cookies 'n Cream in the freezer.* She checks her iPhone. There's an email inviting her to enlarge her penis. She looks around the bar, trying to pinpoint the loudest men — those insecure attention-seekers who imagine having a big dick will compensate for being a dick themselves.

It's only 10.35 and too early to leave without Tara feeling like she's been abandoned. She takes a sip of her G & T. *When this drink is finished, I'm outta here,* she thinks. Suddenly Tara, back from the ladies', grabs Erin's hand and says breathlessly, 'I've just met some guys. C'mon!' Erin raises an eyebrow. Tara's taste in men is, well . . . not Erin's. 'What?' Tara protests. 'They're hot!'

Erin lets herself be led outside to a high table in the courtyard, scans the three guys standing around it. Okay, four glasses of bubbly haven't entirely scrambled Tara's judgement — they *are* cute — but Erin knows she's not going home with any of them – and check it out, one of them even has a wedding ring on. After her last boyfriend, she's over getting her knickers in a tangle for a good-looking man. She should have seen it coming with Gus. Even now, she feels that burning in her chest, the humiliation is what's stayed with her, of catching him – 'it means nothing, I swear it' – texting some girl he'd met at the football that night he didn't come home. It's been eight months since she told him to fuck off – the sweetest, hardest words she's ever uttered. That long since she's had sex. She could end that drought tonight. She takes another look at Mr Into-Myself, Mr Perfect-In-Every-Way and Mr Wedding-Ring. She takes a long sip of her G & T. No way.

Making his way through the crowd, Mitch catches a glimpse of cascading dark hair down a woman's back as he approaches the table where he left his friends Tom, Sam and Sam's boss Antonio, whom Sam is trying to convince to join their football team. Antonio's in his late forties, groomed and toned like a stallion. Sam idolises him. Sheesh, the guys have already picked up two women. The brunette's bra and singlet straps hang on her brown shoulders; her pants are snug over a curvy butt. He has to reach around her to hand the beers out. He looks at Sam's smug face and knows the expression well. Antonio's got the same victorious smirk. The brunette's hot, and the guys are already vying for her. Tom – the last of the world's big drinkers – is still nursing his first beer of the night. He'll be going home to Phoebe, his wife, pretty soon. Mitch thinks he might head home too – there'll be no room for him in what's going on here. 'Excuse me,' says Mitch as he leans past Erin to hand the beers to Sam and Antonio.

Erin sees the hand holding the beers, their bottlenecks protruding like three extra big thumbs. Then she sees the arms and chest. Then the smile.

'Hi, I'm Mitch.' Some beer spills as he hands them over. 'Shit, sorry.'

Erin thinks, *he's kinda clumsy* and something in her goes, *that's kinda cute*. And then, *with big hands like that ... get a grip on yourself, Erin.* 'Hi,' says Erin, and introduces herself and her friend Tara. She runs her fingers through her hair, looking up into his face. He must be about six-foot-three. A whole head taller than her. Mr Perfect-In-Every-Way is trying to make conversation, teasing Mitch about spilling the beer, but then it doesn't matter because he's chosen 'girly-juice', which is probably an in-joke for the premium lights Mitch has opted for. Erin sees Mitch blush under his day-old growth. Tara's laughing like it's the funniest thing she's ever heard. In a hazy moment the two charmers across from Erin both morph into Gus. She turns to Mitch. 'Your friend drives a Porsche, so he's taken pains to let me know. What do you drive?'

'A fire-engine,' says Mitch, smiling awkwardly. He takes a slug of his beer.

She returns his smile. Her eyes are laughing, which makes him feel as though he's walked in on the tail end of a joke, and so can't catch the punch line. But then she's making full-on eye contact and drawing him in as if she's got a secret just for him. The courtyard's busy, people are milling around and past them. She's turned her shoulder so that they're forming their own little circle of two. He can smell her perfume or her hair conditioner from where he's standing. Apricot? Avocado? Shit, what does he know about women's cosmetics? His last relationship ended five years ago. After that, Natasha went on to marry some dude in finance in a big white wedding and already has two kids. Mitch has had some one-nighters since then, after too many beers the night before, but he always wakes up feeling empty and with nothing to say to the woman in his bed.

Now his and Erin's conversation falls about them like a curtain, shading them from the others. She's a marketing manager at a coffee company. Does he drink coffee? He does. What kind? Whatever's around, he doesn't mind.

She punches him on the shoulder. 'You should be more discerning about what coffee you drink. Some of it is crap and full of chemicals.'

He shrugs. 'I guess I'm just not that fussy.'

She wants to know what made him become a fireman. He tells her about studying computer science and hating it, and then seeing a documentary on September 11 and thinking he didn't want to live his life staring at a computer screen. He wanted to do something that counted. He says all this before he realises how much he's said. Spilling his whole life out. But she's laughing at his not-very-funny jokes, and

JOANNE FEDLER & GRAEME FRIEDMAN

he isn't looking at her breasts – just at her mouth and at her eyes that are warm and brown and make him think of that Van Morrison song. Erin – it suits her, that name, sort of unusual, like something out of a fairytale.

He puts his life at risk to save others, Erin's thinking. *That is so frigging sexy.* She wants to ask him if he has a girlfriend, but . . . uggh, nah. That is way too keen. She can usually tell if a guy is interested in her, but with him, it could be that he's just being polite – firemen are probably given some etiquette training, so they know the right sorts of things to say when they have to save old women and children in danger. He's not a poser. He's not trying to impress her. If anything, he's shy. There's no swagger. No real come-on. Just easy talk between them. She can't hear a thing except his voice amid the chatter.

When Tara says, 'Hey Erin, time to hit the road,' she looks at her watch and sees it's 12.20 am.

Mitch looks around, notices that Tom and Sam have gone, leaving only Antonio.

'Well, it's been fun,' she smiles at Mitch.

She's about to go and he says something, she can't quite make it out in the noise. She leans in and he repeats, 'Hey, maybe you could show me what a decent coffee is sometime . . . '

She smiles. 'I'd consider it my civic duty.' He pulls out an outdated mobile and hands it to her. She types her number in. And as she hands it back to him, their hands brush.

Mitch and Antonio watch the two women walk towards the exit.

'Nice work,' Antonio says. 'I'd have given her one, but looks like she prefers men in uniform.' Mitch ignores the remark, and takes a swig of his now-warm beer, his hand gripping his phone in his jeans pocket, his heart kicking in his chest like a wild horse.

They meet for coffee. Erin suggests he drop the sugar; it spoils the taste of the coffee. He's never had coffee without sugar before, but, hey, she's the expert. She tells him about her mum's – what is it, third, fourth? – facelift. She talks about her brother Rob, who's gay and has been in a great relationship with his boyfriend, Tariq, for four years. 'You know how people say gay guys can't be faithful?' she says. 'They've got it so wrong. Rob and Tariq would never cheat on each other – though one should never say never, right?' She natters on about her best friend Tara who can be so 'me, me, me' and silly around men but when you get to know her, she's got a heart of gold. *He's such a good listener*, she thinks. She asks him to come with her to yoga and instead of something along the lines of Gus's 'Only faggots do yoga', Mitch says, 'Yeah, why not?'

And so their second date is a yoga class, followed a few days later by dinner. He remembers everything she tells him, even silly things like the name of her first dog – Denture – who got run over in front of her. He makes her feel like everything she thinks is justified and no, she's not being over-sensitive or petty. So over the main course, a second glass of red in her hand, she finds herself telling him what it was like when her father left her mother for another woman and how, as a teenager, she felt like she had to side with her mum, straining things to breaking point between her and her dad. When she was a little girl she idolised him but then she started seeing him for the selfish prick he is, but maybe that's what her mum always said . . . she's not sure anymore. Thank God for her cousin Stephanie, who was like a big sister to her at the time, and hung out with her when things got too much at home, listening to Nirvana and smoking dope. She can't wait for Mitch to meet Steph and her husband Daniel – they're her role models. Erin was a bridesmaid at Steph's wedding and Erin tells him about the ghastly peach outfit she had to wear. They giggle at the thought of her in her peach outfit. 'Terrible colour on me,' Erin grimaces. Mitch says he can't imagine who'd look good in peach, so although he's agreeing with her, she still feels complimented. And for the first time in a long time – no, maybe ever – she gets this weird fluttery sensation that makes her tearful, and she thinks, *He gets me. Is he going to kiss me tonight?*

Mitch can't quite get over the fact that someone like her – so stunning and smart and full of life – seems to be hot for *him*. He finds himself telling her things, stuff he's never had words for before. Like his recurring nightmare of having to save his family from a fire, the ache of smoke in his throat when he wakes up. And his mum's recent

JOANNE FEDLER & GRAEME FRIEDMAN

revelation that she had Postnatal Depression for the first two years of his life. And Erin touches his hand and says, 'How could anyone be depressed having you around?'

He's so nervous to kiss her, but he can think of nothing else. What if she backs off and says, 'Sorry, you've got the wrong idea'? Walking her from the car to her apartment she leans into him. He instinctively puts his arm around her and she rests her head against his shoulder. And in that moment his nerves dissolve and he stops, turns towards her, and takes her face in his hands. He looks into her eyes before he kisses her, slow and deep and strong, as she wraps her arms around his neck and he feels himself breaking inside like a dam wall cracking.

Inside her place, he cups her butt between his hands and pushes her against the front door. She gasps, feeling his erection against her belly.

Don't leave. Sleep over tonight.

Oh Jesus . . . I can't get enough of her.

OhmyGod, I want him inside me. Those huge arms . . . what shoulders. It's like we were made for each other.

Over the next few weeks, work becomes a breeze. Friends and family take a back seat. Erin ignores Tara's last two texts. Mitch brushes off Sam's offers to join him at footy, even though Antonio has scored them seats in a VIP box. They just want to be with each other. To talk, hold hands, share a bottle of wine, or a hamburger. Objects belonging to each other – a hairbrush left in his car, his football boots in the corner of her living room – take on special meaning. She smells him on her, and doesn't want to wash it off. He finds a stray hair of hers on his jumper and leaves it there. They've never met anyone so good, so kind, so understanding, so unique.

The whole world seems to fall away and all that's left is each other. It's the end of longing and the beginning of belonging, where Rumi's words ring true: 'Lovers don't finally meet somewhere. They're in each other all along.' So as Mitch sees Erin, the deep and eternal recognition, 'it's you – at last,' rouses from its dormant slumber.

༺༻

Sweet isn't it? Maybe a bit nauseating, watching from the sidelines. But when you're inside it, it's fantastic, as if a vagina and penis just met for the first time and realised what the other was for. Falling in love is a giddy, destabilising experience, almost a madness where two people disappear into a timeless zone, making love for hours, only surfacing for emergency ablutions and whatever can be raided from the fridge. Falling. Crazily. Head-over-heels. New lovers can seem a bit mad. We're optimistic and hopeful. Giddy. Open to trying new things – foods we've resisted our whole lives, a day at the golf, horseracing, the opera. It's a state known as *limerence*, coined by the American psychologist Dorothy Tennov. The feeling is so magical it'll test even the most hardened sceptic that this isn't, somehow, all due to fate, the kind Plato described in the *Symposium* in which lovers are two halves of one soul, split and separated from each other, who spend their lives searching for their other half. John O'Donohue, the Celtic poet, writes in *Anam Cara* that when two separate beings finally 'meet', after years, longing for their beloved, this is a profound moment of 'recognition' between two souls, as if an 'ancient circle' has closed between two people. 'Meant' for each other, 'destiny', 'twin-souls', and all that jazz.

This glamorous account will, however, be tested in time, when we're not gazing into our partner's eyes but staring at their dirty underwear on the bathroom floor. Unless we can bear to concede that even destiny makes mistakes. But we're not knocking romance. It's the fuel that launches a relationship, and it's one of life's most exquisite pleasures. But since we're in the business of being adults, let's be clear: romance isn't about getting to know someone. In fact, it's the exact *opposite* – a temporary blindness, perfectly curable as soon as the rose-coloured glasses crack and our projections dry up. Only when the fog of limerence lifts do we start to really see the person in front of us.

The chemistry of love

But what brings two people together? When Erin says, 'We seriously just clicked' and Mitch answers, 'We had instant chemistry,' they're both spot-on. Love is a many splendour'd thing and all that but recent advances in neuroscience have helped researchers isolate three distinct *physiological* processes that happen when people partner up with each other.

9

Lust: The irresistible desire to touch, to experience sensual pleasure; for the boundaries of skin to merge, the gorgeous friction of two bodies moving up against and around and inside each other. All about sex, of course; incessant thoughts of and intermittent experiences of: elevator sex, car bonnet sex, kitchen counter sex, afternoon sex, midnight sex, early morning sex, sex now, sex again in fifteen minutes, sex in the shower, sex in the jacuzzi, sex in the sauna, and anywhere else we have omitted to list.

Romantic love: An ache in the chest area, nausea. Inspired to write songs, writing poetry for the first time. Emotional vertigo, losing balance, shortness of breath. The way Romeo loved Juliet. Sometimes hard to distinguish from a psychological disorder.

Emotional attachment: Companionship, friendship, trust, respect, kindness, generosity. Shared history and experiences. Dependency. Entanglement of one person's history with your own. Sometimes co-dependent. Occasionally suffocating, claustrophobic and difficult to detach from.

The neuroscientists have whacked the poetry and mystery out of love by isolating specific neurotransmitters, the substances that transmit nerve impulses, in each of these processes. Testosterone is the chemical ringleader in the throes of lust (in women too); romantic love is associated with increased dopamine and noradrenaline, along with lowered serotonin; and emotional attachment releases oxytocin and vasopressin. Lust usually elbows its way up front to be first in line, but it's fickle, and has been known to make us want to shag the follicles off someone we actually dislike as a person – someone we'd never fall in love with or want as a long-term partner.

Lust can develop and overlap into romantic love, which can ripen into attachment. Things can, of course, go backwards, as *When Harry Met Sally* taught us – two friends can fall in love and end up in a carnal swelter together. We can also lust for one person, be romantically in love with another and attached to a third, which is a messy muddle of all these urges. We think of sex dozens of times a day in response to passing strangers. People have affairs which 'mean nothing, really'. A wife dismisses the poor sex she's having with a 'passion fades anyway' because her husband offers 'so much else'. Suddenly, over popcorn and DVDs, there's a frisson of desire for a long-time platonic friend. We 'adore' someone one week and take a different route to work the next to avoid bumping into them. We have smouldering sex with a stranger by moonlight and then come daylight prefer to do our tax return rather than talk to them. Intimacy isn't any one of these drives on its own.

Intimacy is when, over time, all three arise — and keep occurring in ever-growing cycles — with the same person. So how do we make this come about? The way anything happens these days — by networking. Deep down in the gristle and blood, these drives are all connected. Having a 'deep and meaningful' with someone while sobbing your heart out can soon stray into licentious thoughts of ripping their clothes off. Orgasms in turn cause us to say crazy shit like 'I love you', and the next thing you know there's a tangled web of brain chemicals, emotions, words and thoughts binding people together. The chemical glue? Orgasms trade in oxytocin, that elixir of wellbeing that makes us feel as if we've just eaten a bar of our favourite chocolate. Every time we shout 'I'm coming', our brains ooze oxytocin. Those wicked little discharges of release in the nether regions are doing secret deals with neurochemicals. So what happens? After the gasps of orgasm have subsided, we look over at the person who just made us come, and we associate the soft warm feelings with them, much like Pavlov's dogs did with food and that bell. It's a treacherous partnership, making us easily (and erroneously) emotionally attach to the strangers in our beds. This is why it can be dangerous to give our orgasms away cheaply (on this, your mother was right). Neurotransmitters cannot tell the difference between bad boys or skanks and the lovers we'd like to keep longer than overnight. To add to this cocktail, while we're falling in love we're being flooded by dopamine, the neurotransmitter of pleasure, which causes us to feel euphoric. We are literally high on each other, becoming more addicted by the day. During sex, our identities start

11

to merge. The walls come tumbling down. Boundaries blur, collapse. Me and You becomes We.

It feels like intimacy. It feels fantastic (of course it does, we're drunk on brain chemicals). But, we're sorry to say, *this* is not intimacy. It's *intensity*, intimacy's PR manager. And we've fallen for the hype. That's why it's called 'falling' in love.

2.
The Spin

EVERY LONG-TERM PLAN NEEDS PUBLICITY. Romance just happens to be intimacy's campaign. But it's just the spin. We cannot trust our own thoughts during this time because, while we think we're getting to know someone, we're in fact doing our best *not* to get to know them – not really. We see what we want to see. The less we truly know about them, the more attractive they seem. Erica Jong took this to its ultimate conclusion in *Fear of Flying*, when she wrote about the zipless fuck, where two people meet on a train and have sex without saying a single word to each other.

It's a heady time of feel-good chemicals in a perfect bubble of happiness. But we know that no-one really lives inside a Coke commercial. They're actors and they were paid. The perfection romance promises us isn't real. We know this, right?

෧෭

They sleep together every night, taking turns at Mitch's apartment and then at Erin's. During these first few weeks, neither of them breaks wind or forgets to flush. Erin finds everything Mitch says hilarious, and Mitch gives her foot massages and plays with her hair for hours without his fingers cramping up. They never say 'no' to each other. Though he's allergic, Mitch lets Erin's cat Frodo sit on his lap while secretly living on antihistamines. Erin can't stand ball sports, but she

13

watches footy with Mitch, nodding as he explains the rules to her. They never tire of each other's company or want time away. Nobody sulks, yells, criticises or gets irritated. Life is wonderful.

After a month, Mitch takes Erin to meet his mum and dad, but he's in no hurry for her to meet Kayla — his sister is full-on at the best of times. He makes sure to let Erin know that Antonio isn't his friend. 'I only met him for the first time that night we met,' he tells her.

When Erin actually answers her phone, Tara asks, 'Has he met your mother?'

'Are you crazy? I'm breaking him in slowly,' Erin laughs.

One morning Erin wakes up and feels Mitch reaching for her. Her breath smells of the garlic prawns they ate last night and she panics — she usually wakes up five minutes earlier than Mitch to go brush her teeth before he kisses her, but it's too late. Mitch lifts himself up on top of her and plants his morning-breath mouth on hers, and suddenly last night's seafood doesn't matter.

∽

In these early romantic days we're on show, like a house on the market. Everyone knows no home is freakishly stylish once people actually live there. But when we fall in love, just as when we buy a house, we're buying a dream.

∽

Erin calls Mitch one day at work in a bad mood, after a chat with her mum. She tells him she's not feeling well and wants an early night. *I don't want him to see me at my worst*, Erin thinks to herself. There's a niggle of doubt about how Mitch will feel about her when he sees her for who she *really* is. And she's starting to get to know a little more about herself since she began meditating after she dumped Gus. Something inside her felt so broken and empty after that. *Get in touch with your authentic self*, the pamphlet at her local café promised. It was just a beginners' meditation course. At least it would give her somewhere to be two nights a week instead of at home, feeling sorry for herself. She's still new to the practice, but she knows this bright cheerful persona of hers that Mitch has fallen in love with is only part of who she is. There's something much more vulnerable hatching, it's just not as lovable as the girl with the sun in her smile. She's not ready for more rejection, so for now she babysits the truth, happy for Mitch to think she's perfect. And besides, she really does feel like a better person when he's around.

∾

So do we fall in love under false pretences? Of course we do – all the time. Romance makes promises real intimacy can never fulfil. It's the foundation on top of the blemish, the airbrush on the cellulite, the minty-chews that hide the halitosis. We're not looking very closely at the other person, blinded as we are by what they're mirroring to us. The reason we don't see the scars and brokenness upfront is simply a function of where we are in the evolution of intimacy. Real intimacy only begins when we embrace what's imperfect too, when bliss is disrupted by ugly information that throws us into a state of emotional and cognitive dissonance – 'You do *what*?' 'Can it be surgically removed?' '*How* many kids?' – and instead of scrambling for the exit, *we handle it*. Jonathan Swift's poem, 'The Lady's Dressing Room', written in 1732, describes one of those freak-out moments when Strephon wanders through a woman's dressing-room while she's not there. In public Celia is a 'tulip', but in private he finds 'a dirty smock . . . beneath the armpits well-besmeared', combs 'filled up with dirt so closely fixt, no brush could force a way betwixt', 'sweat, dandruff, powder, lead and hair, a forehead cloth with oil upon it . . .' He finally comes to her chamber-pot filled with 'stinking ooze' and this is too much for him. 'Thus finishing his grand survey / disgusted Strephon stole away / repeating in his amorous fits / Oh, Celia, Celia, Celia, shits.'

No matter how into someone we are, after seeing them pick their nose or squeeze a pimple, the party can be over before we can say, 'Don't call me, I'll call you.' While we're falling in love, we're overly conscious of how our bodies look, forgetting they're just little sacks of brittle bones, riddled with failings and imperfections, including that fly in the ointment of personhood – mortality. We don't really want a face-to-face with our lover's sweat, dandruff or excrement or other ordinary human flaws because then not only do we have to confront the fullness of their humanity (and therefore fallibility) but our own, too. So we collaborate in the fairytale that neither of us farts, has eczema, or days when we feel so down we can't get out of bed. From the start, we set ourselves up for a gigantic fall.

But here's the deal: as soon as the spin stops, things get real. Behind the scenes and under the veil, where all our shattered pieces lie, is where real intimacy buds. Intimacy *begins* when the ads are over, even though many of us are bailing out right at this moment with repulsion, disillusionment and 'I've-got-somewhere-else-I-forgot-I-have-to-be' excuses. At this stage, we may have good reason for ending it – we realise we have nothing in common, or he's actually a jerk who hits on other women at cocktail parties, or she's not joking when she says, 'If I find out you've been cheating, I'll cut your balls off.' Okay, so maybe we've been blindly 'in love' with a real psycho or creep, but it happens to the best of us, and instead of beating ourselves up about it, we should be getting the hell out.

Then again, what if we're bailing because we can't handle the shattering of the illusion? Maybe it feels like we've fallen out of love but all we've fallen out of is Wonderland. We're giving up just when things are becoming real. Why do we do this? There's really only one reason: we have a bit of growing up to do first. If other people's inadequacies make us take off, we have to first make friends with our own imperfections before we try falling in love again. It's that old gammy cliché about self-love being the foundation of love.

If, instead, we choose to stick around after the fantasy of perfection floats away, and we've come to terms with each other's flaws, been vulnerable and taken risks, we get hit with the next challenge. All this exposure and investment in someone evokes the terror that we might lose them. Deepening intimacy happens in a dance of risks. I'm vulnerable, I wait for you to reciprocate, and that emboldens me to risk a little more. From the first 'will she kiss me?' to the 'how will he respond if I ask him to live with me?' we take the chance that we'll be hurt, humiliated or shattered. Depending on the architecture of our psyches we each defend differently, and are prepared to take different levels of risk. Some of us fling ourselves into love like a surfer into the waves; some stand at the shore only letting our toes get wet. There's no right way. Just your way.

෨

Erin had wondered whether Mitch was going to kiss her. Mitch was worried that if he tried she'd say, 'Sorry, you've got the wrong idea, mate.' In the end, she was the one who took a teensy risk – she'd leaned in towards him as they walked from his car to her apartment, and that was all the encouragement he needed.

A week after that first blissful night, she invites him to dinner with her brother Rob and his partner, Tariq.

Two days after that, he picks out a new bonsai for her, noticing the one in her kitchen is dying.

The next day she buys him new undies, then wonders if he'll be offended. She isn't suggesting he needs new undies, just that these boxers are so sexy.

'Why did you break up with your last boyfriend?' he asks the following night. She tells him everything.

Each risk taken, each reciprocated, glues them tighter and closer together as they move into the province of attachment. Though they probably won't talk about it yet, privately they're each beginning to imagine a future with the other and to mull, consciously and unconsciously: Will she make a good mother? Will he have an affair? Will she disappoint me like I've been disappointed before? Is he really 'special' or just like every other guy I've ever dated? It's a due diligence they're performing on each other, scanning for common ground and bits that fit together, trying to figure out whether it is safe to proceed or better to bail out now, before they're in too deep.

Birds of a feather or opposites attract?

'So what attracted you to me at first?' Erin asks Mitch one night.

'Seriously? Everything.' He pulls out a bar of chocolate – rum and raisin. She plants a big soft kiss on his cheek. He's so thoughtful, never misses a thing, she tells him. She only mentioned rum and raisin as her favourite flavour in passing the other day.

'But what exactly?' she asks.

'Apart from your gorgeous body, face, hair, personality? Is this a trick question?' He breaks off a piece for her.

'I mean, why didn't you go for Tara?'

'She's not my type.'

'What's your type?'

'You are. I might ask you the same thing – why didn't you go for Antonio or Sam?'

'Yeeuch,' Erin shudders. 'Oh my God, we are so different,' she sighs, watching Mitch pick out the raisins. 'Raisins are the *best* part. I guess opposites attract, huh?'

∞

Why do we go for one person instead of another? Why didn't Mitch go for Tara or Erin for Antonio? What makes someone 'our type'?

In Mitch and Erin's case their differences have a lot to do with it – she's all energy and bubbles, and he's shy and introverted. The yin loves a yang. We look for in others what we don't have in ourselves, craving the contrast and the balance. But at the same time we also go for people who are *similar* to us because we're unthreatened by those who share our religion, culture and moral values. Most of us prefer not to have to explain to our new lover why we wouldn't join the Ku Klux Klan or why we choose not to smoke. Or we might feel a deep recognition when we meet someone who's had a similar experience of childhood (say, the loss of a parent). We look to match our partners in important ways, to be freed from the tedium of having to explain the basics of who we are and where we've come from, to know – and be excited by the fact – that their stories echo ours. Too much dissonance can feel unbridge-able. So, though differences (racial, religious, astrological, biological or psychological) excite us, similarities make us feel safe.

Falling in love also has to do with good timing – Erin and Mitch are both ready to meet someone new and settle down after a history of unsuitable partners. After what they've each been through, they know better what they're looking for.

Like all of us, Mitch and Erin are attracted to each other by their differences as well as by their similarities; by what's good and loving in each of them, as well as by their troubled and problematic parts. But it'll take time for them to get to learn how each of them is layered. In the initial flush of falling in love, they only glimpse what awaits in the murky depths of each other's minds. For now, they're exploring their matching and clashing bits by taking turns with intimate disclosures.

Erin tells Mitch about her parents' divorce in detail. Mitch shares that his mum had Postnatal Depression. This airing of dirty laundry is how they test each other's capacity for empathy, gingerly at first, to gauge just how much further they can go without being crippled or frozen with vulnerability. They stroke each other's egos, validate and make each other feel desirable, while they get to know each other's most adoring and adorable bits with a few choice icky bits on display to make it feel real. When we fall in love, it's with two people – our new lovers *and* ourselves.

Will you be my happy ending?

The only other time we got to feel this 'special', and the centre of someone's world (if we were lucky), was when we were babies. Even though the idea probably creeps us out, romantic love echoes how we were first loved (or not) by our parents. We carry this memory of desire – the longing to be loved – with us, into our adult lives, and what we're doing at a deep unconscious level is looking to be loved idyllically again or in a way we've forever craved. Even the way lovers begin to speak to each other echoes this early love, naming each other 'Angel', 'Sweetie-pie', 'Honey' and other variations on diminutives and confectionary. Sure enough, Mitch gives Erin a nickname, 'Bean', and Erin starts to call Mitch 'Babe'.

When we find love later on, it's a kind of 'refinding' (as Freud put it), an emotional recollection, of our original experience of love, which includes our early experience of loss. The more complicated or painful our early years were, the more fraught our attempts to make up for it. Because we've all got unresolved childhood desires to be loved by our parents in a different way, we might look for partners who evoke aspects of these early experiences, so that we can re-enact them in the hope that they will turn out differently. It's how we try to rewrite a happy ending. Yeah, we know – it's freaky.

We can't do this with just anybody – this isn't random magnetism. We're drawn to certain people who trigger us in a specific way; we need to match each other's matrix of experience, like an enzyme locking onto a particular substrate molecule. It's a complex unconscious recipe we're all playing out, trying to answer the question, does my being have a home with this person? It's as though we have a slot in our psyches, formed by our first caregivers, for a very particularly shaped key.

A year ago, Erin thought Gus was The One. He was a near replica of her dad Vince. Part of her unconscious attraction to Gus was the possibility of a re-enactment of her difficult relationship with her father. While Gus showed his adoration for her, she felt again what it was like to be her father's little princess. Then when Gus cheated on her and the re-enactment was complete she got to feel, all over again, what it was like to be abandoned by her father when he left her and her mother for another woman. Many of us are not sufficiently developed in our own sense of self to withdraw from this kind of retelling of our story, and may set ourselves up for a lifetime of betrayal where we get to be the victim of endless terrible partners. Erin had the good sense to tell Gus to get the hell out of her life.

This experience has readied her for a different kind of man. And on the surface, Mitch is Erin's anti-father, a sensitive, shy man who seems like a much healthier choice.

But is he?

Mitch is also the walking wounded and you can bet that his scars will manifest in his relationship with Erin and activate the unresolved pain of their histories. But for now, they're in a haze of happiness, and we don't want to chase it away – just yet.

It's not long before Erin takes another of those little leaps of faith and says, 'I think I'm falling in love with you.' And he breathes a massive sigh of relief, and says, 'Me too. Jesus, I love you, Erin.' Mitch has never felt stronger, handsomer. Erin feels light inside her – even her mother doesn't work her up into the usual ball of anxiety. Everything seems more manageable now that he's in her life. She just wants to never stop feeling this way.

When we can't make the leap

There's nothing like two people freshly in love. But as time passes, the headiness will wear off. The kimono will gape and the kilt will flap open. The fantasy – of the beloved as well as of ourselves – must fall away. If we're attached to the illusion of perfection, like Strephon, we'll flee in disgust and discard a relationship that has shed its romantic skin. But maybe not. Maybe we'll recognise that this is when our relationship has a chance to ripen from immature romantic intensity into real intimacy. How we cope with each other's imperfections as well as our own will determine the course of our intimacy expedition.

Learning to love another person is a gateway, not only to knowing someone else, but to knowing ourselves.

Not all of us are so lucky. Some of us battle to get this far, stuck, like a broken record, replaying the same bad romance stories over and over again, with different people who end up disappointing us. It's as though we keep meeting 'the wrong person' or act in ways that sabotage even the early establishment of intimacy. Or we're already in a relationship, fraught with grief, contempt and disillusionment, and we can't wait to get out. When this happens, it's time to meet ourselves. And for some of us, it's a blind date.

3.
Meeting Yourself

Why does it seem so easy for some to form relationships and so hard for others?

It's not me: Fussy Tara

Tara can't figure it out. Erin could've had Antonio or Sam – both of them were drooling over her. But she chose the guy who looks like he could do with a good night's sleep and a shave. Okay, Mitch had decent biceps and he was nice and all that, but the other guys drive Porsches, for God's sake.

Tara had to virtually lap dance for Antonio to get him to notice her. And then finally, after a chance meeting a couple of weeks later, they hooked up at her place, where she got to show off the spectacular view of the city (and remind herself that the crippling mortgage is worth it). Antonio had wanted her to have that line of coke. She told him it wasn't her thing, she had a meeting in the morning, but he was welcome to go ahead. He'd been so high he'd wanted to go at it all night long. And now it's been a week and she still hasn't heard from him, except that enigmatic text in reply to the one she made up as an excuse to contact him – had she left her Hermès scarf in his Porsche? 'Still looking,' he'd texted back. Not, 'want to hook up?' Not, 'gr8 night Tara let's do it again', but 'Still looking'. What the hell does that mean? And she's been trying to get Erin to find out from Mitch but Erin's so distracted she's not returning her calls and when she eventually gets back to her it's with the news that Antonio is a player and barely ever sleeps with the same woman twice.

To make matters worse, Tara went out for drinks last week with her friend Sally, who's seeing one guy and has another *two* interested in her. Like she's the fucking Bachelorette. 'There are just way too many fish in the sea,' Sally sighed, sipping her martini. Tara had to restrain herself from throwing her margarita at her.

Now she can't stop crying – not a good look for a 31-year-old lawyer on her way to becoming the youngest partner in her firm. She needs some Xanax or something. Instead, the GP, a kind older woman, gives her the names of two shrinks. She chooses the male. Maybe he'll help her figure out how men think and why Antonio hasn't got back to her.

⁌

By the time Tara and the psychotherapist can line up their diaries, it's three weeks after the 'Antonio Incident'. Her tears have long dried, and she's wondering what she's doing there. Everything's fine. She's even got a date with that hot guy who works in maritime insurance across the hall.

She didn't see this coming – bursting into tears at her first appointment. One minute she's telling the therapist about her history of relationships and the next she's a blithering wreck. 'I just haven't met the right guy,' Tara says. The shrink nods. 'Okay, so my friends say I'm fussy. My best friend Erin reckons I go for the wrong kind of guy. But that's crap. My last boyfriend was great. Gabriel. We were madly in love. We even talked about names for the kids we'd have together one day.' More tears.

'What happened with Gabriel?'

'I don't know, I think he had commitment issues. He had plans to go travelling overseas. We met four months before he was due to leave. He wanted me to go with him but I couldn't just leave my job. In a few years I could make partner.'

'You were hoping Gabriel would change his mind about going overseas?'

'Of course. Why wouldn't he? If he really loved me. You have to help me work out how men think.'

'Tara,' says her therapist, 'this isn't about how *men* think. It's about how *you* think.'

This makes Tara wonder if her money wouldn't be better spent on an extra session with her personal trainer.

'There's nothing wrong with the way I think. I had a happy childhood, I wasn't sexually abused, I've never had an eating disorder. Of course, I'm careful with what I eat – I'd rather die than be fat, but I don't have anorexia. It's just there're so many goddamned losers out there.'

∾

Tara, despite her irritation with her therapist, keeps going to see him. She doesn't know why she's doing it, but something in her unconscious (maybe desperation) keeps her there. Meanwhile, she goes out a few times with the spunk from maritime insurance. And then she sees him flirting with a waitress in the coffee shop downstairs and when she confronts him, he says, 'Hey, I just want to have some fun. I wanna date different people.' For the next week, Tara burrows into her work by day and her blankets by night, sobbing inconsolably. Two months later, she meets Ben at a friend's Saturday night dinner party. He isn't really her type – Erin might have gone for him – but he's the only single guy and she realises she's been set up. But they chat and he's surprisingly not bad company. He doesn't talk about himself all the time. He asks questions and he listens. He's got warm eyes and good teeth. He's a software programmer – he claims there's not much interesting about his job *(no kidding, Ben)* – but is very curious about hers, and seems to take it all in, even the complex bits about intellectual property. The more they speak, and the more she drinks, the sexier he becomes. They end up at her place. She's blown away by the sex – he knows how to use his tongue and he takes his time.

When she opens her eyes on Sunday morning, the first thing she sees is Ben, a tray in his hands, standing at the side of her bed, naked except for an apron. He's made scrambled eggs, muesli and coffee. How *sweet*, she thinks sleepily. Then he turns to arrange the tray on her bedside table and his naked, hairy, skinny butt is a metre from her face.

'I don't know why I didn't notice it the night before,' she tells her therapist at her session the following week. 'I can't stand too much hair on a man. Gabriel used to wax everything. And that skinny butt! I couldn't eat the breakfast he'd made. Then he came to sit behind me and moved my hair from my neck and started kissing me behind my ear' – an involuntary shudder runs down her spine – 'and I felt repulsed. I made an excuse about having to meet my mother to go shopping and ran into the bathroom. My *mother*, can you believe it? And now he's been texting and phoning and I don't know what to say to him. I just want him to disappear.'

She looks at the shrink and sighs. 'Why don't I like nice guys?'

And that is a really good question.

When it's time to look at yourself

Why does Tara have such a hard time falling for the right guy? Ben sounds great, the kind of man you'd want to bring home to your parents (who in all likelihood would have no issue with his hairy, skinny butt). Tara began her therapy trying to figure out why all the guys she meets are dickheads and losers. And of course the world is full of weirdos and we sometimes end up in bed with them. But when that pattern continues, we may have to reassess the only constant factor: ourselves. Tara's belief about the goddamned losers *out there* is really a cover for her terror that there might be something wrong *in here*. Tara's not ready to admit it, but she's the one who feels like a failure, though she can't be, can she? Bright, beautiful, successful – *a loser? I don't think so*. And of course it was Gabriel's fault that their relationship ended, because Jesus Christ, why should a modern, liberated woman have to change her life for a man? *He's* the one who wouldn't give up his dream to travel. So *he* must be the one with commitment issues.

As she starts to feel safer in her therapy, she begins to open up a little chink in the door of her denial. Even then, it takes the catalyst of her fantastic night with Ben screeching to a nauseated halt to make her see that maybe her revulsion is a little over the top. Is she really rejecting him because of his *bum*? A thoughtful, intelligent, generous man serves her breakfast after a night of delicious sex. And instead of wanting more, she wants to run away. Finally, she lets herself see that the problem is in her, and asks the question that will turn everything around: 'Why don't I like nice guys?'

It's no surprise that Tara's brief attraction to Ben turned to disgust over an aspect of his appearance. She's stuck in an entirely self-absorbed way of relating, which contracts her vision, not to mention her relationship potential. She's fixated on her wish list when it comes to guys and these are the boxes they have to tick: hunk, great job (i.e. high earner, high status), charismatic, popular, taller than her. But hang on, what's wrong with wanting to be with someone beautiful who works out and dresses like he cares? She takes care of her appearance. She's not going to 'settle', or waste herself on someone who doesn't look after himself or who's too short – she has a wardrobe full of stilettos for godsakes – some Jimmy Choos she had to pay off on her credit card.

Tara's dilemma is familiar – we all want to be with someone beautiful, right? But if at 31 this is our primary relationship objective, we probably haven't fully worked through it in high school. See, it has *nothing* to do with intimacy. We want someone beautiful so that *we* can feel beautiful. This is a clue about how Tara really feels about herself. She wants someone not for who they are, but for what they'll reflect. She's after a mirror, not a lover. So unconsciously, there's something about the way she's going about her relationship endeavours that either attracts men who don't want to commit, or repels those who do. She's envious of her friend Sally, who says she has too many fabulous guys to choose from. But Tara doesn't need a hundred dates with a hundred new guys. She needs to know what it is *she's* doing that contributes to the dynamics that are set up between her and the men she's attracted to.

As long as Tara lumps the problem in the men she meets, she can off-load any sense of herself as being unlovable. But then she remains a casualty in the grip of external forces over which she has no control. Asking the question 'Why don't I like nice guys?' is her turning point. In this moment, she reflects upon herself, owning the fact that she is the one rejecting intimacy. If Tara wants to find real intimacy with someone, she'll have to invest in some self-awareness and take responsibility for her role in the encounters she has with men. This isn't depressing news – it's empowering. It means she's not a victim of the 'wrong guys', or bad karma, or fickle fate, but that she has the power to change what goes on in her relationships.

The question is: will she own that power, or will she let it slip away because doing the inner work is just too hard?

4.

Heart Burn

SOMETIMES WE DISCOVER HOW LITTLE we know about ourselves when we're flailing about like Steph and Daniel, mortgage-and-kid-deep in a half-dead relationship that's going down the gurgler. Fifteen years ago, when Erin was her bridesmaid, Steph had never been happier. But now, despite her family, her big house and Daniel's financial success, Steph has never felt so miserable and alone. What the hell has happened?

∞

Steph is doing her best not to dirty her white pants and polka dot singlet as she furiously chops the Chinese cabbage for the Thai salad she promised her mum she'd bring to lunch. This morning's been a disaster. Someone – not her – mixed the whites with the colours in the wash, and all her white towels have come out with grey streaks on them. Shadow, Daniel's dog, has left four huge turds on the front lawn, and it's not Steph's job to deal with it. Daniel knows this. She won't pick up dog poo. Those were the terms on which they got the dog. The kids swore they'd do it. Daniel promised he'd do it. No-one ever does it! Really, she shouldn't be chopping vegetables in white pants, but if she hadn't dressed before she got into the kitchen, there'd be no time. The kids are nowhere near ready yet, despite her yelling upstairs four times in the past hour for them to get dressed. Justin's playing Minecraft in his room with the reverberations of Coldplay in surround sound, and Georgia's on Club Penguin on the computer in the study, still in her PJs. Just as she's about to shout out again, Daniel arrives back from his Sunday morning cycle. Pumped on endorphins from the ride, he strides into the kitchen, dumps his sweaty helmet on the counter, right on top of the bag of avocados, and circles his arm around Steph's waist.

'Hey, Brains,' he whispers huskily. 'How 'bout some Sunday morning delight? Remember that?' He kisses her neck. The kids are nowhere in sight – not that he's expecting a blow job in the kitchen – although how spectacular would *that* be? He grinds his sweaty crotch up against her butt, which looks goddamned hot in these tight, white pants. It's as if he's forgotten he's been bickering with his wife on and off since Georgia was born.

'Get off me. You're all sweaty,' Steph says, flicking her head to the side. 'Go shower. We're expected in forty minutes.' Brains. That was Daniel's nickname for her in the early days, from his joke that she was the 'brains of the outfit'. But these days, calling an unstimulated stay-at-home mum whose return to the workforce is long overdue 'Brains' is insulting in its irony.

'Oh wow, we might be five minutes late. How could you live with yourself?' Daniel mocks.

'My mum hates it when we're late.'

'You hate it when we're late. Like it matters, Ms Control Freak.'

She elbows him off her. 'If you did something – anything – around here, I wouldn't have to do everything. Like not bugger the laundry up. Or pick up dog shit. Just do something useful for a change. Take out the garbage. Go tell the kids to get ready. Jesus Christ!'

'Whew, you're a bitch sometimes,' he says, suddenly exasperated. Bloody hell. Every time he tries to make an affectionate overture, she blocks him. He wasn't expecting sex now, he's not an idiot, but instead of the vacuum cleaner to the carpets, she could take his cock out one of these days and dust the cobwebs off.

'Shit, Daniel. What do you want? A hero's welcome with my tits on display and a beer in my hand? I'm not the one who's been out with his mates for three hours. Justin's refused to do his homework; he's been on Minecraft all morning. Georgia's eaten an entire bag of chips on her own. The house is a tip. You do nothing around here. I haven't had a moment to myself and then you come home and you're all over me. Just control yourself!'

He grabs his helmet from the counter, knocking the avocados to the floor. 'Fuck it, Steph, you only bitch about what I don't do. I'm sick of it. Get over yourself.' And he storms out.

∽

What's going on here? Why does Steph turn on Daniel so quickly? The stakes seem so low – being a bit late for lunch with her folks – but the result is so divisive. So Steph's fed up with her domestic tasks. And yes, they'll probably be late for the lunch. Big deal. But in this couple's interaction, it *is* a big deal. They can't even interact civilly over the small things. They're both reactive, contemptuous of each other and easily hurt – and they're not even aware of how they're feeling or behaving.

How would self-awareness make any difference? Surely we just have to figure out who's 'right' and who's 'wrong' and get the one who's wrong to apologise? Actually, who's right or wrong is irrelevant. Fault and judgement are pretty unhelpful when it comes to sustaining long-term intimacy. And that's because it takes two to look after a relationship, so being right doesn't solve the conflict. If one person 'loses', the relationship loses. And the 'winner' can enjoy the sights from the moral highground – alone. In any case, judgements about what's right or acceptable are subjective. What works in your relationship may not work in mine. What I may tolerate in my partner (laziness, addiction to porn, OCD), you may not tolerate in yours. Intimacy is what's negotiated between two people who fit together in the way that only they do.

Self-insight thaws self-righteousness and helps us understand what's really going on between us. So Steph would be able to link her anxiety about a messy house or punctuality to her childhood where her parents were always running late and would invariably end up in screaming matches before leaving the house. This means that as an adult, she tries to control her external environment through cleanliness and order, to calm her inner world. Knowing this about herself would help her be less reactive to Daniel. But she has tunnel vision, and so on this particular day, when things seem to be spinning out of control, when Daniel arrives home, she's a grenade about to blow. In he strides, all manly with a sweaty crotch-grind against her perfect white trousers and kaboom! She explodes. Daniel, on the other hand, has no idea what he's walked into. Messy house? Arriving half an hour late? So what? He's in a fantastic mood, pumped up, a man among men, and he just wants his wife to notice him. If we could siphon the testosterone out of the scene, he's actually reaching out – clumsily, admittedly – for some closeness, but the only way he knows to ask for it is by rubbing the last bit of himself she wants anything to do with up against her. Oblivious to the laundry crisis, the trail of dog turds on the lawn and her panic about the time, he doesn't see her, nor does he see how his own expectations of being admired as a stud work against him. All he sees is that the woman he loved and married has frozen into a frigid bitch.

Without self-insight, they're like two blind boxers in a ring, flailing wildly at each other. And nothing can change between them until they can recognise how they're *each* contributing to the situation.

The better we know ourselves, the less defensive we become. If we understand our patterns, we feel easier about asking for help or empathy and in this way, we can defuse fights before they even start. Let's say Steph understood the source of her panic. She might then be able to ask Daniel for the help she needs in this moment: for him to notice and share the burden of her anxiety. And if Daniel were clued in, he'd know that Steph's mood actually has little to do with him, and that all he has to say is, 'Hi hon, thanks for holding the fort. I know we're under time pressure. I'll have a quick shower and tell the kids to get ready. Ten minutes, tops.' Points for mirroring the spouse's feelings and making her feel like they matter. Likewise, if she'd whispered in his ear, 'Hey, you're a sexy spunk in cycling shorts, wish I had time to peel them off,' the man would feel like a man – even without the blow job.

But with the salad half-made, Daniel not yet showered, and neither of their internal worlds illuminated, all they can do is blame and hurt each other.

What lurks in the dark: the problems of ignorance, incarceration and investment

As Freud pointed out, given that so much of the human mind is concealed in the unconscious, we can barely know ourselves let alone someone else. We're hidden from ourselves psychologically, just like our internal organs are unavailable for direct inspection. But ask for a rundown of what's wrong with our partners and we can give you a list. We probably can't explain why these behaviours or traits of our partners drive us nuts. Nor do we have a clue why we keep repeating the same routine over and over when we know it doesn't make us happy or our relationship any better.

Ignorance about who we are is only one of the problems with getting to know ourselves. The other is incarceration: there are bits of ourselves – drifters, itinerants – lurking in the alleyways and dungeons of our unconscious, waiting to sabotage our efforts at intimacy and life in general. And what the hell, you may very well ask, are these homeless vagrants doing down there? In fact, *we* put them there. They're the disowned parts of ourselves we've sent into psychic exile, aspects of ourselves we've not spoken to or even met as adults. They're the orphans of consciousness that are lost inside ourselves: our neediness, selfishness, greediness, loneliness, fear – the whole pitiful playgroup of our wounds.

Finally, there's the problem of investment: because our stories have worked for us all these years, we're in a comfort zone and have an aversion and resistance to change. We're attached to the life stories we've carried with us to explain who we are: 'I was abandoned as a child so I can never trust anyone'; 'I lost my mother when I was little'; 'My father hit me'; 'My father always wanted a boy'. Often these stories are blocking our way forward in intimate relationships because we don't know who we are or could be if we let go of them.

As little kids, we all experienced overwhelming feelings and impulses that terrified us. Thanks to the psyche, which went into rescue mode, we survived them, cobbling together unconscious defences and ways of relating, and pushing the pain from our awareness – kind of like a psychic anaesthetic. As time goes by, these deeply anchored mechanisms become habitual, so we're not aware of them. We never give them any thought, just like we don't tend to notice that we breathe or sweat.

Then we obliviously walk these childhood habits into our adult relationships, as we might saunter through baggage screening at the airport denying we're carrying any sharp objects, only to have security discover a pair of nail scissors at the bottom of our carry-bag. In the tussle of being ourselves and being in a relationship at the same time, the Tupperware of squashed painful feelings, shoved like leftovers out of sight at the back of the fridge, gets dislodged. Suddenly we remember. Denial has a brief shelf life and relationships unsettle our shadows, which is why we grow in self-knowledge through them.

Relationship is how we get inside ourselves. It's the key that unlocks these hard-to-reach places.

So how do we make things better? There's only one road in. Inner work. And it's not just a matter of blowing off the dust. It's a grungy business. Hard, dirty work. It's graft we probably don't want to do and have spent a lot of time in our lives avoiding. Sometimes it's called shadow work, because it's not a picnic on a sunny afternoon. But think of it this way — the only constant we bring into our relationships is ourselves. Intimacy starts with us. We can't control how others behave; we can only control our own thoughts, words and actions. So as long as we're blaming others for what goes wrong in our relationships, we're probably going to have 'intimacy issues'. When we shift from 'Poor me, I'm the victim of your behaviour' to 'I've co-created this situation', we take responsibility for our lives and our relationships. And that's when things start to change. Only then.

Steph and Daniel can't sort out who brings what to their rela-tionship. As they trip over each other's baggage of self-loathing or unwelcome desire, one yells, 'This belongs to you,' while the other denies, 'That's not mine. That's yours!' Without self-knowledge and a willingness to share it, everything we are becomes tangled up in our partner's stuff. Fights get messy and relationships jam, wedged in chaotic, unconscious entanglement.

We can only go as far with someone else as we've gone with ourselves. So, if we've only scratched the surface of our own inner world and are out of touch with how we feel about ourselves, we can only ever know someone else at that depth. But if we've crawled through our tunnels on our bellies in the grime, and reached far down inside ourselves, we know the journey. We're familiar with the territory. We're veterans, and we bring this emotional intelligence into our interactions. So it's really up to us, and how deep we want to go with ourselves, and with others. It's a beautiful partnership: as we get to know someone else, little cracks start opening up in us, which, if we chisel away at them, help us get inside ourselves. And the more we know our interior land-scape, the further we'll be able to cross into the territory of intimacy with our partners.

If we have a history of failed or fraught relationships behind us, if all our bad relationships are other people's fault, if the thought of examin-ing our histories feels overwhelming or something we don't want to do, if we're easily hurt and take everything personally, if we exagger-ate or blow things out of proportion to get attention, if we withdraw and feel sorry for ourselves when we don't get our way, if we play for sympathy, feel smothered or bored, if our partner doesn't understand us and is never there for us, if we're the one always compromising or sacrificing, if we feel dominated and controlled – we can do something about it. We can overcome our inner ignorance, set our inner hostages free and disinvest from our stories. Doing this work is a radical act of self-love.

The young woman who left her sad self behind

There's an ancient Zen story about a young woman, Ch'ien, who was in love with an orphaned boy, a distant relative, who had been taken in by her father. When her father wished Ch'ien to marry a man of rank who had asked for her hand, she ran away with her beloved to a distant land where they had two children. Ch'ien longed to see her father and to ask for his forgiveness, and so six years after running away, she returned to her homeland with her husband and children. She knocked on the door, and an old man opened it. 'Father!' she exclaimed. 'It is me, your daughter. I have returned. Look, these are my children.' The old man looked at her in amazement. 'Daughter? It cannot be you. You have been upstairs in your bedroom grieving for your lost love for the past six years.' And as the father said these words, the daughter saw herself descending the stairwell, dressed in black, her sad face drawn and withered. The two Ch'iens approached each other. They embraced and stepped into each other, becoming one person. Ch'ien said, 'I didn't know I was at home. I dreamed I ran after my beloved. But now I can't say which was really I – the one who ran away or the one who stayed home.'

The question asked when this story is told is, 'Chi'en and her soul are separated. Which is the true Ch'ien?'

The answer is: both. Inner work is about just this merger. When we finally meet up with the parts of ourselves we've run away from, we can 'own' them and integrate them into our psyches. And that's not all – when we take back our messy bits we grow our capacities to think about and manage our feelings, to empower ourselves, to have compassion and empathy for others. All good news for intimate relationships. These are the dividends of 'becoming whole'. These parts may be hellishly difficult to hold together because they probably contradict one another. If we're in an honest relationship with ourselves, we're likely to always be in negotiation with the contradictions, and feel conflicted or torn or muddled. All we have to do is try to become conscious of them and how they play out in our intimate encounters. 'Do I contradict myself?' Walt Whitman wrote in 'Song of Myself', 'very well then I contradict myself/(I am large, I contain multitudes.)' The best we can do is welcome our flaws with curiosity instead of chasing them down into the dogbox of our consciousness and denying they are part of us.

So it's time for us to organise a homecoming party to meet these exiled parts of ourselves. We have to undergo a process of self-retrieval. We have to go back, go inwards, go deep. To solve the conundrum of who we are and why we tend to get stuck in habituated patterns, we have to go back to the factory where we were made. That little hothouse that is our family of origin. Back to the scene of the crime.

So glove-up, get on your gumboots. We're going in.

PART II

When We Go Back

5.
First Love

I've been through some terrible things in my life, some of which actually happened.

— Mark Twain

BY THE TIME WE'RE FALLING in love, we've lost our emotional virginity. That first kiss with the captain of the football team or the girl next door wasn't our initiation into love. It happened long before that. In fact, by the time we're two or three, we've pretty much worked out how love works. The tracks for our intimate relationships later on in life have already been laid. The love stories we play out aren't special or unique, they're versions of the love stories we've been exposed to in our families, communities and culture.

Mitch rolls his eyes. 'Don't tell me those first few years matter. Seriously? I don't remember any of it.'

Erin smiles and says, 'I had a happy childhood. My family only fell apart later, when I was a teenager. And I've been meditating, getting in touch with who I am now. So I don't have to do any of this work, do I?'

Whether our avoidance tactic is infantile amnesia or glossing over trauma with a merry giggle, the past is still in us. If we don't own it, we repress it. It doesn't go away. It just festers, biding its time.

'So if I'm screwed up, that's my parents' fault, right?' Mitch jokes.

It's true that our parents largely shaped who we are (not forgetting siblings, relatives, teachers, and other important figures in our upbringing). And what sucks about this is that we have no control over our emotional inheritance just as we are born with our temperaments or biological histories, whether it's a particularly unattractive set of ears or a propensity for colonic polyps. We got the parents we were given without consultation or any opportunity to exchange them, refund them, or put them on eBay. But there's no point in laying charges, harbouring grudges or rewriting history. A logbook of parental grievances may be great material for a best-selling memoir, but as an internal narrative on repeat, it just keeps us feeling victimised, helpless and embittered. It detains us from becoming grown-up in our intimate relationships. What we need is to resolve long-held conflict, take responsibility for the people we've become, and eventually – when enough work has been done – let the old folks off the hook. Because (psychopaths notwithstanding), our parents probably did the best they could with what they had. Any harm inflicted upon us was, in all likelihood, unintentional and a spin-off from their own crappy upbringings and pressured lives.

Why go there?

If the aim isn't to wreak revenge or persecute our parents, why bring up all that stuff? Why not do the big-hearted 'forgive and forget' routine? And if we're angry, lost and full of pain, we can just have a drink or go for a massage.

Well, we've all tried that, haven't we? Some version of the violent-repression-and-distraction-with-shopping/celebrity gossip/sport/work/television or anything else that keeps us out of our own skins. For those of us more loftily inclined, we engage in a rigorous self-help regime to *om* and 'be in the moment' so we can spiritually bypass the bygone mess. And we all know how that's working for us: the past won't be weaselled out of, dumped or ignored. It insists on a face-to-face. If we go there, we might just find the kind of insight that can make or break our love lives. It's the difference between reading only the last chapter of a book or the whole book. Skip to the end, and we might be able to guess whodunnit but we'll never know who the characters really are or appreciate the elegance of the plotline nor complexities of the narrative. What's worse, we wouldn't know what we've missed.

Even spiritual traditions, like Buddhism, the archetypal in-the-moment practice, send us on a scavenger hunt back to the past, so that we can let go of it. Every moment in the present, says the Vietnamese Buddhist monk Thich Nhat Hanh, is made up of the past. And every moment in the future starts in the present moment. Emotions have birth certificates. Our present pain is umbilically attached to the past. When we overreact, shut down, or respond inappropriately to immediate triggers, there it is: our hurt has a history. Our job is then to understand where that story came from. If we don't, we can't change the way we respond in the moment. Without looking at it squarely, we're in default mode, where the white noise of the unconscious patterns of our past is always playing. When we meet our past, we hold it accountable, so that we don't destroy the present without even knowing why.

There are no short cuts to doing it right. If we really mean business in getting intimacy working, we've got to start with Chapter One: our earliest family environment – the years we don't easily remember. In fact, if there's access to a prologue, that's even better. The dramas of previous generations, the elephants in the room, family myths and secrets, ghosts of lovers past, tendrils of unresolved fears and wishes, have all crept into our love scripts like computer viruses, silently shaping our personalities.

Though some of us were luckier than others, we all got damaged in the journey from childhood to adulthood. Not enough bubble wrap, too many bumps and unintentional careless handling. If our folks were tired, distracted, depressed or ill, and were unable to give us the attention we craved, we may have worked out, 'I'm way too much trouble', 'I'm too intense', 'I'd better be self-sufficient', 'I don't need anyone'. Or if we had too much bubble wrap and our parents were smothering and over-protective, we may have figured out, 'I am responsible for other people's happiness,' or 'I can't be separate from people who love me or they will disintegrate'. If we weren't held or cuddled enough as babies when we cried, we learned that in distress, we have to self-soothe. If we were comforted in times of panic or fear, we became shaped around the knowledge that we're not alone and can depend on others in times of need. As kids we're incredible survivors, adapting to our environments with astonishing creativity, and we spend the rest of our lives living into the fables of our earliest construction.

These, then, become our *getaway narratives*. They help us through our childhoods, keeping us relatively psychologically intact. But in the process of survival, we had to throw off bits of ourselves that were too difficult or heavy to carry with us, the way we might chuck off heavy shoes or a jacket when making a quick escape or jumping overboard. When we felt needy (as we all do) but our needs were not met, we let that part of ourselves go or we locked it away. Like all that we bury or leave behind, these bits of ourselves find their way back to us. They pop up. And when they do, we pretend not to recognise them. This is how we do it: 'Christ, that woman we met tonight was such a pain. She didn't stop talking about herself. It was me, me, me. What a narcissist.'

Whenever other people annoy or irritate us, it's a clue, an arrow pointing inwards. It's a precious opportunity for us to scrutinise our reactions, to see if we recognise them as parts of ourselves that are asking to be let back into the family of our consciousness. And *this* is how we come to learn about ourselves through relationships. Like dental mirrors or X-ray machines, other people force an encounter with aspects of ourselves we can't access on our own. But because we'd rather chew glass than let those dangerous, unpredictable bits back in, instead of falling to our knees in gratitude, we become angry at others who arrange a play date we didn't consent to. So we throw the relationship out, together with the key to our own growth.

But at some point in our lives – often when we're in agony – a pattern alerts us that maybe it's us, not them, and we wake up to the fact that we can't ignore these parts of ourselves anymore. The getaway narratives that helped us survive our childhoods are outdated. They've expired. They're not working anymore.

We can count on the fact that the pain of our early wounds will play itself out in our relationships. So let's come back to Mitch. What happened to him in his early years? What are his survival narratives?

What happened to Mitch
Mitch grew up in an ordinary middle-class neighbourhood. His dad, Trevor, whose promising football career was cut short by a knee injury,

bought a bakery just before he married Connie, a friend of his younger sister. Connie was neat and smart and worked as a human resources manager at a small company. She loved the independence work gave her; it ensured she wouldn't end up like her own mother, who never finished school, but raised four children and sank into depression when the last one left the house.

Trevor was a quiet, introspective man, who would rise for work at 3 am, and stay late to do the paperwork. When Connie fell pregnant in their third year of marriage, she took time off work, hoping to have two children close together so they could be playmates. She gave birth to Kayla, who was colicky and hard to settle. With Trevor hardly around, Connie struggled; her sense of herself as a competent, 'can-do' girl floundered. She was never going to be like her own depressed mother and so she resolved this cognitive dissonance by thinking of her experience as merely hormonally induced 'baby blues'. It will soon pass, she told herself. No-one needed to know how desperate and alone she felt with her new baby whom she knew should be bringing her joy. The less control Connie felt over her volatile baby, the more she struggled with the ambiguity and unpredictability of motherhood. She longed to be back in her neat office with her pile of work and, at the end of the week, a column of satisfying red ticks running down her to-do list. But she put on a brave face and got on with motherhood.

Kayla continued to be 'difficult' – she needed grommets in her ears and became lactose intolerant. Connie felt like she was barely coping as she tried to keep up with her toddler's ever-changing demands, and just when she felt she'd regained a sense of balance, she discovered she was pregnant again. Much to her shame, she found herself crying alone in the bath one night, unable to articulate what she was crying about. She had to endure chronic morning sickness together with Kayla's temper tantrums.

Mitch was born ten days before Kayla's second birthday. The only time Connie ever saw Trevor cry was on the day he was born. He kissed his wife on the forehead and told her she had made him the happiest man in the world.

'Aren't you a lucky girl to get such a lovely birthday present as a little brother!' her aunts and grandparents cooed to Kayla at her party. 'I vont a puppy,' Kayla replied.

Trevor took off a week from work to look after his wife and son. Connie revelled in her husband's attention, optimistic that she'd be able to settle into a routine with the new baby, given that Mitch seemed a much more placid, 'easier' baby than Kayla and the breastfeeding was going well.

But after a week's leave, Mitch's father went back to work and Kayla, ravenous for mum's attention, fussed, cried and threw even more tantrums as soon as she didn't get her own way. When Connie tried to calm her one time, the little girl wriggled free, accidentally kicking her mother in the chest. A day later, Connie's left breast swelled up with mastitis, making breastfeeding unbearably painful. She winced whenever Mitch latched, hardly making eye-contact with him. Sometimes, while feeding him, she'd cry and her tears would spill onto his face. Whenever he cried in distress or hunger, she responded slowly, the effort almost more than she could muster. A big strapping baby, Mitch was constantly hungry, and so he went from being a calm, easy baby to a niggler and a whiner.

Connie had a sense of déjà vu; she couldn't manage 'another Kayla'. She changed Mitch's nappies as quickly as possible, sometimes handling him a little roughly. Dulled by depression, her low energy reserves sapped by the demanding Kayla, she was too tired to stimulate Mitch with baby talk or play. When Trevor finally walked through the door at night, she'd withdraw into passive-aggressive silence, sulking all evening.

The first few months of Mitch's life went like this. Though her mastitis cleared up, and her mental state improved slightly, Connie felt like she had nothing left to give. Of her two kids, Mitch was the least demanding, so it was there that she could cut corners, short-change and get away with the bare minimum. Left alone to cry, often for long periods, Mitch's feelings flew from him like a flock of pigeons and scattered chaotically into an emotional black hole.

He doesn't remember this, but Connie does – when he was eighteen months old Kayla covered him completely in fluffy toys. When Connie came into the room she found the three-and-a-half-year-old girl lying on top of a pile of teddy bears and stuffed dinosaurs. 'We're all hugging the baby,' said Kayla, which was when Connie realised that Mitch was somewhere under that pile. When she pulled him out, Mitch was conscious but frozen, unable to breathe. After an interminably horrible moment when she thought he couldn't inhale, his chest heaved and he took in great gulping breaths and Connie burst into tears of relief and shame.

Kayla and Mitch's relationship did improve over the years – she never tried to kill him again. But their truce relied on Mitch taking a back seat, remaining the quiet, dutiful little brother, not encroaching on his big sister's limelight. It helped when Kayla's natural talent for gymnastics in subsequent years absorbed her desire for competition and kept her out of the house training most days. In time, Connie recovered some sense of her former buoyant self, especially after she returned to full-time work when Mitch was eight years old. Mitch became a latch-key kid who'd come home, make his own dinner and, when he didn't have football practice or a game to go to, kick a ball against the garage wall, looking towards the street every now and then for his father, hoping he'd have the energy to join in the game when he came home.

Why it matters – being contained

Whether he remembers it or not, those early months and years of his life were both critical and formative for Mitch and will tell us a lot about how he might function in an intimate relationship with someone like Erin.

Psychoanalysis explains that when a baby cries, needing relief, he projects his feelings into the world, and to receive relief, they must be accepted or *contained*. When a mother wonders: *What does my baby need? What is he experiencing right now? What is it I must do to soothe him?* she's reeling in those projected feelings and trying to work out what her baby is feeling. As soon as she feeds or changes the baby or figures out how to comfort him, internal fireworks go off at a psychological level for the baby, because he's had an experience of someone else who has:

- survived the feelings that were intolerable to him
- not forced those feelings back at him (no retaliation or punishment)
- held his distress and thought about it.

∽

As pain transforms into comfort, babies start to learn to do a fancy psychological thing called *introjection*. They form inside themselves a mental representation of a figure who can manage difficult feelings. Over time, with enough repetition, there is a growing sense of this figure (who sorts out discomfort) being not just outside but *inside* him. And *this* is how human beings learn to manage pain, fear, panic, anxiety: when someone else does it with us and for us when we're just a bundle of neck wobbles. Eventually we develop a growing capacity to manage our own feelings, not having to outsource our freak-outs for someone else to sort out. Crudely, it's emotional 'copying'. We see it out there, we experience what it feels like, and over time we can reproduce it inside ourselves. We learn how to tolerate painful or uncomfortable emotions in the same way that we pick up the language our parents speak by imitation. Mothers and fathers don't have to pull this off perfectly, but well enough to give their babies the experience of containment. This is what is called 'good enough' parenting. It's a term psychologists use, which doesn't mean second best, but some-thing sufficient, not perfect.

If we've had an adequately containing presence in these times of trouble, we'll have a much easier time processing our difficult emotions because of the presence of the container, which allowed us to feel safe when we felt overwhelmed. So a baby's mind goes like this:

$$\text{Distress} + \text{Mum (container)} = \text{Relief}$$

That's all very well for those of us who had this kind of containment. But what if we had a mother who, as the psychoanalyst Gianna Williams puts it, wasn't *concave* (could contain) but was *convex* (bounced our emotions back to us). Then our psychological algebra goes like this:

$$\text{Distress} + \text{Reflected distress} = \text{Terror of annihilation}$$

It really can feel like the end of the world. Young children have 'magical thinking'; they confuse fantasy with reality. They experience hostility as dangerous and destructive to their world. An enraged baby will also be a very frightened baby, sensing that his world is threatened. Since no-one can tolerate feelings of obliteration and nothingness, kids who constantly feel abandoned will do everything they can to avoid this distraught state. They disown that part of themselves, not unlike Aron Ralston, the mountain climber who, in 2003 in Utah, with his arm trapped by a boulder, severed his limb in order to survive. As kids, we cut off bits of our emotional selves in order to stay alive.

With a mother who was more convex than concave, Mitch hasn't had enough containment. He would always have been competing for attention with Kayla, and as a second child with a demanding older sister, would have got less than he wanted or needed. When his mother winced as he breastfed during her bout of mastitis, Mitch would have learned to associate the satisfaction of his basic needs with his mother's pain and irritation. She was never fully present for him because she was depleted and depressed. He'd mostly have felt that she was leaving, or half-there. When she was slow to respond to his needs, what would have become of Mitch's urgency? When she tried to 'get the feeding over with' as quickly as possible and handled him roughly, Mitch-in-formation would have had no choice but to shape himself around the only force in his world. Without much stimulation from his exhausted mother, Mitch would learn to stare blankly at the ceiling, to cry himself to sleep. Babies are silent witnesses to all the dynamics around them, without any way of processing them or making meaning out of them.

Of course she didn't intend to, but when he was a baby Mitch's mum imparted to him that she was unable to survive any of his demands or feelings that were overly intense. Too full of her own pain, the container of herself had limited capacity for Mitch's projections. So Mitch's survival strategies for getting through childhood would have been to slowly learn to occupy less space, not make too much of a noise or impose too many demands. He'd have locked away or disowned his neediness, his urgency and his intensity. He would develop a persona: Mitch the 'quiet, shy guy'. To anyone who meets him as an adult, he'll seem reserved and introverted. If we told Mitch that inside him was a Kayla screeching to be let out, he'd tell us to get lost.

The whispers of our history

'But even so,' Erin and Mitch might argue, 'what can we do about it now? We don't remember much at all from early childhood.'

Many people remember nothing at all from before the age of four, and most have only a handful of memories from before six or seven. Even then, what we remember is often the memory of an original memory, which may well have been a distortion of reality in the first place. The stories of family members can help, but we may come to this work after our parents have died, or maybe we don't have relationships with parents or siblings where we can sit down and interrogate them about those early years. Also, their stories and memories will be imperfect, contradictory and shaped by their own survival narratives. So 'getting to the truth' (if there is such a thing) probably isn't going to happen. It doesn't matter. What we have to get to is enough of an understanding of the past that fits our experience in the present, which in turn supports our growth towards self-definition and adulthood.

We can work with whatever histories we've inherited and with as much or as little information as we're able to retrieve. Luckily, there are other ways to investigate. Just as archaeologists or palaeontologists examine artefacts, fossils or soil samples for trace elements or structures that will help them work out what was going on thousands or millions of years ago, we have within ourselves clues as to how we experienced and adapted to our early environment. Neurological pathways and brain maps are laid down from the beginning of life, and because the more fundamental of these habituate and resist change, our current behaviours give us clues about what went down in our early years. Our relationships with our partners – or our difficulties finding partners – will highlight the probable dynamics we learned to shape ourselves around. Our wounds will appear in our intimate interactions, like secret messages written in invisible ink.

The Buddhists tell us that while history affects us, it's ultimately illusory, as is the future. All we have is the present moment. If we're not able to go back to the scene of the crime, we can still work with the whispers of our histories which are embedded in our relationship patterns and the triggers that our partners set off in us. Our assignment is to become aware of impatience, anger, disengagement or feelings of abandonment in the present moment and to bring mindfulness and compassion to these feelings. To love the parts of ourselves which have experienced so little love.

෧෨

So, if our responses as babies are set up so early in life, how can we change them now? We can't redraft history, but we also wouldn't be writing this book if people can't change. We can. However, the more entrenched a habitual response pattern, the harder it is to transform, just like a smoker who's been at it for ten years is going to have to work harder to give it up than the person who started last month.

We need compassion – not only for our all-too-human parents or primary caretakers, but for ourselves. All love relationships are frigging hard and test us. But who said they'd be easy? Relationships are humanity incubators. Once we know who we are and how we were first loved (or not-so-well-loved), we stand a better chance of letting go of our attachment to our 'stories' as the 'middle child', 'lonely only child' or 'surviving child'. We may come to understand our impatience as adults when we learn that we were hurried as a child and forced to grow up too quickly and instead of lapsing into self-loathing, we give ourselves permission to slow down now. Wounds from the past just need us to visit and pay our respects. We don't have to shoulder the gravestones into our future. We can just leave a bunch of flowers and move on.

6.

Threesomes

MITCH IS ONLY ONE HALF of the story. What about Erin? How will her history play out in her relationship with Mitch?

What happened to Erin

Vince, a handsome, newly qualified orthopaedic surgeon, and Trish, a model in her early twenties, fell in love at first sight. He was quick-witted. She had an infectious laugh, flaming hair and green cat-like eyes. Charisma oozed off the two of them like butterscotch sauce.

Their wedding pictures made the society pages. You just had to take one look at them to reflect on how romantically inadequate your own relationship was. Trish soon gave up the runway for modelling maternity wear and then, within a week of giving birth to Erin in a quick, neat procedure performed by one of Vince's colleagues, she and her new baby were posing for articles in women's magazines. In between a busy schedule of mothers' groups, music appreciation and swimming lessons, Trish would call Vince to let him know 'I found her the cutest bikini today' or 'She sat up all by herself, you should have seen her!' By the time Erin was nine months old, duties in the operating theatre weren't the only reason Vince wasn't taking calls. Not that he didn't want to hear about his darling girl, but he was a busy man and Trish didn't understand the meaning of 'Keep it short, darling'.

Just before her first birthday, Trish entered Erin into a 'beautiful baby' competition. The prize was a photo shoot and the chance to make it as the face of a new disposable nappy. Erin lost out to a blonde baby with blue eyes, an injustice that churned in Trish for years to come. All that remained was the portrait of Erin in a picnic basket wearing a pink bow around her head, which was framed and hung in the lounge room.

Trish excelled in managing the household and mothering Erin in between hosting dinner parties for Vince's senior colleagues and visiting surgeons, and occasionally her friends from the fashion world. Vince attended international conferences, and applied himself to the learning of cutting-edge techniques. While he was away, Trish brought Erin to sleep with her in her king-sized bed so she wouldn't be alone. She'd whisper to Erin that she was her special girl and that she loved her more than anyone in the world. Then when Vince returned, he'd make a beeline for his 'little princess', presents in hand. But come bedtime, Erin would be returned to the cot in her own room where she'd cry and whimper until her angry mother appeared at her door. 'Naughty girls get no cuddles,' she'd scold, or 'Your face will stay ugly if you keep crying.' And Erin, bewildered, would sink into her cot, alone and bereft.

Because he was part of a team pioneering a new surgical technique, Vince became more and more in demand at conferences. He also started to spend two weeks a year volunteering in Third World countries. Although Trish was proud of his achievements (she took every opportunity to boast about her brilliant husband to anyone who would listen), she never grew used to his departures. 'Why are you leaving me? I need you. I'm all alone when you're gone,' she'd cry furiously. 'You don't need me, you've got Erin,' Vince would sigh, battling to match a tie with a work shirt. 'Do you think the stripes or the teardrops go better with the navy shirt?' Turning to Erin, Trish would say, 'You don't go off and leave Mummy, do you, my precious girl?'

Whenever Vince returned from one of his trips, Erin would be sent off to play by herself while her parents shut her out behind their closed bedroom door. Sometimes she'd sit and wait outside their room, quiet as a snail, picking at the carpet, or scraping her little nails along the grain of the door.

While he was away, Trish talked about Vince to Erin all the time. 'I'm going to have my hair done today so I can be beautiful for when your daddy comes home. Do I look beautiful enough for Daddy?' she'd ask Erin, or 'Do you think Daddy will like Mummy in this new dress?' Erin knew all the right answers. 'Yes Mummy. You're the beautifullest in all the land. Daddy will love you the best.'

Vince was hardly ever at home. On his returns, fights became more vicious, and the activity in the bedroom more audible. Erin heard Trish sobbing one night, 'I really want another one, please Vince, I'm desperate for another one.' When Erin was four-and-a-half, Rob, Erin's baby brother, arrived. The few family holidays were usually organised around Vince's conferences. The last of these was in Barcelona where he paid for a full-time babysitting service to look after the kids while he and Trish went exploring the city or sat around the hotel swimming pool drinking cocktails, Vince excusing himself between activities to take 'work calls'.

A month after returning from Barcelona, Trish picked up the home phone to call her mother and overheard Vince talking from his office on the other side of the house to a woman he called 'honey'. He had never called her honey, not ever.

Vince moved out. Six months later the beautiful couple got an ugly divorce. Trish kept the house and the kids.

After Vince left, Erin slept in her mother's bed with her, until that place was intermittently taken by a series of boyfriends who washed in and out with the attendant drama of serial tsunamis. Erin grew adept at sensing when her mother's latest fling was ailing and, having saved her pocket money for just such a time, would go out and buy Trish tulips from the corner store. She became a little mother to her brother Robert, and taught herself how to boil pasta and make scrambled eggs. Trish would sit on the verandah in her high heels, a glass of wine in her hand, and as she watched Erin water the garden or take out the garbage, she'd call out, 'I don't know what I'd do without you,' and 'You're the best thing your father ever gave me.'

When Erin became a teenager and was invited to parties, things between her and Trish became strained. Asking for permission to go out on a Saturday night with friends when Trish was between boyfriends became an ordeal. 'Who will I talk to?' Trish would ask.

'I dunno, Mum, maybe get a DVD?' Erin would suggest. Then when it came time to leave, Trish would lie on her bed with an icepack on her forehead for her 'migraine'. 'Can you bring me some painkillers with a glass of water?' Trish would croak. As time went by, Erin learned a hundred ways to lie and leave. A hundred ways to hurt her mother. A hundred ways to be a terrible daughter.

Why it matters – becoming triangular

Erin describes herself as 'happy, bubbly and energetic', which is exactly Mitch's first impression of her. Her family history reveals she was an easy baby, and the darling of her mother's world. To say she was loved by her parents wouldn't quite cover it. She'd be the first to point out that she had an indulged, spoiled childhood, endlessly reminded how pretty and special she was, and that it was only in her teenage years that things, for her, began to unravel.

Wasn't this 'good enough'? Shouldn't this augur well for future relationships?

Erin's problem is that she's never had a healthy threesome.

∽

Threesomes have regrettably got a bad name, given how we tend to associate them with sleazy orgies and hardcore porn where three is never a crowd. Intimacy, however, is an exclusive club for twosomes. Conventionally, the couple outranks the trio, which is both sensible and mathematically neat: in pairs, no-one is excluded. But when it comes to developing our capacity for intimacy, everyone needs to know what it's like to be the odd one out.

Thinking back on your wanton youth you may lament that you've never been part of a threesome (making you feel left out all over again), but trust us, you have. You probably don't remember it. Not because you were drunk or stoned, but because you were small. And it was probably an awkward experience.

If we could talk as babies, we'd talk of heartbreak. The moment the universe of Me & Mum is shattered, the horizon changes. We learn there is other life out there. Other big people. Other little people. Human traffic. Non-human 'others': work (Mum goes away for hours at a time); illness (Mum has little energy); other stuff (Mum's dad has had a stroke, there's no money for rent, one of the other kids has to have an operation); Mum's own life (yoga classes, tennis, medical appointments that don't include schlepping a baby along). Through the pain of this terminal knowledge we are inducted into the beginnings of selfhood. We confront the threesome. Our world has shifted from 'It's all about me' to 'Hey, what about me?' and with it we tumble into the abyss of separation anxiety.

Erin was born into a triangular arrangement of mother/father/baby in which there are two separate connections that included her (one with Dad, the other with Mum) and a connection (between Mum and Dad) that excluded her. There are heaps of variations of this arrangement – from same-sex parents to single-parent families, from families with single children to those with many, or merged families. While the family configuration may change, the principle remains the same: a baby has to come to terms with the fact that she is part of several triangular relationships, and that she'll be excluded and isolated at times. This gives us our first experience of being an observer rather than a participant. We look on as a witness. Here we learn that:

- our parents are in a relationship together
- we are in a relationship with each parent and
- others might observe us in a relationship.

Just as introjection is crucial to how we learn to manage our feelings (our discomfort contained, survived, thought about and translated into relief-bringing words or action by a carer, helping us copy a figure who can manage difficult feelings inside ourselves), so we need to experience an outside Observer, so that we can build within ourselves an internal Observer.

Psychoanalysts refer to the mature integration of this capacity to observe and understand that we are being observed *the third position*. While we will use the term 'the third position' in this sense, we will also apply it more broadly to speak about a *strategy* people can use to enhance intimacy. Here we are talking about a psychological manoeuvre, where we juggle several perspectives at the same time: our own point of view, the other person's point of view (empathy), and a bird's-eye view where we watch ourselves interacting. So while we're shrieking at someone, we're able to think, 'I'm not being very kind right now,' the way a person watching us might perceive our behaviour. This is the psychological skill that gradually allows us to see the whole elephant, as well as the blind men touching it.

How a 'positive injury' helps us separate

It's hard enough having to share a slice of cheesecake or a box of popcorn. It's much harder to share someone we love. When our special one-on-one relationship with a parent was crowded out by the presence of another and what we thought was 'Mine! Mine!' had to be shared, we were cut to the core. It's wounding, but it would be wrong to think of it as tragic. It's part of the inevitable hurt we all must go through when growing up, the 'positive injuries' that guide us towards healthy relationships. Threesomes are both painful and necessary; they teach us *how* to be excluded, and in this we learn to do that fundamental move on which intimacy relies: we learn to be separate.

How does this happen? We acquire the ability to bear contradictory feelings without cancelling out or denying either one. Even as we hate feeling excluded, we also (and simultaneously) love our parents (separately). Here is the first lesson in learning to love and hate the same people at the same time. And *this* is one of the keys to successful intimacy later on in life. Tolerating ambivalence, and holding paradoxical feelings without becoming overwhelmed or destroyed by them, teaches us to endure this other relationship, the one that is outside and away from us. It's a kind of internal resilience that allows for things to not have to be one way or the other, but to be both, and for that to be okay. Here we experience feeling safe enough, knowing that at times I am the centre of the world, and at times I will be on the periphery. To sustain an intimate relationship as adults, we accommodate shifts and imperfections in mood, feeling, attraction and desire as inevitable. We allow for seasons. For ebbs and flows. We don't try to freeze or fix anything in stone. But we also have to be secure in the knowledge of fluidity or change. It's about being able to rest in the undulations, to

55

accept what the Japanese call 'wabi-sabi', which means beauty that is imperfect, impermanent and incomplete.

So what did Erin, as a child, learn about healthy separation and holding ambivalence? Unfortunately, not enough. What she witnessed while she was growing up was two adults shifting between moments of connection with each other and where one or the other parent felt excluded, let down and hurt. In Erin's family threesomes couldn't be accommodated. When Erin became aware of her parents as a couple, and herself as the excluded link, she became the 'outcast'. How she managed this early experience of loss – and how her caregivers and environment facilitated this – is at the heart of her psychological development and created the furrows of habitual responses she will later take up in relationships.

Neither Trish nor Vince tolerated being the spare wheel in the triangular family system that is naturally set up when that pregnancy pops and oops, another person arrives on the scene. So when Erin was born and Trish fell in love with her (and herself all over again: 'Look how clever I am, what a beautiful child I made'), Vince was bumped down in the hierarchy of Trish's affections. As an over-praised only-child himself and a successful surgeon ('Oh Doctor, aren't you wonderful, look how you've healed me'), he wasn't used to getting the silver medal, so he devoted himself to the one arena where he could count on being idealised: his work. The more he worked, the more distant he became, the more Trish felt ignored and devalued, with retorts like, 'Do you think I was one of the best bloody models in the country only to be left at home all day to change nappies?' to which he'd reply, 'Settle down, Trish, it's what you wanted. No-one forced you to become a mother.' And so began the fighting and the make-up sex.

As a small kid, Erin was excluded from the excitement of the make-up reunions between her parents and was literally locked out, left alone to process emotions of marginalisation and exclusion. So she yoyoed between feeling loved and adored, to feeling abandoned. This might have been a 'positive injury' – part of a necessary resolution – if her parents had been able to contain Erin's feelings of hurt and anger. But Trish bounced Erin's upset back at her, telling her she was being naughty, or looked ugly. Trish's own sense of lovability rested solely on validation from her husband and the outside world. As soon as she felt lost or unloved, she had to find a mirror to reflect back to her how beautiful and special she was – and if Vince couldn't do it, goddammit, Erin would have to. But let's not hurl stones at Trish, because her narcissism was surely the result of inadequate resolution of her own childhood losses. This is not about blaming but about understanding.

Vince was more subtle in his convex reaction but he too had limited capacity for Erin's angry tears, reinforcing and only being able to tolerate the 'good' Erin. When she was a baby, he'd hand her over to Trish if she became 'difficult', saying he had to go and work. Later on, he'd tell her she wouldn't be getting a present from him when he returned from his next trip if she carried on like that.

So Erin learned early on that there was no space in her parents' world for an angry or sad baby. She devised emotional survival strategies to keep her parents happy. For her mother, she was more like a supportive girlfriend than a child, taking on the job of ensuring Trish felt adored. She was solicited into her mother's narcissism, and got tangled up in all those strings that were attached to her mother's love: treat me as special or I will be hurt; turn a cold shoulder on me, and I will do the same to you. She functioned as a kind of adjunct – an extension – to her mother. Not separate, but merged in the service of her mother's narcissistic needs.

She didn't feel her father's fragility – he acted as if he was worthy of everyone's love – so with him, she took on the role of the cute, engaging little princess. So Erin will have struggled to introject an image of herself as someone able to tolerate the anger and hatred that flows from feeling excluded. Instead, she developed an image of herself as being lovable *only* when she was cooperative, bubbly and sensitive to the needs of others. She needed to defend against – to repress – what she was learning to be the 'bad', unlovable parts of herself.

For many children who, like Erin, 'successfully' become 'narcissistic extensions' of their parents, things come unstuck as soon as the kid starts to express the need to break away. And this is what happened when Erin, in a natural attempt to become more autonomous, tried to pull away as a teenager: her mother was hurt, sick and felt abandoned. Because Erin was denied her own emotions, as a teenager she'd have been filled with ambivalence and guilt, feeling that she alone was responsible for her mother's unhappiness.

Beyond the ego – taking up the third position

> *We do not see things as they are, but as we are.*
>
> —The Talmud

In relationships, our subjective experience can cripple us. We can lose mobility and become rooted to the spot, only able to see as far as our perspective allows. We lose breadth and depth. We forsake curiosity. We become caged in conclusions. *He always comes home late. She never touches me.* When we label someone, we close down their mystery.

We can't help but see things from our own perspective. But Buddhism and other spiritual traditions remind us not to be attached to what we think, because when we are convinced we are right, or that the way we see things is morally/spiritually/rationally/intellectually better, we enter into judgement: my perspective is better than yours. The need to be right is a defence of the 'ego', the part of ourselves that cannot tolerate contradiction, ambivalence, paradox or challenge. The more we act out of our ego, the more we'll push that it's 'my way or the highway'. If we're more intimidating or domineering than our partners, we can impose our perspective on the relationship.

But if one person's right, then someone has to be wrong, and while being right (whatever that means) may give us momentary feelings of self-righteousness, it doesn't advance intimacy. If we can only see things from our own egocentric vision, we get mired in victimhood, blame the other person and continually feel disappointed.

Relationships teach us to accept that someone else sees the world differently from the way we do. We get a chance to really listen to another person, stand in their shoes and tolerate that our viewpoint is just one of many. We give a bit, we receive a bit, we tolerate not always getting our own way, we put ourselves out to make our partners happy, they do the same for us. In the process, the membranes of our perception become permeable and we develop tolerance, empathy, respect, loving kindness, compassion and other qualities that extend us out of our own egos and self-absorption.

Being able to see the whole elephant while still touching only a small part of it – taking up the third position – is one step beyond this. When two people clash, each invested in being right, feeling wounded or blaming the other, the relationship will get stuck. The third position offers a way forward: it's an objective perspective that takes both points of view into account and holds them together, even in the presence of seemingly unresolvable paradox. To do this we have to rise up out of our skins and adopt a different view. We have to look at how we're behaving and at what's going on in the relationship, as if we were an impartial observer. Resolving conflict is ideally done when both partners can take up the third position in one form or another; but there will be many times when one partner is too stressed or hurt or angry to do so, while the other is able to take it up and hold the position on behalf of the relationship. If just one of us can pull this off, it can shift the dynamic between us. If both of us can do this, the intimate transformation can be magical.

But this psychological move, like touching our toes, will be harder for some of us than others, depending on our flexibility, our willing-ness to give it a go, how intact our egos are and how attached we are to being right. It will stretch us, but with practice, will get easier. Some of us literally cannot get there. Even if we're willing, we can probably only manage it on a good day when we're feeling emotionally resourceful. We need to be emotionally organised with sufficient insight, capacity for empathy and understanding of our own shadows. Like an orgasm, for most of us, it's impossible to sustain over any length of time. We touch it momentarily, then we lose it again. Such a human experience. The ability to step outside ourselves is what lies at the core of resolving all our relationship difficulties.

But we can think of it like a harbour. Like all the ways in which we can be present or 'awake', we keep coming back, like the medita-tor returns to the breath, like the priest recites the same prayer, like the gardener tends to the same earth. Intimacy 'breathes' – we are constricted by it, but then we're expanded again. We stumble, we stray, we fall from grace. But the work of intimacy is in how we return.

Just as no-one can tell you how to love, no-one can map your way to the third position or tell you how to get there. It's a path we each make through the partnership we're nurturing.

7.

Dodging Suffering

What is hell? I maintain that it is the suffering of being
unable to love.
— Fyodor Dostoyevsky, *The Brothers Karamazov*

IDEALLY, A RELATIONSHIP GIVES US a context in which to observe how we behave intimately. But some of us will spend our lives avoiding intimacy at all costs. Who wants to be that vulnerable? Who wants to go through all that pain? If we're sidestepping a relationship out of fear (rather than choice) we probably say stuff like, 'I'm just not ready,' or 'I haven't met the right person,' or 'I'm having fun, I like being alone.' To understand what's really going on, let's revisit the night Tara hooked up with Antonio . . .

When it's all about ME

Antonio rolls onto his side. His penis lolls onto his thigh. He just wants to close his eyes and sleep now. The girl next to him snuggles up behind him, spooning him. What's her name again? Tori? Tina? Tara? Something like that. She starts to kiss his back. She stops.

'Hey, what's this on your back?'

'I dunno, what is it?'

She touches something on his upper back just below his neck. 'Looks like a mole . . .'

'No idea,' he grunts.

He just wants to sleep now but she's all over him. What's her problem? She had an orgasm. That's one thing the girls can't complain about; he knows how to please a woman. It must be nearly morning. He can see the first streaks of dawn coming through her window, and if he can just get a few hours of sleep in, he can be back home by mid-morning to feed Vixen and Nixon, his two Weimaraners. The girl has wrapped her arms around his waist. He feels claustrophobic. He presses the light on his watch to see the time. It's 4.57 am. 'Mmm, that was so good . . .' the girl murmurs into his ear. But she's more than a girl, come to think of it. She's way past his usual cut-off mark – she must be over thirty.

'Always happy to please,' he says, 'but I've gotta go.'

As he says this, she retracts her arm. He swings his legs so he's sitting on the side of the bed. She pulls the sheets up protectively around her and turns away from him. She doesn't even ask him where he's got to go or why.

'Got to feed my dogs,' he says. 'If I don't get home, they'll chew the furniture.'

'You've got dogs?' she asks quietly.

'Two of the best friends a guy could ever have,' he says. 'I got to keep custody of them when I got divorced.'

'You're divorced?' she asks.

'Yeah, six years ago.'

The girl is quiet.

'She tried to fight me for custody of them, but I told her I'd have to have her killed,' Antonio chuckles.

The girl doesn't laugh. 'How long were you married for?' she asks.

'Three years.'

'Do you have kids?'

He guffaws. 'She wanted them, but I managed to get out of that one. Lucky escape.'

He starts to get dressed. He's talking too much, giving her too much information, but he wants to get out of there as quickly as possible. He knows he's being a bastard, but look, she wanted to fuck him as much as he wanted to fuck her. In fact, she came onto him. She's not even really his type, not that he has a type. He loves pussy, he can't help it. He's just a bloke.

'Don't you like kids?' she asks.

'They're like breasts. I don't mind them on someone else.' He laughs at his own joke. Ties his laces. Where's his wallet and keys? He scans the room – ah, there on the dressing table.

Since the divorce, everyone's been trying to set him up, but they always try to set him up with chicks who are over the hill – they're all past thirty-five and some are even divorced with kids. As if he's looking for that kind of shit in his life.

He goes over to the dresser and takes his keys and phone. On the dresser, amid the disarray of earrings, necklaces and perfume bottles, is a photograph of a little girl with blonde curls smiling up into the camera. She has a butterfly painted on her face. He wonders for a moment whether this is Tina – no, it's Tara, he's almost sure of it – when she was a little girl, or whether it is some friend's daughter, or a godchild. Something tugs inside him, something between a memory and a wish. Suddenly he is ravenous. It feels like he hasn't eaten in days. He is almost weak with hunger. He'll stop by Maccas and pick up two breakfast McMuffins on the way home.

He turns and faces the girl who is now lying in a foetal position, her eyes peeking out from between her tousled hair and the sheet she has gripped protectively against her body. Her eye make-up is smudged, maybe from their sex, maybe from crying.

'Look, I'll see you around,' he says.

She nods, not looking up at him, just staring ahead of her.

'The dogs . . .' he starts.

He almost reaches out to touch her head of curls, but if he does, he'll just get roped into staying and all he wants to do now is run. He isn't going to feel bad about this. Jesus, if he had to feel bad about fucking and leaving, he'd spend his life feeling crap. He lets himself out and leans forward to start his car. As he does, he feels his belly tight against his trousers. He'll get a bite, feed the dogs, have a sleep and later he'll go to the gym. If he's going to be fucking girls half his age, he's got to keep in shape. Nothing worse than flab.

∞

There's a bit of the narcissistic Antonio in us all, but some of us turn it into our personalities. We don't listen, we talk – mostly about ourselves – and then when we pause for a breath, say: 'So enough about me, what do you think about me?' Everything has to be our way and on our terms – we drive, we pick the restaurant, we don't drink that brand of sparkling water, we call the shots. In Antonio's case, he picks up women and then he dumps them with a 'Don't call me, I'll call you', which he never does, unless it's a booty call or he needs a hot date for a function. But inside every narcissist is a terrified control freak.

Antonio's vanity is twisted up in his womanising. He exerts his power by objectifying women, treating them as extensions of his ego. His flashy car, huge house and colt-like dogs reinforce his own beauty, strength and aggression. What Antonio will never show or admit to are the empty rooms inside his fancy home. Men like Antonio often claim they're not attracted to women their age. Of course not – these women might actually be his 'equals' and Antonio isn't interested in equality. Women his age, women who don't hang all their self-worth on how they look, petrify him. They'd laugh at all his posturing and would invariably see through his defences quickly. So his way of defending against this type of vulnerability is to denigrate them as 'old', and keep going for younger women who are easily impressed by his wealth, his worldliness and his slickness.

Ask Antonio and he'll say he's the happiest guy on earth. He's adopted the narrative that he loves being alone, and won't settle or be with anyone who isn't 'at his level' (i.e. good-looking, well-toned, successful). He's never remained faithful in any relationship and cheated on the wife he once loved. He's always chasing something 'out there', retreating to his big empty castle when it gets too much. He flies now and pays later, either not seeing or not admitting to the artificiality of all his ego-extensions or the consequences of his actions. It will take only one real crisis to shake his flimsy world to the ground.

For now, he's moving from one encounter to another, looking for that perfect woman who can fulfil him. Of course, he hasn't found her yet. And that's because he's chasing an illusion, which suits him perfectly. It means he never has to commit to a real relationship.

When the prince awoke

Before he became enlightened, the Buddha was a prince called Siddhartha, living in India, at the foothills of the Himalayas. Prince Siddhartha's mother died a few days after he was born. To protect him from suffering, his father, the king, kept him within the palace walls so that he never saw a poor, sick or old person. When he was sixteen, he ventured outside the palace walls and for the first time in his life encountered the pain and anguish of old, poor, sick and dying people. He was so struck by what he saw that he spent years searching for answers, vowing to sit under a tree until he understood the cause of human misery. He emerged from his meditation understanding that suffering is inevitable, and that attachment and resistance to change creates suffering.

Buddhist practice encourages us to make friends with mortality – admittedly, not the average friendship. Permanence is an illusion, as is our notion that we are in 'control'. We come to accept our own end (and the end of all beings) as the only inevitability. Knowing that death is inescapable and the moment of our own death an uncertainty, we begin to ask, how then shall I live?

Antonio's palace

Antonio has never asked any of these questions. Like Prince Siddhartha, he has not ventured beyond the walls of the palace or confronted the reality that he – and everyone else – ages and dies.

The key to understanding Antonio is to look at the palace in which he grew up. We might assume his spoiled behaviour as an adult must come from having been overindulged as a child. But this isn't the case. All he has in common with Siddhartha is that he lost his mother within days of his birth – not to death, but to disinterest. He was born to an eighteen-year-old runaway in a state hospital in Rome. Sequestered by her shame-ridden parents in Positano on the Amalfi coast, with her sights set on the high life in Rome, eight-and-a-half months pregnant, Antonio's mother took off, the bus ride bringing on labour so that by the time she reached Rome she was five centimetres dilated. She gave birth and took off for a second time in two days, leaving her infant behind with nuns and spending the next two years snorting, shooting up or smoking whatever she could find, before being rescued by her family.

By then, Antonio was being brought up by his adoptive family – a diplomat, Gaetano Conti, and his wife, Lea, both originally from Milan – who would raise their family citizens of the world in the postings assigned to Gaetano: India, South Africa, Poland and, finally, the United States.

Gaetano and Lea had struggled to fall pregnant, finally giving up and opting for adoption. Thrilled to find themselves the parents of a healthy boy, they packed for New Delhi, arriving when Antonio was four months old and, unbeknown to them, with Lea two weeks pregnant. Lea, feeling nauseous during her first few weeks in India, consulted an English-speaking doctor who palpated her abdomen, nodded at her and the infant in her arms, and said she probably had Delhi belly but, he wondered, could the *signora* be pregnant?

'No,' said Lea. 'My husband and I cannot have children. This beautiful one was given to us by God.'

'Indulge me,' said the doctor. 'I think we should do a test nonetheless.'

Lea and Gaetano, after recovering from the shock of the doctor's confirmation, spent the remainder of Lea's pregnancy joking about her ever-expanding Delhi belly. Lea had two boys, almost twins, she joked, Antonio and Donato, and she gratefully fell into motherhood as if it were a divine gift. When Lea's next bout of 'Delhi belly' – a girl, Sabina – came along, Antonio was three. Two years later, by which time the family was ensconced in Pretoria, Gaetano's next placement, a third natural child was born, another boy, Patrizio.

Antonio, like many adopted children, despite Lea and Gaetano's even-handed commitment and love, couldn't quite shake his early foundation of rejection by his biological mother: it was Donato, whose name means 'donated by God', who was the child his adoptive parents had wished for, and he, Antonio, was a stand-in, a second-choice substitute; this was his intuited narrative, sensed long before he knew it intellectually. The arrivals of Sabina and Patrizio cemented a growing sense of otherness within him, that somehow there was the family, and then there was him, standing apart, a satellite revolving around Planet Conti. The family's diplomat lifestyle was a challenge the three biological Conti siblings met by turning towards one another, forming a tight web of friendship; they treated Antonio with wary affection and curiosity Antonio always believed was antipathy, as if he'd gatecrashed their family.

Antonio went on to adopt a rough and reckless charm. If he was a visitor, he'd act like one, enjoying the hospitality of his hosts with an air of passing attachment. It was a strategy that brought him success in the commercial world, where charisma, brash intelligence and a willingness to take risks reaped huge dividends. Convinced of the temporary nature of everything, his only attachment was to the one constant in his life – his own self. For the rest, it's about what he can touch in the moment.

But below this surface of consciousness, Antonio is searching for a sense of belonging, of being held by someone who's not indifferent to him. The one anomaly in his life was the beautiful Claudette, a young French lawyer, whose constant swinging between Gallic passion and glacial distance tantalised and unbalanced him, as if she were his lost Madonna. They fought like mad. Eventually they battered each other into resentful submission and parted company. Antonio reverted to his pre-Claudette strategy, defending against the pain of indifference by being indifferent towards everyone else. Not remembering Tara's name is one of his ways of projecting away from himself the terror of abandonment.

Antonio can continue in this way for a long time, chasing his illusions and pursuing pleasure, but this is no substitute for intimacy. Pleasure for its own sake is fleeting. It doesn't nourish the parts of ourselves that long for meaning, and will invariably be followed by some kind of pain or hardship. Events in Antonio's life – a health scare or simply growing older – will inevitably undermine the superficial meaning he has created, and make him confront his lack of connection. If Antonio cannot stay when things get difficult, he'll be swallowed up by his own emptiness.

8.
Lost Parts

WHILE ANTONIO SPENDS ALL HIS time avoiding intimacy, someone like Tara spends all her time chasing it. Could it be that she's chasing the wrong elephant? Maybe there's something inside herself she needs to find first. Just like Ch'ien had to return to her father's house to be reunited with the self she left behind, so Tara, after too many painful encounters with guys like Antonio, needs to go back before she can move forward.

When we want what we can't have: Tara revisited
Tara tells her therapist about her friend Sally. How come it's so damn easy for her? Three men are after her, and they're all really great guys. And what about Barbara, whom she works with and sometimes has lunch with? Barbara came out of post-grad, married one of her classmates who's on a mega-salary, and now they have two beautiful kids, a gorgeous house in the suburbs and a perfect life. How come someone like Barbara got it so right? Not that she's being judgemental or anything, but Barbara's not even that pretty.

৩৩

Tara sticks with therapy. She wants to figure out why lust turns so quickly to disgust. Slowly, over a few weeks, she begins to accept the idea that maybe she has to change. She starts to unpack some of her history in therapy, and to understand the pattern she creates in her interactions with men. There comes a time when we can no longer delegate the responsibility for our unhappiness onto the long list of jerks we seem to have dated. Time to take a long hard look in the mirror.

What happened to Tara

Tara's mother liked to knit at night in front of the TV and play bridge on Thursday mornings. She sighed whenever Tara's dad tried to be helpful around the house, muttering things like 'God, you're useless' when he couldn't assemble the new television cabinet from Ikea and she had to call in a handyman. In turn, he would offer to do the grocery shopping, water the garden, and would have offered to walk the cat if cats needed walking. He brought her tea on a tray with a doily when she was watching her favourite TV show, with two shortbread biscuits on a little plate. 'You're standing right in front of the TV', she'd gripe.

As a little girl Tara would put on plays and make things out of felt to show her mother. Her mother would say 'Not right now' when Tara asked if she could perform her play, and 'What is that?' in response to Tara's creative efforts. Not a mean woman, Tara's mother always had a decent meal on the table at night, mended Tara's clothes and picked her up from school, though she seemed to be permanently in a rush to get somewhere else. What made her irate was having to 'wait around' for Tara if Tara was running late for any reason.

Looking back on her history, Tara begins to recognise that in her household, her mum was always right and no matter what Tara or her dad did, they could never win her favour or get approval from the dictator-mother/wife. Experiencing her mother as aggressive and critical would have left Tara hungry for her love and approval. At an early age, she turned to her father, a shy, placid biomedical engineer, for affection. He was attentive, gentle and loving, and seemed to thrive on the 'special' relationship with his daughter, where he enjoyed the human warmth that was sorely lacking in his marriage. But as Tara grew older, the closeness with her father grew more awkward. And besides, she would constantly be reminded that her mother called the shots, and couldn't rid herself of the feeling that, regarding her father's love, she was getting a poorly valued consolation prize. What she really craved was her mother's love and acceptance.

Little girls tend to identify with parts of each parent, usually taking after their mothers in ways fundamental to their growing gender and sexual identity. Tara's unconscious solution to feeling pushed away by her mum was to identify with her, to grow closer to her by taking on some of her characteristics. Her powerful mother would project her thoughts and emotions in her words, her moods and her body language, which were taken in and adopted by her daughter. As an older child and teenager, Tara began to find herself irritated with her father. Bitchy in her criticism of his failings, she sided with her mother.

This, then, is the scenario she re-enacts with 'nice guys' — men who are attentive and kind. From the scripts in her family of origin she's come to see all good guys as powerless, wanting her more than she wants them, and, essentially, as some version of her father. So any sexual excitement invariably turns to repulsion. Men who remind her of her father trigger the mother part of her, invoking her disdain and desire to distance herself from him. Conversely, the high status man who withholds his affection, who might act coolly towards her, reminds her of the parent whose love she craved. He evokes neediness in Tara, the little girl yearning for the love and attention of her mother.

When it comes to relationships, Tara lives in a binary world: one person takes up the role of the needy, weak pursuer, while the other is powerful, denigrating, and too good for the pursuer. When she's with the nice guy, he falls into the weak pursuer role, and she feels too good for him. When she's with the hot guy she becomes the needy little girl desperate to have him share his power and beauty with her.

What would the Buddha say?

Tara claims she's looking for love. That's what she's saying. But how is she acting? What would the Buddha say? Especially about that little freak-out over Ben's skinny butt. The Buddha had the biggest belly. Would she kick him out of her bed? (Sadly, she probably would, with a 'Go easy on the cream puffs, Sid.')

The Buddha would whisper to Tara that maybe her difficulty in finding love is because she's not *behaving* with a lot of love. All her hyper-criticism and judgement isn't serving or empowering her. What mortal man can come close to meeting her standards of exacting perfection? Tara spends a lot of time 'perfecting' her own (mortal, fallible) body and image, believing imperfection is failure. Of course she can't quite comprehend why Gabriel buggered off – she was 'perfect' and yet still not enough for him. To her logical lawyer mind, she is the 'perfect package'. How, then, is she still alone? If she's 'perfect' and nonetheless was rejected, she can continue to believe there is nothing wrong with her and the problem is Gabriel. And the guy before him. And the guy before him.

If something's got to change, Tara will have to examine the ways in which she judges people. She needs real power – not the I'm-a-hot-shot-law-firm-partner kind but the deep, internal solidity based on self-knowledge and self-acceptance. To get there, she needs to stop judging herself and others. 'But hey,' Tara might say, 'I'm just being discerning. I can have my preferences, can't I?' Sure she can. But the process of judging is the cause of much human suffering, all self-inflicted. Everything that exists, both 'good' and 'bad', is part of 'what is'. And, so spiritual teachings go, criticising the way things are is as useful or wise as shouting at the thunder for being too loud. We can keep doing it, but it's not going to get us anywhere.

When we constantly judge things as 'pleasant' or 'unpleasant', we learn the habit of evaluating, categorising, pigeon-holing, scrutinising and criticising (just another day in the life of a law firm, right?). But this mindset creates inner turmoil and dissatisfaction in our ordinary interactions and dealings. We become connoisseurs of dissatisfaction – restaurants are too noisy, busy, overheated, staffed by incompetents . . . nothing ever satisfies us as just being okay for what it is. Never mind our inflated sense of entitlement or expectation.

So what can Tara do?

Here's one suggestion: she can learn to meditate. Meditation teaches us how to quieten the incessant judgements that arise spontaneously, making space between these thoughts. Over time, these spaces grow and we can reach peace of mind that flows from the stillness. Or, if meditation doesn't appeal to her, she could try Deepak Chopra's suggestion in *The Seven Spiritual Laws of Success*, of spending an hour a day, at first, with the intention of not judging anything, and then extending it to a few hours, and then a day at a time.

By placing herself in a world devoid of judgement, where the birds and the spiders are simply themselves, she could learn to connect with a balance that's so often missing in the human world. Given who Tara has become, chances are she'd try to get her meditation or tranquil outdoor time out of the way as quickly as possible so she can get back to her files and her missed calls. Her biggest challenge will be to meet her resistance with compassion – not more judgement, as in *I'm such a failure at meditation*. As soon as we label things, we stop the conversation with them. We shut them down with our judgements. We stop getting to know them. We refuse their mystery.

By practising non-judgement outside her relationships, she'd get better at it and could then bring that skill back into them. Let's say she decides to call Ben back and give him a second chance. The next time she sees him naked, she'd quietly notice, 'Oh, look, Ben's got a hairy, skinny butt.' She'd observe – with curiosity, not judgement – her own repulsion. And instead of over-identifying with it (*OMG, that is so disgusting, I am so turned off, yuck! How could I have slept with him?*), she could greet it like a temporary visitor and remind herself that all emotions arise and fall away. They do not have to set in concrete. If she was able to simply state 'what is', without a positive or negative verdict, she could then take the next step and turn her attention to her own body. When she finds a bit she's not deliriously happy about, she could try this: 'Check it out, there's that cellulite on my thighs. Oh, look, a grey pubic hair. Far out, is that a wrinkle?' And again, she could note her own self-loathing, *without judgement*. Notes to self: repulsion, self-loathing . . . as if she were compiling a shopping list where nothing matters all that much.

What can potentially shift in this process is that the imperfections of her lovers can become the path to her becoming more self-loving. The degree of her repulsion and lack of forgiveness for small imperfections in her lovers reflects the perfection she demands of herself – both in her body and her work. So she'd come to see that all her judgements of Ben are, in fact, *self-judgements*. When she's able to recognise that she cannot tolerate imperfection in others because it's unbearable in herself, she may move to the next stage, which is to offer herself some compassion for her human failings and to embrace those as okay and forgivable. Every offering of kindness she can show herself will have a corresponding offering of generosity to her partner. And so, as she grows her self-awareness and self-compassion, she will open herself to being able to tolerate imperfection in others.

'Everything that irritates us about another,' said Carl Jung, 'can lead us to an understanding of ourselves.'

෯

Spiritual teachers, such as Stephen and Ondrea Levine and Harville Hendrix, teach us to think of our relationship as a spiritual practice. Some even suggest that it is our beloved who is our 'guru', or teacher, because they reflect back to us everything we need to learn about ourselves.

Tara fundamentally has no firm sense of who she is separate from the events, people or circumstances outside of herself. If she's not successful at her job, immaculately dressed, wearing the right clothes, drinking the right wine, who is she? In spiritual terms, she's cloaked the ego with all the trappings of material and status-based 'things' (just like Antonio). She's always seeking the approval of others, unconsciously or consciously, and to this extent is not well differentiated. 'Differentiation of self' is one of the key concepts of the pioneering family therapist Murray Bowen. If we have 'low differentiation', we either conform with others or need others to conform with us and we may be stricken with the need to gain the approval or acceptance of others. Understood like this, Tara is 'fused' with her family's dysfunctional way of managing emotions.

When Tara appreciates that her 'perfections' are also only temporary 'achievements', all of which will fade in time, or through circumstance, she'll be able to see that the ground on which she is trying to build a relationship is a shifting terrain of quicksand. That in order to build something firm and solid, something that will withstand the inevitable transitions of a life – sickness, ageing, bereavement, misfortune – she has to be more grounded. She will need to work to find a place of non-judgement and compassion inside herself. Perhaps become the affirming, maternal voice for herself that she was always denied.

The world of 'I am what I wear' has not equipped Tara for intimacy. She's illiterate in the language of affection, and low in generosity, kindness of gaze or forgiveness of imperfection. While she's stuck in this way of being, she'll struggle to experience intimacy with anyone else, and will remain cut off from herself.

∽

Does this mean we should never have a fantasy about what our perfect partner should look like? Do we set real people up for failure if we dream up our ideal mate? What's the balance between having standards and pricing ourselves out of the dating market? Are we jinxing our luck by only dating people of a certain race? Religion? Age? Height? Weight? Income? Is it okay for us to want a non-smoker? Someone without a bald spot?

Fantasies are great as long as they don't interfere with real life. Standards are appropriate as long as we acknowledge that 'having standards' is not a neutral position, but has a judgement lodged inside it – *I am better than you*. Judgement is one of the key ways we sabotage our relationships – not only with our partners, but ourselves. The things we tend to judge others for, or the 'standards' we hold to, often have to do with surface characteristics as opposed to people's inherent value or worth as human beings. We will be evaluated by the same standards by which we judge another. So if looks are important to us, then we're making looks part of the language of our relationship. Though we might think we're an eight out of ten, we should ask ourselves whether we want to always be held to such high figures. Women might like a bit of leeway for the indignities and distortions of pregnancy, or the unglamorous sweaty years of menopause. Men could do with some understanding when they can't get an erection, or for that depressed stage of their lives after a retrenchment. Or if money matters to us, how will our relationship fare during a financially unlucky time in our lives? We are making the terms of our intimacy simply by bringing ourselves – our values, desires and history – into the relationship.

Good looks and youth are an unstable economy. They're short-term and will erode. People we fall in love with will get sick. They'll have bad hair days. So will we. Things will fall apart.

In her novel, *The Post-Birthday World*, Lionel Shriver writes that our decision about who to marry is ultimately a decision about choosing who we will help die. Gulp. Who said anything about dying and does that involve bedpans? Most of us never think beyond the deep-tongue kissing of the moment to consider that we are about to make a sacred choice about who we would like to have holding our hand when we give birth, lose a parent, get retrenched, sued or a bad Pap smear or prostate result. But that's the fact of it. When we get married or commit to someone long-term, we're making a choice about the first person we'll call in a crisis, the one who'll sign consent forms if we need surgery in an emergency, and the one who'll be the sole guardian of our children if we die first. We love more fully when we can bear the pain of loss, when we can see that our relationships will bring us joy and sadness, and that there is beauty in the full spectrum of how we experience our lives and lovers.

If Tara is serious about intimacy, she has to let go of her attachment to some of her beliefs that are chaining her to a life of loneliness.

PART III

When Love Gets Tough

9.
Deeper

YOU'VE DONE IT. YOU'VE ACTUALLY fallen in love. You change your Facebook status from 'single' to 'in a relationship'. Seriously, this could be it. The sex is still great, but you're ripening into deeper affection as you encounter each other's 'shadow side'. You've lived through farts in bed, PMS, him snapping at a waiter, her 'incessant' texting. But still you hang in there. Something inside you relaxes – you don't have to be perfect to be loved. The balance between lust and an ever-growing emotional attachment starts to shift. There are flashes of real intimacy and a deepening understanding of your connection beneath the surface of your initial attraction.

Revisiting attraction

It's a few months in and it's become clearer that the intermingling of Erin and Mitch's psyches and personalities is more mysterious than just 'opposites attract'. Whatever's really going on between them won't fit any neat formula.

Robin Skynner, a British family therapist, noticed couples often share a history of similarity in their families of origin – maybe they each lost a parent at a young age, come from divorced families, had disciplinarian parents or cold, withholding mothers. What's freaky is that people come together without actually voicing these similarities or even being aware of them. It's as if the unspoken stories of our psyches carry limbic resonances that are literally picked up by each other, like pheromones.

Mitch and Erin both grew up in households of uninspiring marriages where intimacy shrivelled like unwatered pot plants. As kids, they each learned to stifle their neediness. Their sets of parents, for completely different reasons, couldn't tolerate their children's emotional demands or put up with any kind of opposition. In both their families, sad was bad. Both were rewarded for being good kids, for getting on with it, taking care of themselves. This shared history makes Erin and Mitch recognise something of themselves in each other, as if they're speaking the same unconscious language, and are on the same wavelength.

We often choose people who have a similar capacity for independence and intimacy. When people are on completely different levels of differentiation, someone invariably screws things up, either unwittingly or on purpose.

Take Erin's ex-boyfriend, Gus: he signalled his commitment issues by sleeping with another woman. Maybe he was drunk or wasn't thinking, but unconsciously he knew he couldn't keep up with Erin and stay with her at the same level of attachment and intimacy that she's after. So, good for Erin – she ended things.

So far, Erin and Mitch have met each other step for step. Though they were both the 'good children', they expressed it differently. Mitch did it by burying emotion and rationing his demands. Erin did it by expressing herself – as long as she was happy and cheerful. They each see something in the other that they long to develop in themselves: Erin loves Mitch's sense of purpose about his life's direction and his commitment to doing 'good work'. He seems so solid and certain, and it balances out her own flightiness (she's got no idea what career path she wants to follow, really, and knows she's disappointed her dad by being so vague). Mitch represents the stability, safety and strength that Erin lacks beneath her sparkling, confident exterior. She also loves that he's not needy and judgemental like her parents were. He seems satisfied with little. He won't demand that she be faultless; she's so tired of being her parents' perfect child. Yet he's interested and curious and does that cute thing with his eyebrows to show he's listening. And

Mitch has been well-trained at the hands of his mother's depression. He loves to feel helpful, to be experienced as the 'understanding' one. Because he's naturally reserved, Erin picks up how special it is, what it means for him to be feeling so intensely. It's clear he rarely gives his passion away, and yet she's won it.

For Mitch, Erin's playfulness and spontaneity and her seemingly uninhibited passion are like sunshine in the shadows of his childhood, an antidote to the depressed and unavailable parts of himself, the parts of his parents he internalised as a child. Erin comes across as strong and independent. He feels so free and unburdened with her. He doesn't have to work at containing his own needs. He can let go. She won't be overwhelmed by him. She's curious about how he thinks. She wants to know what he feels, and she doesn't flinch when he tells her. He seems not only to be getting to know her, but himself as well. He's felt excited by women in the past, but he has never before been able to think the words 'I love you', let alone express them. They each feel enlivened and strengthened by the other, a state of mind that acts as a kind of superglue, bonding them together as a couple.

Secret gardens

With deepening intimacy comes greater responsibility. The dating stage is cupcakes compared to the croquembouche of what comes next. We have to brace ourselves for *Loss of Eden: The Sequel.* The original premiere, long forgotten, is embedded somewhere deep in our psyche – the pain of being ousted as the centre of our mother's world. Shit, now we have to get over this all over again and accept that we don't own our lover (*we don't?*); we don't have exclusive licence to their affection or focus (*we don't?*); and they have lives outside of us (*they do?*). At some point in every love affair, the encapsulating glow wears thin, not because we haven't loved each other well enough, or we're not doing something right, but because, like all living energies, it flares, subsides and transforms. We have to make peace with an otherness both within our partners (the darker, unloving parts, including their gaze, which sometimes wanders away from us); and without (their interest in other things out there, like friends, family, work). All of a sudden our partner wants to have a boys' weekend, or a girls' night . . . *Don't they love us anymore?*

It's hard not to feel and act sixteen at this juncture: *OMG, he/she's just not that into us anymore . . .* We *have* to lose each other in this way as a relationship progresses. Intimacy is a rhythm of contraction and expansion. We want to be free and to love free people. Chains and handcuffs may work in the bedroom, but not in everyday interactions. Love isn't a leash or a muffler. It's proved in the ways in which we surrender the people we love, so that they can enjoy their secret gardens: early morning walks alone, friendships, sports, book clubs, email correspondence, beer or bubble bath.

There's a beautiful ancient Sufi story about a man called Nuri Bey. One of his servants whispered in his ear that his young wife was acting suspiciously and wasn't allowing the servant to look inside an old chest in her room. Nuri Bey then asked his wife if he could look inside the chest. She said she would prefer him not to. But she offered him the key to the locked chest on condition that he got rid of the servant. Nuri Bey did as she asked. But seeing that his wife was troubled, he ordered his gardeners to take the chest to a distant part of the garden and bury it.

What's moving about this story is that Nuri Bey could have done the 'I'm the boss of you' thing and ripped that chest open. But instead, he chose to respect his wife's wishes and her privacy. When we protect someone else's privacy, far from losing self-respect or power, we gain it. We can't bully people into sharing themselves with us. Our lovers tell us their stories, share their secrets, their fantasies and regrets only when they feel safe with us. This takes time and we don't get there by wheedling, manipulating and nagging for attention. Privacy is not necessarily secrecy. If someone we love needs time alone, that is not a rejection of us: it gives us time to be alone, too.

୭ର

Four months into the relationship, Erin moves into Mitch's apartment. Heartbroken but resolved, she gives Frodo to Rob and Tariq. She's figured out that Mitch is allergic and she loves him more than her cat. Tom and Sam, Mitch's friends, tease him about how quickly things have progressed – 'she's got you on fast-forward, hasn't she?' – but he jokes that it just came down to the laundry: he got tired of running out of clean clothes when he was at Erin's. Of course he'd never joke like this in front of Erin, because (a) it would hurt her and (b) it isn't really true. But he's a bloke and he has to keep up appearances. The truth is that he was beginning to find it difficult to be apart from her. And the more he felt like that, the more he started to fear losing her. Maybe she'd wake up one day and the fact that he's a fireman wouldn't impress her all that much anymore.

So, they go out and choose a new sofa together, in Erin's favourite blue. They buy a funky light for the bedroom. They talk about maybe getting a puppy, one that won't send Mitch into sinus lockdown. As the intensity of those first few sizzling months starts to dim, they each privately nurture their own nagging anxieties. *How will this play out? Will we stay together? Will s/he get tired of me?* As this unfurls, we look for ways of bringing certainty to the unknown. Moving in together cements the relationship. It appeals to our other unspoken needs – emotional attachment, the desire for children – by fostering a sense of security. So you trade a little independence for a little safety. You make sacrifices (you give up your cat ☹). Suddenly you're accountable for your movements – *what time are you home tonight? Who are you playing squash with?* What *are you making for dinner?* But you don't mind. It feels good to have someone interested in everything you do.

You begin to do things together, to create routines and rituals, to lay the foundation stones of a stable relationship. Sunday mornings he brings you coffee and croissants in bed with the Sunday paper. Tuesday nights you go out for Cheaper Tuesday steaks. Saturday afternoons, you make love and go to dinner or a movie. You take turns at choosing what to see. Your pet names for each other become the only names you use. No-one else calls your partner by these names and so they stamp a mark of possession. You own sole naming rights.

With the creation of shared history, home, friends – and later, bank accounts and children – the seesaw shifts in the other direction. Now, instead of making love every night, passion gives way to tiredness, or the need to watch a late-night movie. The balance of lust, romance and attachment begins to shift.

When two histories twist

Just as a baby is the new result of a couple's combined DNA and never an exact replica of any single parent, a relationship is the product of two people's psychological histories coming together. It's a third entity, more than the sum of the two individuals' parts, a dynamic interplay of those parts, creating a new, shared world. Mitch's vigilance to Erin's state of mind and his undemanding nature make him a rare guy in Erin's view, dependable and strong. Erin's capacity to look after herself comes as a great relief to Mitch. He can let go and enjoy her. She's a happy, stable woman. In some ways, Mitch and Erin both believe this is who each of them is, and who the other one is. But it's not so simple. Beneath these alluring qualities are hidden dynamics which could easily lead to conflict. What would happen to their attraction if it turns out Mitch isn't really that dependable and in tune, and Erin is not as self-sufficient and buoyant as she comes across? Will they fall out of love? Will their relationship come apart at the seams?

So far things have been blissful. They have yet to have their first fight. Now let's introduce a simple irritation and see what happens.

10.

First Fight

MITCH LIKES TO KEEP THINGS neat. Erin finds that cute. 'Aren't only gay men supposed to be neat?' she giggles. Rob and Tariq's place is like a museum. Mitch agrees. Rob and Tariq's place is pretty awesome. 'Awesome?' Erin crinkles her nose. 'It's sterile.' Erin can't even remember to close drawers or pick up yesterday's gym clothes from the floor. She'll get to it when she does the laundry. When she lived on her own, she'd let the dishes pile up in the sink for two or three days until she literally ran out of crockery. Since living with Mitch, though, there's not much chance of this happening – he's at the sink in a flash.

Mitch recognises that disorder unsettles him, but doesn't know his inner landscape well enough to connect this anxiety with his childhood where, among other disturbing things, he was frightened by Kayla's explosive outbursts and tantrums. Back then, he unconsciously attempted to soothe himself by putting things in order; his games frequently involved building towns with neat little lines of cars and people. At the fire station, he's a stickler for keeping his fire engines clean, the equipment checked and double-checked. On a call, faced with chaos, his job is to contain it, to go into damage-limitation mode. It's what he did in fantasy with his early environment. He was a firefighter in nappies.

∾

It's a Tuesday and Erin's just come back from the gym. She's in the shower when Mitch lets himself into the apartment. It's been a stressful shift at the fire station. He walks into their bedroom, and the bed is as neatly made as he left it this morning, with the pillows carefully stacked two and two at the head of the bed. Erin's gym clothes are strewn all over the floor. For the first few weeks of their cohabitation Mitch picked them up and put them in the laundry basket.

But today he finds himself standing over her clothes, clenching his fists. Erin walks into the bedroom, her hair dripping down her back.

'Hi, babe,' she says.

'Hi,' he says, his voice clipped. 'Can't you put your clothes in the laundry bin?'

Erin stops. She's never heard him talk in this way.

'Excuse me? What's got into you? I've just come back from the gym. I'll get to it.'

'I know exactly where you've been. I'm sick of coming home and cleaning up after you.'

'Well, don't! I can do it myself.'

'Then why don't you? Don't you have any self-respect?' he says, already regretting the words as they tumble out of his mouth.

By now, she's fighting back tears and a horrible, niggling thought – *Who is this man? Have I made a mistake?* She doesn't trust herself to speak. Her own words might loosen her tears and she doesn't want him to see her crying. She picks up her gym clothes and leaves the bedroom, taking her hurt to the bathroom where she dumps the offending items in the laundry basket and blows her nose.

The big meaning beneath the small things

We've all been here. How easily we hurt and are hurt. Over dirty clothes. The smallest of things. If two people really love each other, would these things matter? Isn't Mitch sweating the small stuff? The truth is they *do* matter, but only because these little fights hold the key to understanding where our relationships might go off the rails.

The more two people get to know each other, the more they become twisted up in each other's deeper stories, hooking each other into a strange and mysterious script they're unconsciously playing out.

Our attractions are never a straightforward 'opposites attract' or a bunch of hormones and pheromones; it's a complex interplay between each person's history and the way the two histories 'dance' together. We're drawn together by the way our wounds speak to each other or fit together, as well as by the way our humour and joyfulness do. Often the difficulties create the most powerful chemistry as we start forming patterns of relating and get stuck in repeating these. We each take up a role or position that complements our lover's: one rescues while the other is wounded; one pursues while the other withdraws; one is critical, the other humiliated. These positions may flip back and forth, or remain fixed, but they become predictable and allow the couple to remain together, functioning in relatively expectable ways. They may also escalate. What's kind of crazy is that these patterns that end up feeling very painful have often arisen from the very things that attracted the couple to each other in the first place – the apparent differences.

So how can we unpack Mitch and Erin's fight so we can understand what's really going on behind the neat freak's freak-out?

Scene 1: As he walks in, feeling on edge, Mitch is aware it's been a stressful day, but if you'd bumped into him on the stairwell and asked him 'How are you?' he'd say he's fine. Nothing a beer won't sort out. Many of us operate at this unconscious place of 'it's fine' without being in touch with how we're really feeling. But after the day he's just had, whether he knows it or not, his internal container is full. He can't hold any more demands being made of him. He's been on a job in which his team had to use a jaws-of-life to free a driver from his crumpled car, which took two hours and in which the paramedics almost lost the patient a few times. But hey, he's seen a lot worse. He's trained for this stuff. He's a fireman doing his job. But deep down, when he walks through the door, Mitch needs relief from the tension he's been carrying all day. He needs to be looked after.

Scene 2: Mitch walks into the bedroom and there are Erin's gym clothes on the floor. It's nothing he hasn't seen before. She always chucks her clothes on the floor, and really, we're talking about a tank top, some lycra shorts and a pair of socks. But these strewn items of gym-wear trigger an unconscious response in Mitch that (a) he has to pick up her dirty laundry and (b) because she's so messy (literally), she won't be able to take care of him in his moment of need (just like his mother couldn't give him what he needed when he was little). In Mitch's world, a woman in disarray can't be there for him. That's his story, his script. Of course he doesn't know any of this consciously, so what does he do? He locates the fault in *her*.

Scene 3: Now here's where couple dynamics really get interesting. Mitch, unaware of the complexity of his response to Erin's mess, and to defend against these vulnerable feelings, does the only emotional manoeuvre he knows – to become critical of her: 'Can't you put your clothes in the laundry bin?' To Erin, this is like a slap in the face. Who *is* this person? She's never seen this side to him. This . . . this . . . angry, aggressive, critical ugliness. Up until now, he's only ever made her feel safe. And right then, she reacts to him, not as Mitch, the man she's getting to know (there's no known hook yet for this judgemental, critical tone; she can't figure out where it's coming from) but as a hostile man. The only experience she's had of aggressive men is from her past, chiefly her own father. That's her story, her script.

See how the scripts get tangled up together? Mitch projects onto Erin because of his particular life-script (feeling overwhelmed and responsible for messy women) and she defends herself through a combination of her own story (the teenager reacting to her critical father) and the projections being thrown at her by Mitch.

Scene 4: All hell breaks loose. They argue, hurling horrible words at each other. They're both on shaky, unfamiliar ground. To protect themselves, they reach for the defences they know, falling unconsciously into the patterns set up in their psyches from when they were small. Like two porcupines, they ball into themselves, spiked to ward off danger.

And so a couple enters into a particular dance in their relationship, triggered by one person, and met and matched by the other. It's become a messy tangle of stories.

When what we think becomes what happens
In the field of quantum physics, scientists over the past few decades have been forced to concede that when it comes to understanding how the universe works, the observer affects the result. The wave particle paradox that confounded researchers (is light made up of waves or

particles?) shifted the inquiry to a different level: the answer depends on who's watching or doing the experiment. How we observe things determines the outcome. This is a profound understanding to take into our relationships.

Psychology has a way of explaining this, revealing just how powerfully we create the dynamics in our relationships. When Mitch thinks that Erin won't be able to look after herself (her dirty bits are lying all over the place) and therefore won't be there for him, he not only projects this onto her but *into* her. He literally shifts her internal state so that she plays out exactly what he fears. By *expecting* her unavailability, he acts out a script that ensures that she becomes exactly that. It's a self-fulfilling prophecy. What he anticipates becomes his experience. He unwittingly sets things up to evoke a response in her that will very likely lead her to withdraw from him in tears. Erin then acts out the role of his tearful, withdrawn mum, Connie. Mitch has an internalised image of this mother and, in attempting to disown it, has put it into Erin. This is known in psychoanalytic terms as *projective identification*, which happens when an internal aspect of ourselves we cannot bear and wish to disown is split off and enters into the *interpersonal* space between us and our partners, and is taken on board by the other. The second partner unconsciously accepts the disowned, projected aspect of the first partner, and behaves as if it belongs to him/her.

Mitch splits off and projects the 'unavailable, chaotic nurturer' part of himself into Erin. Erin then acts the part. And when Mitch relates to her in this state, he isn't seeing her as a separate person, he's relating to the part of his own self but as if it is her. Mitch's sense of self is depleted and Erin's is distorted.

Breathing

Later that evening, over dinner, unable to bear the jagged, threatening silence and Erin's tormented eyes, Mitch looks up and says, 'We almost lost a guy today.' Erin asks him what happened. He tells her how stricken the driver was. 'You should have seen the look on his face. He was terrified. I swear, he thought he was going to die. I kept telling him that it was going to be okay, that we were going to get him out . . . just breathe, just breathe . . . but fuck it, that was bullshit because we both thought he was going to die.' As he talks, easing some space between them, breathing some air around the congested energy of their fight, Erin's compassion for Mitch revives. 'I guess I should have taken my own advice, when I walked in . . . and just breathed . . .'

Erin smiles at him and puts her hand on his. She knows, from her meditation practice, how just by focusing on inhaling and exhaling, you can ground yourself and hold steady. She tells him that she understands he dumped on her because he had such a traumatic day. He apologises for being a prick about her gym clothes. She accepts his apology, and tells him that she can't imagine how tough it must be to work with life and death issues. 'Next time,' she says huskily, sneaking her hand up his neck, 'just tell me and I'll make you feel better. I know just the way . . . And I promise you, you'll be breathing very deeply when I'm finished with you . . .'

They don't embark on an in-depth analysis of their interaction – neither at this point in their lives has sufficient insight to put it into words – but there's enough unspoken understanding. And as he talks about the vulnerability of the driver who nearly died, and Erin reinforces his masculinity as the rescuer, she sees a depth to Mitch's vulnerability that he has not yet been able to show her. She can almost reach out and touch it, but it's like a fish underwater. Just as she approaches, it darts away to hide among the seaweed and rocks. But in this moment, she comforts him, asking him how he feels, listening to everything he needs to say and praising him for saving lives. Though they're only at the outset of their journey of intimacy together, Erin understands Mitch finds it almost unbearable to be vulnerable. So she finds a way of gently telling him off about the way he went about things – by making a joke and suggesting she'll take away his angst next time by making love to him. It's a nifty creative resolution to their first tiff. But it's only going to work for so long. They'll need to deepen their knowledge of themselves and the other if they are to unlock the mysteries and challenges that are ahead.

As things progress, Erin and Mitch can do one of two things: they can act as if this fight was an aberration; they can apologise, make amends and smooth over the creases that it's created in their silky-smooth love affair, and promise not to fight over silly things again. Or they might start to think of it as a peephole in their interaction that allows a view of something deeper. And the questions they might ask are:

- *Who am I?* (This is the 'self' I bring into the relationship, the part of me that is differentiated from you and that I must hold onto at all costs.)
- *What is mine? What am I bringing to the relationship?* (What must I 'own' in the relationship?)
- *What is yours?* (What must you 'own' in the relationship?)
- *In what way do the parts of our selves interact? What do we create together?*

We can only pull this off by knowing what our own stuff is and owning it, and knowing what our partner's is and offering it back to them, as if we were separating colours and whites for the washing machine: *right, this belongs to me, this belongs to you.* Knowing where you end and someone else begins is the border of intimacy.

Friction, disagreements, upsets, impasses — all these interactions can be used as a catalyst to explore what's going on at a deeper level of our relationships. The fight is a messenger, a call of the invisible patterns between us, even something beautiful, like an aggravating grain of sand around which, with enough time and patience, a pearl might form inside an oyster.

৩৩

Just breathe — it's a great circuit-breaker when two people bump up against each other in a moment of crisis. Science has finally caught up with Eastern yogic practice, showing that the chaos of our beta brain waves in times of stress is calmed as soon as we start to breathe deeply; breathing deeply activates our alpha brain waves causing us to relax.

Emotions, like the breath, come and go. So when Mitch walks in and is confronted by mess, stopping and breathing will help him notice his feelings of anger and irritation, and he can see them for what they are — temporary states that will pass. He might also recognise that his anger and irritation hide underlying terror evoked by his sense of help-lessness earlier in the day as the traumatised driver hovered on death's threshold. But even those feelings are temporary. They will pass. By breathing into the constrictions in his own heart and his fight with Erin, Mitch unknowingly allows himself some third position perspective. And what felt unbearable just a while ago, doesn't feel so hard anymore.

II.

Jealousy

WHETHER WE CONSIDER IT A perk or a liability of monogamy, the fact is, we get exclusive rights to a certain kind of bodily and emotional interaction with someone to the *exclusion of others*. That's the promise, anyway. Like an original one-off artwork, our commitment to one chosen person is special because even though each of us may very much want to dabble on the side with other appealing candidates – we don't. There's a RESERVED sign on our hearts and genitals, creating territory only the two of us have access to. It's private property and trespassers will be prosecuted.

॰॰

At some point, when the romance bubble pops, we become aware that we're not alone and that there are pre-existing constellations of people and factors around us, encroaching onto our reserved territory. Families, yours and mine. Histories. Mothers-in-law. A kid from a first marriage. Stress at work. An ex-spouse. Friendships with other people. There's a world of curve balls out there waiting to pelt down on us. And once again we have to shift the dynamics to make space for a third presence.

Any new relationship threatens existing friendships – we don't have the same time or need for them. Friendships can dwindle, be neglected and die of malnutrition. But friendships and other close relationships are essential in maintaining balance. They help us hold onto our sense of individuality and differentiation of self. We rely on friends some-times to help us get to a third position, such as when we talk about our relationships or invite them into the dynamic to help give us a different perspective. So how can we make space for these existing relationships and manage these intrusions skilfully?

Even for those of us who might be more than happy to allow our partners platonic feelings of love – with family or friends – and plenty of space for activities separate from ourselves, somehow when sex is involved, it's as if we lose our adulthood and regress to high school. We happily pretend that our lover doesn't get turned on by others, doesn't want to flirt or wish for a free pass even for just a night.

But it happens – we excuse ourselves to go to the loo, and when we come back our partner is texting somebody called Pamela ('Just a friend at work,' he shrugs). Or we see her chatting to the guy in the singlet at the gym, the one barely distinguishable from Brad Pitt, who has his hand on her shoulder. ('Who? Josh? He's just a sweet personal trainer.') You know, however, that sweet isn't the right word for a man with sculpted pecs and calves like a racehorse. Enter jealousy, commit-ment's ugly sister.

Robert and Tariq

Robert and Tariq have been together for four years. They met at a gay pub one night, went home together and haven't been apart since. Tariq's parents moved from India when he was six years old. He isn't a practising Hindu and has even given up vegetarianism. When Rob introduced him to Trish, she took Rob aside and said, 'I raised you for this? So you could end up with a black man?'

'Would you prefer it if he were Jewish?' Rob responded.

'What? I have nothing against the Jews,' Trish said. 'I think Daniel is marvellous.'

But as Trish got to know Tariq (and his exceptional culinary skills), she grew to adore him. The guys live in an apartment they bought and renovated together. Rob is a history teacher at a girls' high school and Tariq is an architect.

Tariq's best friend is a guy called Steven. They were lovers a few years ago for a brief, disappointing two-week period. With sex out of the way, they found they really wanted to stay friends – they had a lot in common, and so much to talk about, given that Steve's also an architect. Robert's been fine about Tariq and Steve remaining friends – he's got friends too. Steve's a great guy. Tonight, they've invited Steve and another friend of theirs, Corey, for dinner at their place. Rob's cooking lamb, Jamie Oliver-style, and Tariq's making a salad and a raspberry white chocolate cheesecake for dessert. In the middle of preparations, Corey calls to say he's been dumped with an urgent deadline for tomorrow and won't make it over tonight; he's really sorry to cancel at such short notice.

'No worries, Corey, hope you make the deadline,' Tariq says. 'Take it easy, mate.' He looks over at Rob. 'Corey can't make it.'

Robert, peeling the garlic for the lamb basting, frowns. 'We need to invite someone else,' he says, an urgency in his voice. 'We've got all this food . . .'

'Leftovers,' Tariq says casually.

'No, seriously. We have to invite someone else. To round up the numbers.'

Tariq shrugs – it's already too late and anyone invited now is going to feel like they're a substitute for a no-show. Anyway, he's happy to have undiluted time with Steven – they haven't caught up in ages.

'Three's not a good number, T, it just doesn't work. We *need* a fourth person. How about Gavin?' Robert insists.

'Forget it. He's all brawn and no brain. Do you really want to spend the evening listening to football stats?' Tariq can't figure this out. They've entertained single guests on several occasions. Robert's being silly and annoying.

Rob turns away, confused and hurt. Why is Tariq making this such a big deal? They could call up his big sister Erin and have her over with Mitch – they haven't seen them since their housewarming party, and they won't mind the late invitation. He suggests this to Tariq.

Tariq shakes his head. 'Just drop it, Rob, you're being totally childish,' he says. 'I don't have time for this. I'm going to the bottle shop to get some Merlot.'

'I don't have a good feeling about it,' Robert persists.

'We often have only one person for dinner.'

'But not bloody Steven!' says Robert, surprising himself a little.

They both stop.

'What's wrong with Steve?' Tariq asks.

'Nothing, he's a top guy,' says Robert. He can't articulate it, but if Steve is the only guest tonight, Rob's going to feel left out.

'So then . . .?'

Robert fumbles. 'Well, how about I invite one of *my* ex-lovers? Like Joel?'

It's a low blow. Robert's ex-lover, Joel, tried to sabotage Rob and Tariq's relationship early on by sending Rob gifts and texting him relentlessly. Joel is also six-foot-four and a triathlete, while Tariq, at a sleek five-foot-six, has often expressed to Robert how hard it some- times felt to 'compete' in the gay community with Joel-types.

Tariq grimaces. 'You're being horrible and immature – you're really acting like a baby. I don't understand why you're trying to hurt me. Sometimes I just don't get you,' he says, before storming off to the bottle shop.

∾

We all know how it feels to be left out, and acting like a grown-up is difficult when we feel threatened. We sometimes regress into that little child who was excluded, especially if we didn't have great role models to help us introject a healthy and robust image of ourselves able to tolerate feelings of exclusion. In this moment, Tariq and Robert are far from the third position; each can only see the situation from his own point of view. Rob isn't even conscious of feeling threatened until way into the interaction. They've had Steven around several times before – and Rob has felt okay with it. The trigger, though, is that with Corey dropping out, this will be the first time he and Tariq will be alone with Steven. Rob is aware that Tariq and Steven have been lovers in the past, and have a close relationship now based on their common profession. He's scared that at dinner, Steve and Tariq will constitute 'the couple', and he'll feel marginalised. Having a fourth at the table won't only dilute things but, in Robert's unconscious mind, sets Steven up with a 'partner' for the night, thus making him less of a threat. Is he being petty and ridiculous? It doesn't matter. What does matter is how he's feeling and how he and Tariq manage it.

Tariq, on the other hand, is oblivious to how Rob's feeling. He's very sure of his and Rob's status as a couple and he's so not interested in Steven in *that way* anymore. He can't track Rob's logic or make sense of the urgency behind the request. He feels like he's being manipulated, and so reacts defensively. Then when Robert lets slip that it's because it's Steven, with the implications of Steven being a threat, Tariq really begins to act out Robert's exclusion script by telling him he's behaving like a baby. Tariq takes up a judgemental, critical parental voice, reinforcing the fantasy in Robert's mind of him being the abandoned child with Tariq and Steven as the adult couple.

By trying to restore his state of comfort and security with Tariq, Rob has only succeeded in experiencing even more distance and threat. On top of that, he now feels humiliated, making him angry with, and critical of, Tariq. He doesn't want to feel infantile and wrong. If he can relocate Tariq as being the 'bad', insensitive one, then he can take up the role of the unjustly victimised one. And so begins a fierce argument, one which still hangs in the air when Steven later walks through the door.

As a result, the lamb is overcooked and no-one has a good evening.

∽

What might things have looked like if either (or both) Tariq and Rob could have accessed any form of the third position?

When things become unstuck like this we can just breathe, so that we can become aware of what we're feeling. If we don't know how we're feeling, we can't expect others to. As babies we're entitled to expect our caregivers to interpret our needs – in a sense, to read our minds – but growing up means that we gradually take on this job for ourselves. We have to learn to regulate our own moods and contain our anxieties. It's the private inner work we have to do as we prepare for adult intimacy. If it's just a big emotional mess inside us, we'll make a mess outside. Most of us will need our partners to feel things on our behalf, but when we overload them they're going to throw that load back at us. So if Rob had been in tune with his own mind, he'd be able to know that he was anticipating feeling excluded by Steven coming for dinner on his own. That there would be in-jokes between Tariq and Steven that he couldn't share, and that there's a history between them that he only knows from what Tariq's told him. There may even be secrets between Tariq and Steven he'll never know.

Recognition leads to ownership – once Rob recognises his feelings, he can own them. He might decide to let Tariq know how he feels and say something like, 'Hey T, I'm feeling a bit spare. You and Steve, well, you know . . . you guys have a history. I know it's silly and that's all in the past and all that . . . but I want someone else here so I won't feel jealous and left out.' Tariq might have then found it easy to reassure the man he loves that there is absolutely no reason to feel threatened, and that he'll make an effort to ensure that he and Steve don't go off on tangents talking about things Robert isn't interested in.

And yes, it *is* bloody hard for most of us to process things this quickly. But if Rob had been able to notice the red flag of his anxiety, he might have pressed the pause button, taken time out, a few deep breaths, a gulp of wine, or gone for walk around the block. He could have sat with his feelings, reminding himself that they'd pass. Any form of meditation would have helped him to 'be with what is', and to notice, kindly and compassionately, that he's feeling vulnerable. He could have drawn on his knowledge that Tariq loves him and held these paradoxi- cal feelings at the same time – his jealousy together with the comfort of knowing he's loved.

Tariq, instead of getting distracted by Rob's 'unreasonable' insist- ence on another guest, could have summoned empathy for Rob's psychological state and just noted that he was upset. With some insight, he'd have noticed how things moved from Rob's conflicted *intrapsychic* state to the conflicted *interpersonal* state in which Rob's internalised feelings of exclusion are acted out between them. Tariq could have adopted the third position by being neither the critical parent (Rob's script) nor the unjustly put-upon partner (Tariq's script), by not acting out but rather being a container, a mind able to reflect on Rob's internal state while Rob can't do it. He could check the annoyance in himself, recognise that Rob's anxiety acts as a trigger for his own, and respond from another, more compassionate part of himself.

It's a big ask, and often even the most aware couples only manage it after the argument has erupted and at least run some of its course, but it's the kind of understanding that can stop things from spiralling out of control. All it would take from Tariq would be to hug Rob and tell him, 'I've been there and done that with Steve. He's no competition. It's you I love and want to be with.'

Buddhists would view Rob's jealousy as an expression of unhealthy attachment, and encourage the pursuit of non-attachment. But what does non-attachment mean and how does it fit with love, which involves such a big dose of emotional attachment to another person? It's impossible for any of us not to feel like our hearts have been crushed if someone we love leaves us or dies. When we adore someone, we want them in our lives. But our love can manifest as a desperate grasping of their presence, bubbling with possessiveness, jealousy and the terror of losing them (to another person or to death). If love becomes a form of emotional owner-ship, that's the 'attachment' Buddhism tells us causes suffering. But we can also love (or learn to love) freely and without conditions (including the condition of being loved in return or even of the other person being alive). When we love someone with an open hand, supportive of everything they are, our emotional bond with them is deepened, not weakened.

When lovers look elsewhere

Choosing to be in a monogamous intimate relationship with one person does not, unfortunately, eliminate our attraction to, or desire to have sex with, other people. We're all attracted to many people. Monogamous intimacy places pressure on us to (a) almost never speak of such things, and (b) certainly never act on them.

So we make-believe that our partner is the only – and most desir-able – person we want to be with or have sex with. It's easy to feel threatened or jealous when our partner looks at another person with the same desire we once saw in their eyes for us.

༄

'I'll have the soft-shell crab,' Mitch says.

The waitress smiles at him, and writes it down. She's tall and blonde and her cleavage is a phenomenon all on its own. A double D for sure.

Erin watches as Mitch's eyes flick over her shape. 'Yes, and I'll have grilled salmon,' Erin says tersely.

When the waitress leaves, Erin looks quizzically at Mitch.

'What?' he asks.

'Thought I saw you eyeing her breasts,' Erin says.

'Well, they were hard to miss,' Mitch says.

'So . . . what do you think? Is she hot?' Erin asks.

Mitch takes a long slug of his beer.

Of course Mitch thinks she's hot. She *is* hot. So what's Erin doing asking this question? Is it a trick question? Is she trying to back him into a corner? If he denies she's hot, Erin will know he's lying. If he says she's hot, Erin will feel hurt, because Mitch desires another woman other than her. He's fucked. And he knows it.

'Yes, I think she's hot,' Mitch says. But he knows Erin's feeling excluded and vulnerable and because he loves her, he wants to reassure her that though he's just a guy and he'd have to be blind not to think the waitress was hot, it doesn't mean he wants to have sex with her, so he follows it quickly with, 'but you're hotter.' He puts his hand on her knee and leans forward to kiss her lips, 'My beautiful Bean.'

The genesis of jealousy

Unless we've managed to resolve our childhood feelings of jealousy when we were excluded, or anxiety that we weren't good enough, they'll tag along with us into adulthood, stowaways in our consciousness where they'll continue to make us feel inferior, resentful or hateful of others who have what we want.

Envy and jealousy, the psychoanalysts will tell us, are not the same. Envy originates in infancy, when the baby is clueless about relationships that exclude her/him. It's pre-threesome (the loss inherent in triangular relationships). Envy happens between two people, when someone has something we covet: I envy your success, your figure, your intelligence. It's when a third person pitches up that jealousy makes its grand entrance, as it did when we were kids and Dad crashed the Mum & Me party or a new baby ushered in sibling rivalry. As grown-ups, this manifests as anxiety, suspicion, mistrust and worry about losing the love or affection we want from someone, which will then be given to someone else. The 'third' or 'other' becomes a rival and what we truly fear about this intruding Johnny-Come-Lately is that we'll be compared unfavourably and come off second-best.

In this case, Rob's afraid Tariq will see Steven as sexier, cleverer, wittier than him (and probably with a bigger cock or as a better lover). Erin sees Mitch admiring the hot waitress and needs validation of his exclusive desire of her in order to guard against the threatened loss of her own self-esteem.

Jealousy is a beanstalk. A seed can easily erupt into an obsession. It becomes obtrusive and stubborn, and won't let go of us. When we're jealous, we obstinately accuse our lover of having an affair, almost as if we want to be told, 'Yes, I have betrayed you.' Even if our lover denies this honestly, jealousy doesn't buy it. It persists, as if we'll only rest if our worst fears are confirmed. It's the only answer we'll trust to be the truth. Erin's question to Mitch is a test – she won't be satisfied with a denial. She wants him to say that yes, the waitress is hot. Because the truth is, she is. But even if Mitch did get a rush of blood to his nether regions, he won't act on it because he loves Erin. Jealousy doesn't let us parse our emotions out like this, it conflates our anxiety with an objective fact (the waitress's hotness) and allows only one conclusion: we'll be cheated on.

Jealousy can be tenaciously adhesive. It's often a shield, protecting something that will be felt to be even worse, like unresolved guilt, shame and aggression that are rooted in past wounds. It could be a projection of our own desire to be unfaithful, or our own feelings of inferiority. (*Surely I'm going to be unmasked for the fraud I am. I am unlovable, so how can he/she truly love me? She/he must surely prefer someone else.*) Erin's eyeing the waitress too, and she's the one comparing the waitress's body to her own. Mitch may be harmlessly enjoying the view.

So what happens if we find ourselves overly jealous and possessive, or wanting our partners to feel that way about us? That's kind of a problem for intimacy. If we're entangled in jealousy, not able to make a move without straining the tethers, we may have to go back a few spaces and do a bit of that inner work on ourselves to let it go. Relationships steeped in jealousy can be fatally attractive because of how a lover's possessiveness mimics passion. *He can't have me out of his sight. He doesn't like me to talk to any other man. He likes me to dress in a specific way. I have to let him know where I am at all times.* At first this kind of attention makes us feel special, but this is really one of those cases where what we feel and what's really going on doesn't match. It starts getting really creepy when partners question our whereabouts, go through our pockets when we're not looking, check our text messages or, most terrifyingly, declare that they can't live without us. That's not intimacy. It's obsessive attachment which has nothing to do with how special we are, but everything to do with how jealousy is being used to control us. To make things worse, jealousy often morphs into aggression. Turn the notch up on this behaviour just a fraction, and what you have is a full-on abusive relationship. No matter the circumstances, where there's brutality there can be no intimacy. When things get violent, it's time to locate the exit signs and run for our lives.

The blessings of jealousy

Shouldn't we deny our attraction to other people to spare our part-ner's feelings? Reassure them that they are the only ones in the world we're attracted to? Wouldn't that be the loving response to our partner's jealousy?

We could do that. But let's not kid ourselves. In reality, (a) it's a lie (we're all potentially attracted to other people), (b) by denying our attraction, we're repressing our non-monogamous energy and (c) it's patronising if we're doing this only to placate the fragile egos of partners who feel threatened. It's healthier to rethink the role of the 'third' or the 'other' in our intimate relationships and to try to find a creative way to bring it into our partnership.

Jealousy alone is not inherently destructive. In fact, it's essential for our psychological growth, teaching us to tolerate relationships that exist separately from us. Through the pain of working through jealousy, we must compare, bump up against others, feel excluded and navigate the transitions between connection and being on our own. All this leads to a differentiation of self and other; there is no other way for it to occur. Jealousy is a sign of a strongly felt love. Hey, it's *normal* and, if we manage it well, it's got a place in our relationships.

If we do something that makes our partner jealous, instead of shutting them up or belittling them, we can have compassion for their ego frailties (sheesh, we have enough of our own) and we can contain their jealousy instead of letting it spiral out of control. By seeing jealousy for the opportunity that it is, we can figure out a constructive way to manage it. We might adapt our behaviour to reassure them that while we want connections with people outside of our committed relationship, and we may even want the freedom to flirt with others, there's no big threat, and we have no intention of leaving them. But there are never any guarantees. We cannot give nor extract a monogamy warranty from each other — and that, too, is one of the terms of commitment: that within the bond that ties us together, there is also the freedom to leave. The real danger, if we continue being jealous, is that our partner will get the shits with us and things will break down to the point where they might actually want to walk out (talk about self-fulfilling prophecies). So the best we can do is to work on deepening what's between us, because that's the barometer of whether there's any real risk our lover might be unfaithful.

We can try to make sure jealousy keeps better company. When it hangs out with low self-esteem, projected fantasies and other rogues of the unconscious, it's dangerous. But when it hooks up with humour, a solid sense of self, imagination and feeling worthy of our partner's love and desire, it can be a lot of fun. There are a hundred uses of jealousy, and titillation is just one — *yeah, Mitch* (Erin might smile wickedly), *when we get home, fuck me like you'd like to fuck her*. If we can joke about the third person, use the idea of 'someone else' as flirtation between us, it gives licence to this form of playfulness. It paradoxically robs it of power. When it's not lurking in the shadows, it can't sabotage our relationship. In fact, the couples' therapist Esther Perel, author of *Mating in Captivity*, would say that invoking the strangeness of a 'third' into our own lovers reignites eroticism. If we imagine our lover enjoying the idea of someone else, and can be curious about what he/she's thinking or feeling, that's steamy territory for us to explore. And if we imagine someone else lusting after our partners, can view our partner through their fresh eyes, keeping us alert to their 'otherness', there's no telling how hot and horny things might get.

12.

Flatlining

PHOEBE CAN'T DECIDE: THE ITALIAN place around the corner (Tom's favourite) or Ubuntu, the new African restaurant in the city she's been dying to try since reading that glowing review. It's offering dishes from Morocco to Malawi, she'd read, including those from Ghana, where Phoebe was born to an Australian aid worker and her Ghanaian partner. Phoebe's parents took her to live in England when she was nine years old, but nine years in Accra was enough time to embed the tastes of Ghana, along with the echo of an African accent, on her tongue. Just thinking about *fufu*, the West African staple made of pounded yam and plantain, makes her salivate.

She wants somewhere special for their sixth anniversary. She's about to text Tom and ask him, but then maybe she should surprise him. Though he's not big on surprises. She chuckles as she sends the text. The only real surprise would be if she were pregnant. They're both still young – she's thirty-one and Tom's thirty-three, both in well-paid, high-pressured jobs, so hopefully they'll have paid off the mortgage on their terrace in a few years' time. She loves Tom and knows he loves her. He's respectful and the easiest company. She only has to think, *I'd love a cup of coffee*, and he'll appear holding one for her.

Phoebe is grateful that Tom's in her life. God knows she could have ended up like her friend Serena, who leaps from one relationship crisis to the next, and seems to be a magnet for impossible men. But then,

Phoebe supposes, having had an ardent feminist for a mother probably safeguarded her against Serena's fate. The thought of any man telling her what to wear, or not to talk to other men, never mind raising a hand to her, is ludicrous. Phoebe grew up reading black women's literature – Bessie Head, Toni Morrison, Maya Angelou. Books like Tsitsi Dangarembga's *Nervous Conditions*, about displacement and colonisation, eased the confusion of her mixed heritage during her years as a black-identified teenager living with a white mother in village Yorkshire. We're all human beings, after all. And in any case – she'd point out to the sea of white faces in her classroom – the fossil record proves that we're all African under the skin. That was part of what drew her to Tom – he didn't make an issue of her dark skin. Previous white lovers, oblivious to their reverse racism, had ooh-ed and aah-ed at the contrasting colour of their entwined limbs, as if they'd caught an exotic fish. She wasn't going to be a koi in anyone's pond.

Phoebe's phone beeps with an SMS: 'Happy to try African xoxo.' Bless him, but Phoebe knows Tom has no appetite for the hot spices and smoked fish of her birthplace. He prefers the garlic of Mama's Trattoria. Garlic breath: is that going to shut down the chance of post-dinner romance? It *is* their anniversary. Maybe with some wine, he'll be able to relax, they'll go home, he'll . . .

They've hardly had any sex for four years and none at all since that last time, eight months ago, on Tom's birthday when he couldn't get a hard-on. She'd held him and told him she loved him and it didn't matter. That she was sure he was right: it was just stress. That's when they booked the end-of-year trip to Hawaii. Perhaps it'll come right over there.

Phoebe looks over to the framed photo of her and Tom on their wedding day. She'd lost five kilos to fit into that wedding gown. Damn, she looked good. And the sex wasn't too bad in those early days – maybe it was even good. She'd been the one with more experience and a higher libido. Tom's sexual tastes were conservative, as if he was shy of his impulses, unable to really relax into them. He'd go down on her but she always felt as if he never really enjoyed it and was just doing it to please her, which kind of robbed her of the pleasure. What was clear was that he never liked her to give him head. At first, she found that weird. What guy doesn't love a blow job? Was it her technique? No man had ever complained before. And Tom wouldn't let her keep trying. 'I just don't like it. It's not you, it's me,' he soothed. Most of her girlfriends' complaints were that their husbands and boyfriends seemed to want endless blow jobs. Call *her* weird, but she *enjoyed* giving blow jobs. She used to love sex. A shiver of frustration runs through her.

What had gone wrong? In the early days, they'd both have satisfying orgasms. The frequency just dropped off after the first few months, becoming fortnightly, then monthly, then rarely. Didn't he want her anymore? In the early months of near-celibacy, she'd tentatively raise the topic, but he'd reassure her that he still found her desirable. He was just tired, stressed, had some health issue or another, or had to get up for work early in the morning. Over the years she had gradually put on weight, though Tom assured her she was still attractive even if she was a dress size larger. 'I love you just the way you are,' he'd always say. Darling man.

The discussions about sex were always tense. He'd turn away from her, stung by her simply raising the issue. And then her sexual urges withered from the lack of supply. She'd go through phases, often prompted by a man – at work, or a party – coming onto her. Of course, she'd brush them off. But she'd go home horny as hell, only to be stonewalled by Tom's unavailability. Eventually she went online and ordered a vibrator. It felt unfaithful to Tom, but her guilt gave way to frustration. Now she uses it when she needs some release. At least it never fails to get a hard-on. And she tries to forget that it's not images of Tom getting her wet, it's fantasies of one of her colleagues, Jake, an arrogant, dismissive prick, who knows just how to push her buttons. He's the absolute antithesis of Tom.

But maybe tonight she'll get lucky. Maybe Tom will make more of an effort. Phoebe calls the Italian place and reserves a table. She texts Tom back: '7.30 at Mama's. Happy anniversary, honey x.'

Tom smiles at his phone, relieved that he won't have to scour the menu for something he can eat. Phoebe understands him. He's a lucky guy. He's bought her a pamper package for an expensive beauty spa, which he knows she'll love. Seven-thirty is early. It means she's planning to get home before ten. She'll have had a few glasses of wine. She's going to take him by the hand and look at him with those deep, soulful eyes. She's going to say, 'It's our anniversary, let's celebrate.' Tom sighs.

He loves his wife. It's just that he doesn't get turned on by her like he used to. It has nothing to do with her; she's beautiful, really gorgeous. Don't you stop wanting it after a while? Isn't that what people say about marriage? Actually, he doesn't get horny much anymore at all, and when he does, a guilty one-minute wank to some pornographic images will relieve him.

He slumps in his chair, a cold, empty feeling in his belly.

∽

Ouch. What's going on here? Do Tom and Phoebe, with all their thoughtfulness and respect for each other, have a happy marriage? They *never* fight. Isn't that a sign of a successful relationship? They also *never* have sex. Does this mean they have an intimacy problem? If he loves her why can't Tom get it up for Phoebe? Can Phoebe have a satisfying long-term relationship with her vibrator? How can they work it out?

No fighting, no fucking
Couples that don't fight don't fuck.

Passion needs a bit of grit. In sex we grind, thrust, pull and scratch each other. It's what psychoanalyst Margaret Crastnopol calls 'the rub' — 'a constructive friction, of healthful pushing against' the other. *This* is what creates excitement, not only during intercourse but in all parts of a relationship. So to keep the thrill happening, we have to bump up against each other — and that's why making up can feel so intense, and the sex that follows can be so bloody glorious. Who of us hasn't manufactured fights, or pushed our partners to create conflict, so we can evoke a connection, come together, emotionally and sexually? But if we haven't learned how to fight, or don't have a healthy way of expressing our aggression, where does it go? Right down into the unconscious where it gets repressed or disowned. Right now, this is where Phoebe and Tom are.

To define ourselves, we need to feel both the support and love of our partners *as well as* resistance. Obstacles in our paths trigger aspects of our personalities vital to our growth as human beings. Tension, arguments and conflict enliven and circumscribe intimacy; and are not simply problems caused by faulty communication we need to stamp out like a fire. If harmony is the result of repression or denial of our inherent natures, we lose our selves, and the relationship becomes a kind of anti-love, an absence of real connection. For psychic growth and change we need the other as both vehicle *and* obstacle.

Phoebe and Tom are so busy pleasing and placating each other, they have polished any friction away. What's happened in the process is that they've lost a sense of differentiation of self. It's not only narcissistic, uncompromising and controlling people who are poorly differentiated. People-pleasers also have a slippery selfhood that runs through their fingers like water, always deferring to other people's opinions or ways of seeing things ('What do you think?' 'What would you like to do?' 'I don't mind, as long as you're happy'), people-pleasers have a hard time asserting, or even knowing, what they feel or think, and so allow others to decide for them. Between these two poles is a place of a healthy differentiation of self, where we are neither 'yes-men', nor obstructive for the sake of being oppositional, where we can hold onto a sense of ourselves while remaining connected to our partners.

What happened to Phoebe

Phoebe's mum, Alice, died when Phoebe was twenty-one. Alice was an engaging, lively feminist with an explosive temper. Phoebe's dad, Akwasi, would try to pre-empt fights by being compliant and agreeable, behaviour which often evoked Alice's scorn and sharp tongue. Occasionally, his compressed frustration would cause him to storm out of the house and disappear for a few hours. As a child, Phoebe cowered from her mother's rage, retreating to the arms of her father. Without siblings, she was exposed, with nowhere to hide.

In her teenage years, Phoebe started answering back. The arguments between mother and daughter became ever more vicious, from which each would retreat to her own bedroom, fuming. In the morning, Alice would be her chirpy, engaging self, as if nothing had happened, leaving

Phoebe feeling that she'd been trumped and shamed – why couldn't she be generous enough to 'forgive and forget' (her mother's favourite phrase)? Phoebe would withdraw into a helpless sulk for a day or two, straining for politeness in the face of her mother's ebullience.

When she was seventeen, her father left the house on one of his walk-outs and never came back. Akwasi waited for Phoebe outside the supermarket where she worked part-time, and explained that he could no longer take Alice's rages; he had tried to make things work in England but with Phoebe finishing school and now accepted into the London School of Economics, he was returning to Ghana, where he hoped to resume his position in the civil service. He sent money for her airfare and she visited him during her first university holidays, and then didn't see him for the two years her mother fought a losing battle against breast cancer. Alice's diagnosis evoked in Phoebe a guilt-ridden patience, which had her on the train for home whenever she was able, to nurse her dying mother.

Phoebe's family life left her with no experience of a space outside either the dramatic fight or the chirpy denial of the fight, no experience of angry conflict being resolved between two parties. The triangle of dynamics between Alice, Akwasi and Phoebe taught quite the opposite: that anger and hatred must exist in a separate place to love and affection. Phoebe could rely on her mother to comfort her in the face of perceived injustice – a bully at school, or a teacher who'd drawn red lines through an essay – but if she cried after grazing her knee, or after a fight with a friend, she was told to 'toughen up'. With her mother as the source of hurt and fear, it was to her father's gentle but emasculated arms she turned for solace. She was unable to introject a sense of love and conflict coexisting within the same relationship. Conflict had to be denied in order for love to exist. If there was conflict, there could be no love. She both loved and hated her mother, but it was as if she had two mothers, unable to bring them together. Finally she buried her internal conflict along with her mother's cancer-ravaged body.

What happened to Tom

Tom was born into a devout Catholic family, the youngest of three boys. For reasons the doctors were never able to explain, his mother's first three successful pregnancies were followed by miscarriage after miscarriage. His mother, ordered to bed by her doctors, would remain there, praying stoically, until the spotting on the white linen announced God's will for her foetus. Tom's parents lost eight pregnancies before Tom was five years old. The last of these was followed by a hysterectomy. This, too, was accepted by Tom's parents as God's will, and they got on with the business of raising their three boys.

Tom's father took his boys on camping and fishing trips. The family attended church regularly and the children each became altar boys in their turn. The church held picnics and ran soup kitchens and other charity drives. Tom's parents were friendly with Father Brian, the parish priest, and when he moved on, they befriended Father Danilo. Tom learned his respect through Biblical injunction: 'honour thy mother and father' and 'treat others as you would have them treat you'. No-one needed to 'turn the other cheek' because rarely did anyone in the family slap another – metaphorically or otherwise. The slightest hint of anger was immediately doused.

Tom's older brother Michael was the imp of the family, and because he made people laugh he was given some latitude. But even he knew not to swear or take the Lord's name in vain. Around the dinner table, Tom and his brothers came to know a relaxed, human side to their parish priests, especially Father Brian, whose Irish sense of humour would scandalise Tom's parents with quips like the one about Sinéad O'Connor who 'even the tide wouldn't have taken out'. The boys loved it when he came over.

It was a safe world in which to grow up, like soaking in a warm bath.

∽

Now that we know something of their histories, Tom and Phoebe's situation makes more sense. In Tom, Phoebe found a mate who would collude with her unconscious attempts to quash conflict from her relationships. They both repress disagreement and default into politeness until they feel companionable again. Their friends and family would describe them as a loving couple who treat each other with immaculate respect and care.

But beneath the surface both Phoebe and Tom are terrified that their anger might destroy the one they love. While Phoebe fought endlessly with her mother, Tom doesn't push the same buttons in her that Alice did. What he does is trigger an enactment that puts him in the role of Phoebe's gentle father, Akwasi. In this unconscious arrangement, there is a couple sheltering from persecution. In the past it was Phoebe and Akwasi, now it is Phoebe and Tom, and any hostile feelings that exist are projected outside themselves, into a third entity that acts as a kind of black hole, sucking up expressions of disappointment and anger.

As a couple, they literally don't know how to fight. And this has a spillover effect into their sex lives – they also can't make love. Tom's fear of his aggression, complicated by other aspects of his childhood experience, means he can't get the 'the hots' for Phoebe. Erections elude him; his potency is completely disarmed. Phoebe represses her frustration and anger for fear of losing Tom. If she confronts him, she's afraid he may collapse, counter-attack or leave her. She has no faith that confronting him will bring about a good result because she has no experience of positive, robust confrontation that ends well. The feelings of lust and romantic love they were able to muster in the early phase of their relationship have long since been extinguished, leaving emotional attachment as the sole survivor of the troika of urges that brought them together. Despite Phoebe's feminism and Tom's respect for her independence, they have been smothered by a dictatorial state of co-dependency.

When intimacy kills eroticism

'This marinara sauce is delicious. How's your fish?' asks Tom.

They're in a secluded corner of Mama's, a squat candle dripping its red wax through a gap in the crater formed at its top. 'Not bad,' says Phoebe, just managing to hold back the next words, which would have been, 'Pretty boring, actually. The fish at Ubuntu would make this pasta seem like it came out of a dehydrated packet.' She takes another sip of her wine.

Over the course of the evening, Phoebe drinks four glasses while Tom nurses one. They walk home, Tom's arm around Phoebe's shoulders, stabilising her walk. 'Thanks for the anniversary gift,' Phoebe says, and then giggles. 'My body could do with some pampering.'

'I thought you'd like it.' He smiles nervously.

Phoebe's words are a little slurred. 'Tom, my darling, you are *very* thoughtful.' She tugs the tail of his shirt out of his trousers and reaches her hand underneath, against his skin.

She's still holding him as they squeeze awkwardly through the front door. He reaches automatically for the light, pushing the door closed behind them. She's tugging the rest of his shirt out, and is pulling at his belt.

'Hey, the blinds are open, people will see!'

'I don't care,' she says. She has his trousers down now, her hand inside his underpants, her fingers working at his limp penis.

'Phoebe, wait!' Tom blurts out, his hand reaching to grasp her wrist. 'I can't, not like this. The lights, people . . .'

'Jesus, Tom!' Phoebe pulls away from him, losing her balance. 'Who gives a shit about people! What about *us*?'

But there is no 'us', not in the erotic sense, and all Tom can do is look at her blankly, drained of any explanation for the terror her desire evokes in him.

∽

Committed partnerships all face the challenge of keeping passion alive in the long-term. Monogamy is a relative newcomer on the human scene and we have to fight for its rewards in the face of our genetic inheritance. Two people may adore each other, feel loved, respected as equals, and have zero activity between the sheets. It's really not hard to understand why good marriages flounder and why fault has very little to do with it. It's got to do with a flaw we don't often talk about in marriage.

In her book *Mating in Captivity*, Esther Perel holds that the agendas of love and passion are often at loggerheads. Love brings security, respect and commitment, whereas passion invokes adventure, conflict, uncertainty, and sometimes even domination and power. To reignite the erotic imagination, she says, we have to enter the murky shadows of the erotic underworld.

Feminism has shifted the dynamics between heterosexual couples. These days the notion of women being subservient to men is mostly regarded as a preposterous hangover from patriarchal times. But Phoebe, like other emancipated women in respectful relationships, is starting to question whether her insistence on being treated as an 'equal' in the marriage is starving her of the ingredients for long-term erotic subsistence. The closer and more familiar Tom and Phoebe became with each other, the less they sizzled sexually. Being best room-mates is no great shakes when raunchiness putters into abiding fondness. Phoebe longs for the person who knows her better than anyone else to want her in that aching way we want someone we can't have. She doesn't want to watch her sexual relationship fizzle out in bed-death, only to become an erotic casualty of their familiarity and companionship.

Though Tom wouldn't think of taking an envelope out of her drawer without asking her permission, she doesn't want him to show the same consideration when it comes to cupping his hands around her breasts, prefacing it with a 'May I?' or 'Would you like to, um, ah, well, you know, have a little intimate relations tonight?' That question will squelch any carnal enthusiasm rather than fire it up. This is an intriguing conundrum. Why doesn't respect translate into the erotic?

Perel says it's because in love we merge with the other, and the erotic works through separation. We have to be able to see the 'stranger' in someone else for desire to take hold. It's one reason people have affairs – to keep the erotic charged in their lives. To be truly sexually alive, we have to be imaginary adulterers, to be seducing our partners as if they were strangers, to invoke their otherness, their inaccessibility.

The problem is that Phoebe can't get beyond thinking of Tom as the person who strokes her hand when she has a migraine or makes her a hot-water bottle when she has her period. She needs to see him as a passionate stranger who would grab her, push her up against the kitchen counter and talk the kind of dirty she's only ever heard voiced in porn (which she watched at university, purely as research for a feminist paper on the subject). And though the feminist in her might be fuming, bingo, baby. Those floodgates will open. There will be a monsoon.

Phoebe knows this is not how it should be. But feminist theory isn't helping her have marital orgasms. At times, she wonders whether Tom really is the right man for her. Maybe those guys who marvelled unabashedly at her dusky skin could more easily enter into the lustful heart of darkness. Having a man handle her roughly and speak to her like she's a sex object may be a function of her 'false consciousness', where her desire mirrors what patriarchy has taught her to desire – at least that's what feminism taught her. But Phoebe doesn't give a damn. Right now, she wants hot sex with her husband. And she's looking for clues, one of which is that the hottest sex they ever had was five years ago after a rare but nasty fight. When she liked him least.

When she masturbates with her vibrator, she fantasises about her colleague Jake, with his disdainful jawline and provocative quips. Though his cavalier masculinity almost repulses her, it also arouses her. When she was single, she would never have dated a guy like him, wanted to wake up next to him or even be his friend. But when she thinks about him thrusting into her, her nails digging into his back, she is so turned on it's embarrassing.

When Tom masturbates to images of women who call themselves 'sluts and whores' he is taken into a place of dark and uncharted desire, which makes him feel dirty and ashamed. He'd never hold hands with, or kiss, any of those women.

What Phoebe and Tom desire, if they could be honest with themselves, doesn't play by the rules of equality or political correctness. This excitement that comes from a secret place in the body has no language. It's a complex undisclosed sinew of myth, dream, fantasy, conditioning, upbringing, biology and mystery. What many of us imagine, in the sacred shadows of our erotic kingdoms, is irrational, inexplicable and a little scary. Women don't really want strangers to tie them up, call them names or make lewd comments about their body parts. In the safety of their marriages, though, they may desire experiences that would freak them out in real life. Without feeling safe enough to speak these truths, they'll continue to be repressed and tamed into the ever-after of erotically flatlining marriages.

Fabulous sex can be courteous and respectful. But in partnerships based on mutual respect, there has to be space for excitement and passion. When we can have gentle lovemaking with the same person who can take us to a differently dangerous edge, when we can have passion in the place we also come to for love, support and comfort, that's hot intimacy. Perhaps one of the unexpected gifts of feminism is that it's made us strong enough women and enlightened men to face these strange and disquieting forces that tremble in the darkest forests of desire.

In our everyday lives, we all want equality and respect. But behind a closed bedroom door, we also want to reserve our rights to a bedboard-slamming shag.

13.
Boredom and Boundaries

THOUGH NEITHER TOM NOR PHOEBE has crossed the line into the territory of an affair, both are looking elsewhere to satisfy sexual urges. They're both having imagined sex with others, whether it's getting off on porn or fantasies of a colleague. There's no conflict or edge to spark their relationship back into life. But it's not only boredom that can slowly euthanise a relationship. Too much aggression can ramp up a sense of hatred and/or danger that can overwhelm the boundaries of intimacy, killing eroticism. It's one thing to have a robust rub and another to rub each other out. Healthy threesomes are not the same as a toxic triangle.

∾

Steph is tired. She feels tired most days.

She's watching re-runs of *Friends* when Daniel walks in after work. She doesn't look up from the TV.

'Guess what happened to me today?' Daniel says, throwing his jacket over the couch. It slumps down into a creased pile.

Steph exhales impatiently. 'I'm too tired for children's guessing games. Just tell me.'

'Christ, Steph. I thought maybe you'd be interested since it's what puts a roof over our heads . . . never mind.'

'What about what happens under this roof of ours? You're not interested in my day, so what makes you think I should be interested in yours?'

Honestly, Daniel's nattering feels like more clutter for her to have to clear away.

'Bugger this, I'm going to take Shadow for a walk,' Daniel says, storming upstairs.

Steph channel surfs for a few minutes, but it's all ad breaks. Fucking washing powders. If she has to see another happy housewife singing the praises of another detergent . . . don't these people have lives? She sighs and switches the TV off. On her way through the kitchen to the back garden, she grabs a box of matches. At the far end where the washing line stands, she takes a cigarette from her pocket. She lights it and inhales deeply. She gets a small thrill at these transgressions, knowing how furious Daniel would be if he caught her.

The weeds are overgrown. She's been nagging Daniel to pull them out for the last three months. She sinks to her haunches and starts to pull them out one by one, puffing on her cigarette. She mustn't forget Justin has an assessment by yet another educational psychologist this week. Wow, another report to look forward to. More psychobabble. More ways of telling her that her son has 'issues'. Don't we all? She used to think of herself as such a can-do girl . . . but that was so long ago, when her life spread out in front of her like a blank canvas, and she imagined she'd get to choose how to fill it. Special moments. Adventures. Overseas travel. Making love in romantic hideaways.

Ha! Sex. One of the thorns between her and Daniel. She had boyfriends before he came along and none of them ever complained. And she's *not* a prude; Daniel just says that to be cruel. She couldn't climax with Nathan because he . . . well, he wasn't very experienced and she didn't want to hurt his feelings. Daniel used to turn her on. But now she's just bored. Tired of his hassling her, and fed up with feeling like she's letting him down. After Georgia was born she just stopped wanting sex. She figured the urge would come back, you know, when the kids got older and she had more energy. But instead of taking a vacation, it went missing in action. In the meantime, Daniel just kept putting the pressure on. Like anyone wants to be nagged into blow jobs. She knows he goes into the study late at night when he thinks she's asleep, probably to watch porn, and while part of her is disgusted by the thought of it, she's also relieved. At least he doesn't bring his erections to the bedroom.

In the past, Daniel joked a few times about 'having a threesome' but she knows it's no joke. All she'd have to do is give the green light and before you could say 'cheap whore', there'd be one in their bed. She doesn't know why it creeped her out so much when he suggested they use a dildo to 'spice things up'. She's used one before in private. But with him there, it would seem so sordid. He likes to watch her touch herself – he used to ask her to do that a lot in the early days. She would only do it if the lights were off, and she can't count how many times she's faked orgasm to get it all over with so she can go to sleep. There were times in their early sex life when Daniel would intimate the sorts of things that turn him on, and she remembers once he confessed he'd like to be dominated by her. She'd burst out laughing. 'Too much infor-mation,' she'd said. He got quiet after that. It was the last time they ever talked about fantasies.

It's not like she doesn't have erotic dreams, but somehow the reality of her sex life with Daniel doesn't do it for her anymore. He's just not the man she fell in love with. Or maybe he is, and *she's* the one who's changed. At the start, they seemed so destined for each other. They had a perfect wedding. Everyone said so. Nowadays, her mother thinks the sun bloody shines out of Daniel's arse. Once she saw what a great life he gave Steph and the kids, his faults all became invisible to her. Between Steph and Daniel, even the religious differences didn't get in the way – they agreed early on to raise the kids without religion, except for Easter eggs, Christmas trees and *matza* on Passover. So when did it become *this*? This endurance of each other. This talking past each other. This ongoing irritation and frustration, like an illness with a terrible prognosis. Daniel, the man she was so in love with, has become someone she can't stand. Shit, if it weren't for the kids . . .

Christ, maybe she should have married Alistair. He'd have made her so happy. She should have followed her mother's advice and waited for him to get back from LA instead of getting carried away by Daniel's self-centred charm. If she'd been waiting for him, maybe Alistair would have come back instead of staying there. She looks at her watch and wonders what time it is in California. And whether Alistair still wonders about her. Does he lie awake thinking he'd have been better off married to her instead of his wife, whatever her name is?

∞

Pretty sad, huh? For hope to desiccate into such antipathy. Plenty of marriages survive the stress test of raising a family, which for the woman includes bludgeoning sleep deprivation, unwelcome changes to her body, a wilting libido and a sacrifice of her working life and career if she's a stay-at-home mum. It's a full-frontal assault on romantic love, leaving gaping chasms in many relationships characterised by women who're just 'not in the mood' for sex, and men who are sex-starved.

Steph's lost all sense of herself as a woman of the world. She lashes out at Daniel without being able to see that when we hurt someone else, we also hurt ourselves. The conflict between them, instead of providing a frisson for eroticism, has become a diseased space of antipathy, devoid of kindness or compassion. Even though Steph and Daniel have a few extra curve balls – Justin has learning difficulties, Georgia's overweight – many couples have far worse to deal with and manage to stay connected to each other lovingly. The problem is that Steph isn't emotionally in her marriage anymore. She lives in the past (romanticising a previous relationship and the early days of marriage) or the future (how life might be if her circumstances were different). She keeps comparing now to then, when they first met. She's not unlike Tara, critical of every man she meets, except Steph is married to the guy she's judging. This is just one way in which she's struggling to be fully present in her relationship. The small-print terms of intimacy are like those of life: that we will have to love someone who is imperfect; love them and be loved incompletely and love them through the rapids of impermanence, where nothing stays the same. Marriage vows hint to this future: 'for richer, for poorer, in sickness and in health.' Our suffering germinates in this inability to accept that nothing stays the same. Beyond lust and romantic love, we confront the overwhelming questions of intimacy: Can I love you if you get cancer? Lose your hair/a leg/your teeth/your mobility/your job?

Become dependent? Incontinent? Morbidly obese? Senile? Intimacy forces us to ask ourselves: What is it I am loving? Can I only love what is pleasing and beautiful?

Steph is struggling to cope with loss – the loss of her romantic ideal, her working life, and her image of a perfect family. She wants things to be different (actually, for Daniel to be different). Why should *she* change? Her relationship has become a scapegoat, a living metaphor for everything she feels she's been denied or has lost out on. Who cares what's going on for Daniel?

And this is the crux of it. The tendrils of connection between them have snapped. She doesn't give a shit about him anymore.

∞

Daniel closes the study door. It's 11.43 pm.

He logs into his private account and clicks into his favourite chat-room. Even as he's doing it, he's filled with self-loathing. He can almost hear his mother say, 'Is this any way for a nice Jewish boy to behave?' He knows his parents would be proud of his career achievements, but wouldn't be so quick to boast about the state of his marriage. Would it have been any better if he'd married a Jewish woman? He'd never been attracted to them. They seemed to expect too much from him. He hasn't been inside a synagogue since his bar mitzvah. The whole religion thing gives him the creeps. He doesn't believe in God ('Who could, after the Holocaust?' his mother always used to say). He wanted to run as far away from his roots as he could. His parents' dying freed him. He threw everything of his history away when he married Steph. There's such a gaping emptiness inside him, and right now all he wants is to fill it with – something. Shantelle will do.

He hangs around inside the chatroom for half an hour, hoping that Shantelle will be online. Last time they connected was the best orgasm he'd had in a long time. She spoke all the dirty stuff he wishes Steph would say to him. After he'd climaxed and she had too (or so she said), he'd ended with, 'Elope with me.' She'd responded, 'Ha ha, I wish. Don't think my hubbie would let me. But meet you again here? Xx.'

Daniel keeps looking for Shantelle. He wonders who she is in real life, and whether her husband feels as hollow and frustrated with her in bed as he feels with Steph. He can't find Shantelle tonight. If he met her in person, would she sleep with him? It's not just the raunchiness he craves, but to be held, touched all over, kissed in all his aching places. He's not proud of what he's doing. It's just that a guy can take being fobbed off so many times before something's got to give. He just wants to be desired by a woman. It'd be enough to simply *know* he can have sex with someone. Someone who really wants him.

Are we from different planets or just sexually immature?

Could it be that men are arseholes and Daniel is just one of them? If he really loved Steph, would he be trawling chatrooms? Should we blacklist him and award her the medal for the best victim? Maybe he's gone about things in a reckless way, but is it true that he doesn't crave intimacy? Everything he's doing – from the way he approaches Steph, reaches for her (ineptly, admittedly), and then sinks into his aloneness online – is a howl for love. Of course his approach is unskilful and damning his cause. Contemporary researchers such as Bettina Arndt have shown that in modern times, men like Daniel, who are on survival rations in their relationships, are deeply dependent and will put up with little or no sex and intimacy to avoid losing their families, and because they know there's nothing much better waiting for them 'out there'. Daniel's been forced into the habit of begging for sex, and bracing himself for endless rejections from Steph, which have bludgeoned his self-esteem and wilted his sense of masculinity. And what about Steph? Is she just the poor casualty of Daniel's libido? Has she really lost hers? Is her pettiness, bitchiness and nagging justified?

Maybe Daniel and Steph's situation leads to the inevitable conclusion that men and women are fundamentally estranged – men are hornier and want more sex than women do and women want more cuddles, talking and emotional intimacy than men. For a long time, Daniel and Steph embodied a common dynamic: she needed to feel connected to him before she could feel sexual (foreplay begins in the morning with him unpacking the dishwasher), and he needed sex to feel close to her. Maybe the sexes, like stripes and spots, are simply profoundly mismatched.

We certainly can't deny gender differences. But stereotyping the sexes can also be a lazy form of understanding, contracting and flattening complexity as a way of explaining relationship anxiety. The question is, does intimacy apartheid expand or limit our ability to connect through the testosterone-oestrogen jungle? We know men want intimacy, and women want sex. How we express it, and fumble our way there, will probably be different and we should be vigilant to those gender dissimilarities. But they're not gospel. As culture and history evolve, so too does human sexuality. And within each of us, these differences change over time: young men generally chase sex first, intimacy later. But the older men get, the closer their desire for a balance of sex and intimacy comes to resemble their female partners. Gay, bisexual and all other non-heterosexual relationships seem to suffer from the same sorts of difficulties as heterosexual ones. So focusing only on biological differences doesn't really take us very far.

And really, the us/them scenario is an old script. These days women are getting better at stating what they want in bed ('not too much of that/a little more of this') and men are befriending their own pink bits. Thanks to Dr Kinsey, Shere Hite, Eve Ensler and other sexual crusaders, we know that everyone's on-button is mysteriously located. You may like girls who look like boys, while I go crazy for big breasts. Some hanker for whips and chains, others would call the cops. Some want to go down, some from behind. I may get into a veritable froth over suspenders; you may get worked up by wearing nappies. It's not as if we have to sign a turn-on treaty that binds us for life. Our libidos and sexualities change as we grow. Some of us spend half our adult lives heterosexually inclined, and the rest homosexually. Our sexual identities are unique, just like our fingerprints. Most of us don't have enough erotic experience or maturity to truly know the landscapes of our internal desires, until we've been with ourselves – and another person – long enough to go there. In our relationship we get to explore our own sexual territory, together with our emotional one.

But of course we need to feel safe enough in a relationship to go there. We all take sex very personally because it's so inherently tied up with our identities. Rejection, poor performance, failure to please, being too quick or too slow all take on a whole new level of sensitivity when it comes to shagging. Never mind how desire is so often overlaid with shame and guilt, given the histrionic erotophobic messages of Western culture and Judeo-Christian religions. Are we frigid if we only like sex one way? Are we perverts if we like it any other way, involving objects, outfits and video cameras? Will we go blind if we masturbate? Does it mean we're gay if we want same-sex sex? So instead of talking about our desires and fantasies, we suppress them. Who wants to be laughed at, rejected or told we're 'sick'?

Daniel did try – remember? He voiced his fantasy about being dominated. And Steph laughed – probably because she was nervous. But without realising it or intending to, she shut him down and closed off that avenue of discovery between them.

Part of the problem is that sex is such a big player in the early phases of lust and romantic love, and gets shoved to the back of the freezer as a relationship goes through its first adult cycle of emotional connection. When this happens, we think it's gone, never to return, instead of realising it's just on sabbatical. We could do with some Post-its around the marital bed during this time, reminding us to 'HOLD ON'. Holding on through this drought and staying with what's difficult or unpleasant in our sexual and emotional relationships is what brings us into a new season of intimacy. Even when our sexual lives seem to match the 'Mars-Venus' stereotype, things do change, and other dynamics become possible: the older women get, the more sexually free they become; the older men get, the more intimacy they seek. What's so exciting is that as we mature, as we stay with each other through the gritty times, finding ways to accommodate each other's different desires, the potential for us to become more and more compatible, both sexually and emotionally, grows.

When a kid comes along, a woman's libido will often putter into slow motion, if not stall altogether – and that's healthy for the child-mother bond. And yep, that displacement of the man (or partner in a same-sex couple) as the object of affection – that's going to happen too. It's a natural ebb in the tide of intimacy. But here's where a man really gets to prove his heroism and emotional largesse – by the way in which he negotiates this displacement. He's got to figure out how to be in a healthy threesome, to learn to feel excluded and separate, while remaining emotionally connected. Sulking, withdrawing or getting angry are human, ego-based responses. A third-position response might be to feel the rejection, and at the same time to hold on to the whole picture of the relationship – which includes the new baby. The rejection is only a small part of what's happening. But it doesn't mean that the couple has become sexually incompatible.

In his book *Passionate Marriage*, Dr David Schnarch says that most sex is 'leftovers'. Sexual compatibility is not finding someone who wants to do what you want to do and doesn't want to do what you don't want to do. Each of us wants different things, sexually, and compatibility is about accommodating someone else's sexual preferences.

So how can couples remain emotionally connected through this sexual starvation diet? We can always express our frustrations to each other lovingly: 'I'm longing to have time alone with you. Do you know how much you turn me on?' To talk dirty. To talk intimacy. To touch each other – with hugs, strokes, foot rubs – to remain connected physically and psychically to each other.

Because Daniel has struggled to negotiate this displacement, he's acting out and seeking other outlets for his sexual needs. It's easy to think of him as the villain since he's the person acting out. But acting out is a response to a particular emotional dynamic, and in the context of what goes on between *two* people. What's happening between Steph and Daniel has as much to do with Steph as it has to do with Daniel.

෴

With Shantelle unavailable, Daniel clicks onto some porn and comes quickly. He shuts down the computer, wretched with a nameless feeling, and starts the long climb up the stairwell to bed. On the landing, Georgia is standing sucking her thumb like she did when she was a little girl and holding one of her stuffed teddy bears.

'You okay, sweetheart?' Daniel says.

'I had a horrible dream,' she says, her eyes wet and bright.

Daniel leads her back to her bed where he tucks her in. He lies down on the floor next to her bed, holding her hand in his, until his entire left arm goes numb.

Addiction: what's love got to do with it?

Can we blame Daniel for going online to find Shantelle or look at porn? Online pornography and dating sites can bring relief and pleasure. Occasionally, these sites may even lead to love and intimacy. Right now, they're all that give Daniel any sexual release – but there's a cost. While Daniel is looking at his computer, his brain is reinforcing the association of porn images with sexual reward, and he's being dosed with dopamine, the neurotransmitter that gives pleasure. The danger with dopamine is that it also acts as a kind of adhesive, securing neuronal pathways around the behaviours or thoughts involved in its release, which is why sex is so addictive. This is fabulous for couples when it's gluing their relationship together. But Daniel's growing addiction to trawling chatrooms for virtual sex, while a symptom of his unhappiness in his relationship, is at the same time silently eating away at the heart of his relationship. It has become a bad habit. And all of us who have them – whether nail-biting, overeating, smoking, drinking, gambling – know what a bitch they are to break.

The neurological activity involved in a habitual pattern literally colonises brain real estate – the habits take over what neurologists call 'brain maps'. Every time a 'bad' habit is repeated, it gains more control of the brain map, taking over space that is no longer available for a 'good' habit. Once established, bad habits are tough to break. It's as if the habit obeys the rule of 'occupation is nine-tenths of the law', making it much more difficult to unseat than it is to learn in the first place.

If Daniel continues to be excited by this risky activity, it's possible his attraction to Steph will change, that she may no longer excite him. Like termites, his addiction could erode their intimacy and the possibility of its repair.

◌◌

How do we know if we're addicted to porn or just using it to enhance our sexual relationship? We're porn-dependent if we can't get turned on by our partners without porn, or we imagine having sex with porn stars while we're actually having sex with our own partners. As we orgasm, the spurt of dopamine reinforces the link. Our sexual pleasure then comes from imagining humping the porn star, not from making love to the person in our bed. (And how many of us can compete with a porn star?) Our addicted brains are being changed in the process so that we forge neural pathways that associate these images and activities with pleasure. Fabulous for a couple consensually doing it together and both enjoying it, but what if one is and the other is not?

We also develop an addictive tolerance over time, which means we need ever-increasing levels of stimulation. To be competitive, porn sites continue to push the limits of titillation. If hot chicks masturbating did it for you last week, this week you're going to need teen lesbians having an orgy, and the next week, something more. Antonio has developed this kind of conditioning when it comes to real women, because for him, 'No matter how hot the babe, someone is growing tired of fucking her.' We need something stronger. The drug isn't working for us any longer. So we advance from sexual marijuana to cocaine.

Looking for porn to satisfy our sexual hunger is a search for an exciting 'other' when what's going on in our own relationship has become stale. We only get bored with what's static. Sometimes a relationship that's stuck needs a third element to invite a new dynamic into the twosome. Some sex therapists recommend that couples fantasise about an ideal lover, imaginatively invoking that third presence. Though this might help bring about orgasm, it creates distance because it's the image of the fantasy lover that's building our new brain map, rather than the partner in our bed. This takes us away from an intimate space, not towards it, and is like using our partner's body as an extension of our own hand or vibrator – just a vehicle for sexual release. The 'third' can be healthy or unhealthy for intimacy. Only we know if it's bringing us closer or pushing us further apart.

When it comes to using porn or fantasies of ideal lovers, we need to ask: Is it enhancing or eroding my intimacy with my partner? Does real sex excite me or only the fantasies imagined? If we can't be with the one we love mindfully and wholeheartedly because we're imagining shagging the one we can't have, we're not present.

Dr Ian Kerner, author of *She Comes First* and *Passionista*, suggests there are plenty of ways we can reignite the joy of naughty sex and find pleasure in our partners, including recounting sexy dreams to each other, having sex or arousing each other in public places like a restaurant or taxi where you may be seen by others (without getting arrested, although that might add an interesting option of sex in a police cell), using sex toys, filming yourselves having sex, role-playing and planning a threesome but not necessarily having one. This is inviting a 'third' into the bed but as a shared activity that can provide a shared excitement, a means of sustaining excitement as part of intimacy.

There's nothing inherently problematic about sexual objectification in the context of a loving connected partnership. Playing with objectification in fantasies can be fun if both people are playing the same game, but not if I am in bed with you and you are in bed with Jennifer Lopez. Finding that place together is what contracts the distance pornography can create.

Being present and the wisdom of wabi-sabi

Neither Daniel nor Stephanie is present in their relationship. She's already leaving him and he's looking elsewhere for sex. Both are starving – him for sex and intimacy, and she for a different kind of life. They're each accumulating grievances against the other, locked in the past. Without them knowing what's going on inside them, they'll continue to flail around, whacking each other in a continuing cycle of attack and counter-attack, laying waste to their intimacy.

Infidelity, secrets and lies spawn in these absences between people. We can only stray from a relationship we're not really in. We can't be fully in one relationship and dabble in another. Some part of us will have to escape in order to manage the deception.

೦ᴏ

Daniel slides into bed. Steph has pulled the covers up over her, her back towards him. He can smell her on the sheets, the distinctive odour of her Steph-smell, a combination of her perspiration, her shampoo, her perfume, and that indefinable sweetness that so intoxicated him when they first met. Something wells up inside him, and he lifts his hand to reach out and touch her, maybe stroke her hair. He wandered into a Tantric sex site the other night and spent hours reading about something called sacred touch – to touch someone as if they were the most sacred thing on earth. Something in him is desperate to know what that might feel like.

But he stops, retreats.

He rolls over on his side, and there they lie, unspooned, marooned from one another. He closes his eyes and is surprised to feel a tear trawl its way down his cheek before he sets the alarm for 6.00 am.

Steph is awake. Her head is full. She hears Daniel coming up the stairs and pulls the covers over her shoulder. She senses him slide into bed beside her. She tries not to move. She feels him coming closer and she holds her breath. She hears him sigh and roll over. And she lies there, her eyes wide open in the darkness, thinking, 'I mustn't forget we're out of mayonnaise.'

The choices we make moment by moment set a world in motion. A world of connection or a world of distance.

PART IV

Love Triangles

14.

The Toxic Triangle

INTIMACY NEEDS RESISTANCE. SEXUAL ENERGY can't spark off cotton wool and cushions, as Tom and Phoebe have discovered. By contrast, Steph and Daniel have too much friction, making their feudal system as untenable as Phoebe and Tom's fuckless one. For years now, their sex has been laced with aggression, withheld punitively and devoid of intimacy, finally withering to nothing over the last year.

If we're not getting creative conflict and tension in our relationship, driven by desperation, excitement or anger, we may look for it off site.

Under the spotlights, in the dark
His left calf is tight. Mitch slows down. He hasn't exercised in almost a week, having missed the weekend game so that he could take Erin to a show she didn't want to miss. But he's ridden much further than his usual twenty-kilometre loop. That bottle of water he drank before he started has made it to his bladder and he needs to take a leak. He's not that familiar with this suburb, but he knows there's a park a little way up, tucked in a backstreet.

He turns a corner towards the park, entering at a sidegate. He rides around its perimeter looking for the toilets, but slows down as he sees a single BMW convertible, parked in the small parking lot. Looks exactly like Daniel's new car, the one he took Mitch for a ride in last

Sunday. Roof down, Daniel had opened up way beyond the speed limit. 'I guess when you do this in your fire truck, it's legal,' Daniel had said, his mouth stretched in a solicitous grin. 'Must take some of the fun out of it. But then, you've got the fire to look forward to.'

Daniel's comment had brought back Erin's first words to Mitch. 'What do you drive?' He'd instantly but wrongly summed up his chances with the gorgeous stranger as nil. All he could muster was a self-deprecating, apologetic, 'A fire-engine.'

As it turned out, he'd said just the right thing. Go figure.

By then, Mitch had long given up on a high-earning career. He wasn't ever going to own a Porsche like his friend Sam. How long, he wonders, will Erin continue to be charmed by his fireman's salary? And when they have children, still living in an apartment while their friends put in swimming pools and extend their homes and go on overseas holidays . . . not that Erin's a princess or anything, but how will he meet her expectations for the future?

Hang on, that *is* Daniel's car. The personalised plate is visible: DMAN1, as if there's a fleet of DMEN at home. Maybe Daniel came out for a ride on his bike, but he wouldn't have driven in the BMW – no bike rack on that baby. Maybe he's brought his dog out for a run even though the signs clearly say 'NO DOGS'. Daniel doesn't give a shit about rules he hasn't made himself.

The pull in his calf is niggling him. He stops alongside the BMW and hops off his bike, leaning into a stretch beneath an oak tree. The place is deserted in a way that makes you feel weird stuff could go unnoticed. It's dark now, but the park is illuminated by occasional spotlights. All of a sudden a man and a woman pass beneath one. Mitch shrinks back into the shadow of the oak as he recognises Daniel. He's caught in the protection of the tree, wondering why he's hiding. It's Daniel. Why not say hello? It's because Mitch doesn't recognise the woman Daniel's with. And Daniel has his hand firmly in the small of her back.

Daniel's walking towards his car, a path that will bring him and the woman right up close to Mitch. Beneath the next spotlight Mitch can see Daniel's companion more clearly. She looks young, fresh-faced. Her hair is platinum blonde and she's in stilettos and a purple body-hugging dress. Mitch sidles around the oak's large circumference, dead leaves crunching underfoot. Daniel is talking in hushed tones to the woman, leaning in towards her. Mitch can't make out what he's saying, but it looks . . . intimate? All he catches is her name, Shantelle, and her tinkly laughter, which makes Mitch feel as if his body is crawling with lice. His chest feels tight. It's like he's ten years old again, tip-toeing around a creepy cellar in a game of hide-and-seek. He hears the beep of the car's alarm being deactivated, sees the glow of the tail lights bathing the grass orange to either side of the oak.

Daniel's voice drifts around from the other side of the tree. 'This is the chariot,' he says. 'Turbocharged. Lots of thrust. Hop in.'

Daniel and the woman get into the car. Mitch swallows, unsure of what he's just seen. *It's probably his cousin or his niece*, he thinks. *I should go.* He edges his bicycle further into the embrace of the thick trees, and climbs back on. He's about to leave but turns once more to look at the car where, even in the crepuscular darkness, he can see the woman's head has disappeared from view. If it's Daniel's cousin, Mitch is sure that what's going on in the car is illegal and the family ain't gonna like it.

He rides home as fast as his legs will go, almost wetting his riding shorts. He never did get a chance to take that leak.

∾

There are some secrets we'd rather not be privy to. Secrets that scorch us and, if let out, can rip through the space around us, leaving a changed landscape. Mitch is not the sort of bloke to meddle in other people's affairs. He saves people from fires, he doesn't set the bloody fire. But he knows that whatever he saw is going to hurt Erin, and that does matter to Mitch. Erin has always regarded Steph as the big sister she never had. Erin's even closer to Steph's mother Jenny. This thing could blow that family out of the water.

Mostly, Mitch is furious with Daniel. His fists curl and uncurl – Jesus, if Daniel were in front of him . . . But he's not even sure what he witnessed. Maybe he's got it all wrong. Ah, that's crap, he knows what he saw. Daniel was picking Shantelle up. Was she a prostitute? But *Daniel*? Shit, who'd have guessed? The guy plays such a good role as husband-of-the-year and devoted father. He wonders what Jenny would think of her perfect son-in-law now.

Should he tell Erin? That would be like knifing her in the chest. What's the right thing to do here? If he shuts up about Steph getting done behind her back, that makes him complicit. An accomplice – and to what? Adultery? What if Daniel picks up a sexually transmitted infection and passes it onto Steph? Steph has a *right* to know. Maybe Mitch should confront Daniel? But what the hell would he say? 'Saw you in the park the other night. You go there often?' All he knows is how to talk shit about football and politics with Daniel over a few drinks. And the guy always puts himself above Mitch, being ten years older, with the big house, the big bucks and living in some financially engorged egosphere blokes like Mitch won't ever reach – partly by choice, which isn't how Daniel sees it. Mitch wouldn't know how to have that conversation. His own father was spare with his words, and when he wasn't, it was about sport or how the supermarkets were squeezing his margins so tightly he'd soon be giving them free bread. What's Daniel going to say anyway – *you must have me confused with your mate Antonio?*

Mitch needs advice, and the person he's always gone to is his level-headed, wise, faithfully married friend Tom.

∞

In Daniel's mind, his behaviour is justified. He's not getting any sex at home. And as long as he's careful (he brought condoms – he's not an idiot, okay?) and no-one finds out, he's not hurting anyone, right? Steph isn't interested in him. She's bloody glacial and he tells her as much. If his words hurt her, good – she needs to hear some truths.

In the beginning her aloofness turned him on – he loved the sense of hunting her, of finally owning her, having her melt beneath him. Now her coldness just shuts him out. The more she doesn't give him access, the more he becomes paranoid that she's getting it elsewhere. He's found himself saying a few times: 'Why am I the only man at the party who thinks he's not going to shag you tonight?' Fuck her. She undermines all his feelings of being a normal sexual being.

Steph, on the other hand, finds Daniel predatory – and the way he pushes her into satisfying his needs leaves her feeling violated and depleted. He warps her reality. (Is she really frigid? Did she never enjoy sex?) It's a subtle sado-masochistic dynamic of small but potent cruelties. Each is in pain and can't own it; they deal with it by projecting it into or onto (blaming) the other. They both lack the capacity to think about what they're doing, and to figure out a way of working through their problems creatively. Because of this, they're on a path of relationship implosion.

But catch either of them alone, in the quiet of their thoughts, and they'll both tell you separately: it wasn't always like this. In the early days they knew their libidos weren't a perfect match. He wanted sex daily – even twice a day if he could work it. Once or twice a week was enough for Steph. For a while, he used to say, and believe, that 'it's not the sex, it's you not wanting to have it with me'. They were like opposite poles of a magnet at first. She was awed by his audacious spirit. His impulsiveness and carefree approach to life was in such contrast to her straight-laced upbringing. It was like nothing she'd ever known before. He thrilled at her seriousness; her conservativeness he could destroy by having her moaning under him, as if he'd just banged a nun or the headmistress. She had the air of the head prefect at school, and he loved nothing more than to see her come undone.

After the kids arrived, Steph regressed into the more established parts of herself – the controlled, withdrawn tidier-of-mess. He still expected to have sex on holiday in a hotel room with babies in it. 'What's wrong with you?' she rebuffed, calling him a 'special needs teenager'. She became less impressed by him, lost her sense of competence as a career woman and told Daniel she needed him to 'act like a man' and become a responsible husband and father. The more she withdrew into her natural conservatism, the more he sank into what comes naturally to him: his impulsivity; acting and speaking without thinking.

Steph the mother just can't let go in the way that Steph the young lover could. Daniel is mindless and disorganised, so to recognise his wild success would be to acknowledge it's in no small part due to his taking risks; all she sees are the risks inherent in his impulsivity, and that he might lose it all in an instant – the beautiful home, the money in the bank, the children's education fund. She's right, he might. But she's not been blameless in this. Her need to control him has contributed to his recklessness and his recklessness has fuelled her need to control him.

If Steph understood how she was shaped, she'd be able to see how and why she's become this woman she doesn't want to be.

What happened to Steph

Steph's parents were young when they got married. Her dad, Mike, was a plumber, a loud and funny guy who was considered the life of the party. Her mum Jenny went to university and became a pharmacist. For this reason, Mike believed that she always thought she was 'too good for him', and this enraged him. Jenny was bewildered by Mike's sense of inferiority, but had no time for it. With Jenny 'on her high horse', as Mike always put it – whether it was her going off to her book club, or wanting to watch a documentary on new advances in the sciences or Stephen Hawking – Mike turned to Steph for emotional support, manipulating her into taking sides. He staked his 'right' to Steph's emotional support, and even when she was a teenager, he'd barge into her room and the bathroom when she was in there, and when she'd exclaim, 'Dad, do you mind?', he'd say 'For goodness sake, stop being so uptight, I'm your father!', making her feel as if there was something wrong with her for wanting her privacy. Often, he'd come into her room and spill his heart out to her, including his problems with Jenny, who was 'up herself', unlike Steph, who was the 'only one who understood him'. This was supposed to make Steph feel special and that was their story, that they had a 'special connection'. Mike would take Steph to the races instead of Jenny, or to watch football, and when she didn't want to go with him, he'd say things like, 'getting too good for your old man, huh? Just like your mum,' and manipulate her into coming with him.

Steph felt more like Mike's partner than his daughter, angry at her mother for lumping her with this role. She became overly vigilant of her own boundaries, rigid to keep out loose forays, to the extent that she could no longer be spontaneous or playful. She has learned to protect the space inside her, feeling that if she lets any man into that space, he will plunder and violate it.

Rolling through all things

We all have our secrets. So maybe if no-one finds out, there's nothing wrong with what Daniel is doing behind Steph's back? How's he hurting her, if she doesn't know?

Of course we all have private spaces that keep us differentiated and whole. But what Daniel is doing strays beyond the boundaries of self-nurturance because it's ultimately destroying the intimacy in his marriage. While he's cruising and straying, he's creating unbridgeable gaps between him and Steph, laced not only with sexual cheating but deceit, often harder to come back from than the infidelity itself.

Daniel's justification is built on the old notion that each of us is a discrete and separate entity, insulated from others around us. Even if Mitch hadn't seen him, Daniel's actions do have consequences, not only for his marriage, but for everyone he is connected to.

Quantum physics has exploded the illusion that we're all separate beings. The universe is a field of vibrating energy and each of us is just part of that vibration, to a denser or more rarified degree. The molecules of which we're all made are in constant motion. The realisation that we're all interconnected is simultaneously a wonderful and terrifying thought. The consciousness that threads us all together is what Jung called the collective unconscious. It's the warehouse of all the experiences of humankind into which we can tap at an energetic level. It's similar to the Hindu concept of the Akashic record, the reservoir of all human experience. In some tribal cultures, it's called ancestral memory. In Buddhism, it's known as Indra's Net. No matter how we choose to frame it or understand it, there is an invisible artery that connects all human beings in a spiritual internet. In chaos theory, the butterfly effect (the notion that the flapping of a butterfly's wings can cause a hurricane on the other side of the world) shows that small change can result in large differences despite physical distance. Whether we choose to call it the domino effect, or *chi sem,* the Dalai Lama's Tibetan word for universal consciousness, or the 'over soul', as Ralph Waldo Emerson called it, what each of us does affects everyone around us at an invisible level. The results may be manifest or unseen. One divorce or suicide in a community often sparks others. When people we know lose a foothold in their relationship, we bring questions back into our own relationships. Joseph Campbell says that when people hear a story, they see themselves in that story; they say, 'That is my story.'

Daniel's about to find out just how connected he is to everyone who knows him and how his dalliance with Shantelle will rip through his community like a bushfire, hurting more than just Stephanie and his kids. Our stories are strung together with others. We're co-authors not only of our own destinies, but of those around us through which ours are threaded.

15.
The Spillover

DANIEL'S NOT THE ONLY ONE keeping a secret. Mitch, the unwitting bystander, is keeping it too. Daniel has, without intending to, hooked Mitch into his deception.

What happens when our secrets spill over into other people's lives? And what do we do if we stumble into someone else's secret? How does someone close to us having intimacy issues affect our own relationship?

Boundaries and secrets

After seeing Daniel with 'that woman' in the park that evening, Mitch's response, initially one of shock, settles into anger. But honestly? There's a word for what he feels – *schadenfreude*. Daniel's treated him like a kid ever since Mitch came on the scene, puffed up with big talk about his business and investments. Mitch has kept quietly envious of Daniel's place as the golden boy of Erin and Steph's family, with both Erin's mum and Steph's parents fawning over Daniel. He's not gloating, but there's something satisfying about seeing Daniel come apart, imperfect.

Over the next few days, Mitch freaks out quietly. What he's seen burdens him, and implicates his own honesty in his relationship with Erin. Not one for gossip, Mitch understands the power of the information he has and needs to make a decision about whether silence or sharing what he knows is the appropriate response. For the next week or so, he thinks the situation through. He lies awake at night replaying what he saw in the park; it has opened a million questions inside him about what integrity is. *I'll never do something like that*, Mitch thinks. But then, isn't that what everyone says? He knows all about Milgrim's famous experiment where ordinary people knowingly administered 'lethal' electric shocks to strangers (who, unbeknown to them, were actually actors). People are capable of all sorts of things, given the right circumstances. *But still . . . I couldn't do it to Erin. Could I?*

∽

Mitch meets Tom at the bar. Between keeping an eye on the cricket on the huge screen and eating his steak and chips, Mitch tells Tom about what he saw.

Tom hesitates for a minute. 'Look, I guess it's up to your own conscience, but do you want to know what I would do?'

'Yes,' says Mitch.

'I'd forget I saw anything.'

'Really?'

'Yeah, when in doubt, don't interfere. You just don't know what you're unleashing. And in any case, who are we to judge? Let those without sin cast the first stone.'

Mitch nods. Their friend Sam would have laughed at Tom's conservative values, but Mitch is used to his mate's Biblical references. Tom can't help himself. And this one has Mitch suddenly ashamed of how much he's privately delighted over what he knows about Daniel. Who's he to judge Daniel? He takes a long slug of his beer. He just wants to do the right thing here – screw Daniel, but what about Erin? He feels like he's been lying to her, finding it hard to hold her gaze, in case she sees it in his eyes. That he knows something she doesn't. His and Erin's relationship is built on trust; they've told each other all their secrets – all the important ones. It's been two months since their wedding and their magical honeymoon on the Serengeti. Not even two years since they met. Steph and Daniel have been married for, what is it, fifteen or sixteen years? Maybe love gets stale after all that time. He shouldn't be quick to make judgements –

it's so easy to get things wrong. He should focus on his relationship with Erin. Keep himself grounded in the knowledge that he never wants to end up like Daniel and Steph, headed for divorce court.

'But Tom,' he asks, 'what if it was Phoebe? Look, I know it would never happen to you guys, but let's say Erin had information about Phoebe having it off with another guy. Wouldn't you want to know?'

Tom looks stung, as if Mitch *had* told him something about Phoebe cheating. 'Phoebe would never do something like that,' says Tom quickly, and looks away at the TV screen. The moment passes, both men silently agreeing to let it slip, whatever *it* is.

'Yeah, but what if . . .'

Tom cuts him off, grimacing. 'You really ought to leave this alone, Mitch,' he says. 'Stay out of it. It's none of your business. Sometimes secrets just need to stay where they are.'

∽

Healthy intimacy relies on boundaries – the invisible energetic border that lets people know that the space beyond it is not a free-for-all. These boundaries exist for each of us in our personal space, within families, between 'subsystems' (the couple, the children, or various combinations thereof), or between the family system and the broader family (grandparents, aunts, cousins) and others in the community.

But some of us are better at managing boundaries than others. We might understand and respect boundaries or blithely burst in on other people's space, inappropriately assuming we have a right to be there.

Boundary violations may include, for example, a 12-year-old child sleeping in his parents' bed, or an affair, or a mother-in-law telling her daughter-in-law how to discipline her child. These boundary violations arise out of unconscious dynamics, they may serve some unconscious purpose (for example, the couple avoiding intimacy) but then become entrenched and often exacerbate problems. An 'other' can be used creatively by a couple to enhance intimacy, and can also play a role in reducing anxiety. In the process, though, it could have destructive consequences – not only for the couple, but for the person who's been recruited to play a role for the couple. The family therapist Murray Bowen put forward the concept of 'triangulation', where a two-person system coopts a third party in order to reduce tension. Triangles (three-person relationships) are naturally more stable than two-person relationships because the anxiety can be shifted around. The 'third party' may not necessarily be another person – it could be an issue, or drugs – but is basically something that takes the focus off the two-person relationship.

Why is it important for each of us individually in a relationship to have boundaries? Without them, we have no firm sense of self. With poor boundaries, relationships become confusing, projection takes place unmonitored, and we end up not knowing which bits belong to whom.

The yoga class

Erin breathes deep into her belly. She looks over from her yoga mat and smiles. Tara and Phoebe are both curled up on their mats in *balananda*, the child's pose. Erin's happy that she's finally managed to get Tara and Phoebe together after Tara's ridiculous avoidance of Phoebe since the wedding. Bloody Tara was offended when Erin made Phoebe – who was 'just Tom's wife' – a bridesmaid. Tara actually voiced that places in the retinue should be reserved for 'real friends', ones that go all the way back to high school. Erin was annoyed with Tara for making her feel like her mother's managed to do her whole life – that she's not allowed close, separate relationships with others. She'd ask whoever the hell she wanted to be her bridesmaid.

She managed to convince Tara to come to yoga because of Vadim – the Russian yoga instructor. 'He's *hot*, he wears these really sexy shorts, it's practically naked yoga . . .' she told Tara.

After the class the girls go for a coffee. Tara reckons with all that yoga and the way he can bend his body Vadim's got to be a great bonk. 'Reckon he can do the fireman's lift even,' she says, smiling at Erin.

Erin catches the sexual innuendo in Tara's tone and can't stop herself from smiling.

'Tara,' says Phoebe jokingly, 'you need help.'

'Actually, I'm getting some,' she says, exchanging glances with Erin. 'From a shrink.' Erin knows all about it. Sometimes she gets a blow-by-blow account of Tara's weekly session. 'I always thought this therapy thing was for screwed-up people,' Tara continues, 'but actually it's helped. I had no idea what I've been up to.'

'That's fabulous,' Phoebe says, covering Tara's hand with hers. 'You deserve to be happy. Any guy would be lucky to be with you.'

After Erin and Phoebe drop Tara-the-yoga-convert at home, Erin notices Phoebe is quiet. 'Everything okay, Pheebs?' she asks.

Phoebe's face is drawn taut, her brown eyes staring through the windscreen dejectedly. Erin pulls the car over and takes her friend's hand. The words trip out of Phoebe's mouth. 'Seeing Tara all excited like that . . . and knowing what you and Mitch have . . .' she stumbles, 'I . . . it's just that Tom and I haven't had sex for the last two years.'

'No sex *at all*?' Erin asks. She tries not to look horrified.

Phoebe shakes her head forlornly.

'God,' says Erin. 'Why? I mean, I know people can manage without sex. I didn't have any between Gus and Mitch and that was a good eight months' worth of drought. But it's kinda different when there's a body right there in the bed with you . . .'

'I have a vibrator,' Phoebe says forlornly. 'I use it a lot.'

'That's not, like, the way marriage is meant to be, is it?'

'Everybody says the passion dies down a bit after the first year, but they still make love, right? He can't even get it up anymore. God I feel so disloyal telling even you. He'd be absolutely mortified if he knew I was talking about it . . .'

'Don't worry, I'm not about to tell anyone.'

'Not even Mitch?'

'No, not even Mitch.'

'The first time it happened, Tom got so upset he went off for a full health check. I don't think he even told the doctor why he was there, just said he wanted a check-up. Came back and said all he needed to do was to get fit. I did everything I could think of to help. I told him it didn't matter. I didn't put any pressure on him. I spent a small fortune on sexy lingerie. On the night of our last anniversary I tried to get something going but he wasn't interested. I thought maybe he just wasn't attracted to me anymore and he's just too caring to say anything, so I went on that crash diet and lost seven kilos – you remember, last year.'

'Pheebs, how could I forget? You said you were dieting to get into your bridesmaid's dress for my wedding.'

Phoebe wipes the tears from her face, her laugh muffled by her palms. 'At least I looked good at your wedding, because it sure as hell didn't do me any good at home. He just made the same excuses about how tired he was, or that he was sick, or he had to get up early in the morning. That's what our trip to Hawaii was all about. It was supposed to give us a new start . . .'

'And?'

'It was a disaster. We fought. Well, I fought. He wouldn't even fight with me. Do you have any idea how frustrating it is trying to fight with someone who won't fight back? Christ, how are we ever going to have kids if we don't have sex? IVF? Can you imagine going to see a fertility specialist and they want to know how long we've been trying for? We'll be the first super-fertile couple to have to get IVF because we're not actually having sex!'

'Super-fertile?' Erin asks. 'How do you know?'

Phoebe's eyes well up. She can't bring herself to speak.

Erin squeezes her hand. 'I'm sorry,' she says. 'Was it his?'

Phoebe nods. 'About four months in to our relationship. We knew we wanted to be together but it was too soon, just too soon. We thought . . .' She looks away. 'We need help. I spoke to my father last week – I just said we're having marital difficulties and I think he understood. He suggested we speak to a tribal elder. He must be losing it. He thinks this is Ghana. I reminded him that we don't have such things here and he said there are elders everywhere. He said we needed a healing ritual. Grief! Can you imagine me suggesting that to Tom? Throw some bones and chant some words and he'll get stiff again . . .' Phoebe trails off.

'Hey, you know, your dad's right,' says Erin. 'There *are* elders everywhere. They just come in different forms. Counsellors, ministers, meditation teachers . . . Mitch and I consulted a witchdoctor. What did they call him in Swahili – an *mganga*? – when we were in Tanzania, just for fun. But he was great. There were people queuing up to be cured of anything from lovesickness to AIDS.'

'Yeah, and what did the *mganga* tell you?'

'Two children,' says Erin, smiling apologetically. 'A boy and a girl. And the girl's going to be musical. The funny thing was, he knew Mitch is a firefighter. Weird, hey?' She still has Phoebe's hand in hers, and tightens her grip again. 'Pheebs, you and Tom need someone both of you can trust and look up to. We can find someone like that. Your dad's right.'

Phoebe leans over and hugs Erin. Right now, being able to share her pain with her friend is balm for her loneliness.

'It's not meant to be so hard, is it?' Phoebe asks sadly.

∽

It's not easy for a couple to seek support. Invariably, one person feels the urgency to get help, while the other is resistant. The members of the couple may switch positions over time, passing the hot potato of urgency between them. It may be an unconscious conspiracy, the system's way of avoiding transformation. It's not lightbulbs we're changing here but deep, habituated patterns – it takes two in a relationship (and often with the help of a third) to change the dynamic. It's even more difficult to admit the need for help when the problem is sexual. People are often filled with humiliation and shame, heightened by the thought of sharing these very private matters with a third party.

Whatever the presenting issue, if serious enough, at least one person in the couple will become so disaffected, so frustrated, that he or she cannot continue. Phoebe's frustration, despair and anger, built up over several years, can't be contained any longer. The taboo she shares with Tom of bringing conflict into the space of love has been overridden.

Tom, for his part, can feel Phoebe shifting. He knows he's in trouble. It's why he reacted with such a jolt when Mitch posed the hypothetical question about Phoebe being unfaithful. Suddenly Tom found himself looking in the mirror of Steph and Daniel's seemingly happy, successful relationship, just like his and Phoebe's. *And if it can happen to them, why shouldn't it happen to us?* The disastrous anniversary dinner and flopped Hawaiian holiday have begun to shake him from his denial. Now Mitch's story about Daniel has triggered paranoid thoughts in Tom's mind. He's begun to wonder about Phoebe having to work late, and finds himself alerted and nervous when her phone signals an SMS. He can't please her, so maybe she, like Daniel, is taking her needs elsewhere.

They've been brought to the edge. A step or two more, and they'll tumble over. So when Phoebe comes home from yoga and sits Tom down and says, 'I can't go on like this, we have to get help,' Tom agrees.

'You're right. We need help.'

She stifles the urge to say 'actually, *you* need help', knowing he'll only become defensive and she'll lose this opportunity. Besides, she's come to so distrust his capacity for self-reflection that she feels she must be there to make sure he addresses his difficulties. She's reached the point where she has to know what he's capable of – if he can't desire her or give her the life she wants, she's going to have to face a hard choice.

16.
Secrets, Sex and Shame

SOMETIMES WE HAVE TO WALK through the door we've been pretending wasn't there. What happens when we confront the corrosive dynamic we've tried to smooth over, or rationalise away?

Phoebe and Tom consult an elder

It took a few weeks of research to find Father Gareth Keane, a priest in his early sixties who is also a psychotherapist. Despite his habit of quoting from the Bible, Tom has not been religiously observant since leaving home (he can't remember the last time he went to church). Meeting Father Gareth brings him back to sitting around his family's dinner table with Father Brian and Father Danilo, the two parish priests who sometimes joined them for a meal.

It's their first session. Tom is swamped by embarrassment, but prodded by Phoebe's deliberate silence he explains they are having difficulty with their 'marital relations'. As he says this, he glances at Phoebe, knowing that she's thinking, *he can't even say the word 'sex'*. Tom offers a few sketchy details. When it's her turn to speak, Phoebe chooses her words cautiously, mindful of how easily Tom feels judged. They carefully list for Father Gareth all the 'blessings' of their relationship and everything they appreciate about each other. They both reiterate how much they want to make things work.

After a while, Father Gareth says, 'On the surface, it's all very polite between the two of you. I'm wondering whether that's for my benefit or whether this is what you're like at home?'

Phoebe jumps in. 'This *is exactly* what we're like at home.'

'Father, what you see is what you get,' Tom agrees proudly.

'Well,' says the priest, 'could that be why you're here? Maybe you need to get some of what you don't see?'

Tom looks puzzled, and Phoebe sighs impatiently. *Why doesn't he get it?* her strained eyes implore. Father Gareth turns to her. Tom is quiet. Finally Phoebe meets the priest's gaze, and she can't hide the mixture of anger, sadness and relief on her face.

Addressing Tom, the priest says, 'Tell Phoebe what you don't like about her.'

Tom laughs. 'Nothing. I think she's fantastic. In every way.'

'There's nothing about her that annoys or angers you?'

Tom shakes his head. 'She's really the ideal wife.' He reaches out for Phoebe's hand.

Phoebe pulls her hand away. 'No, Tom,' she says. 'Think about what Father Gareth's asking. Tell me something that you disagree with, or that you don't like about me.'

Tom shifts uncomfortably. 'Sweetie, why are you behaving like this? You know there's nothing –'

Phoebe interrupts him. 'That's the trouble, isn't it?'

'But,' Tom says, astonished, 'how can the fact that I adore you be the trouble?'

'I think,' says Father Gareth gently, 'maybe what Phoebe's saying is that if you can't express anger or disagreement, it's going to be difficult to express other kinds of passionate feelings.'

'Exactly!' Phoebe exclaims. 'It's not just that we don't make love anymore, it's all so . . . *bland*.'

Tom winces. 'What does that mean?' he says stiffly.

'You know how I like my eggs. I know which fish you prefer. Actually, you're happy with anything I cook even if it tastes like burnt leather. We choose movies for each other. But, you know, I don't really like those action movies. And I booked that friggin' boring Italian restaurant for our anniversary when I really wanted to go to the African one. But we never complain about each other's choices. There's no . . .'

'Tension?' says the priest.

'But Father,' protests Tom, 'what's wrong with having a harmonious relationship? Isn't that what Christ taught?'

'It's called flatlining, Tom!' Phoebe's voice is shrill. 'It's boring. It's dull. I don't like all this niceness all the time. I've put no pressure on you about . . . having sex. We went all the way to Hawaii and *still* nothing happened. You were too tired. On *holiday*!' Phoebe begins to cry. 'You're just not attracted to me anymore! Why don't you just say so? Tell me you hate the dinner I made! Tell me I'm fat and undesirable! Just *tell* me!'

Tom looks on helplessly.

After a minute or two of tense silence, Phoebe, reaching for a tissue, says to Father Gareth, 'This is what happens whenever I try to bring something up. He just withdraws. We can't talk.'

'The two of you can't fight,' says the priest.

'Why would we want to fight?' says Tom. 'I don't like conflict.'

༒

Hallelujah! Tom's just owned a piece of himself that could potentially shift the mountain between him and Phoebe. What he does with this knowledge will determine the future of their relationship. Why doesn't he like conflict? What happens to him emotionally when there's disharmony? And how does Phoebe feed into this dynamic? These are helpful clues, and skilful questions, but they've only just begun, and they need time.

༒

When the session ends, Father Gareth asks if he can 'bring God into the room'. His practice is to end with a short prayer. Tom readily agrees, and Phoebe, despite having grown up as a child of an atheist and a Sunni Muslim, leaving her pretty much in no-man's-land, says she's happy to go along with it.

They all close their eyes, and the priest begins. 'Oh, Holy Spirit, we humbly ask for your presence in this time of difficulty. We ask that you come into this room, and help this couple, Tom and Phoebe, who are struggling with their relationship and cannot find a way through. We ask You, oh Heavenly Father, to heal the wounds from their past so that they may find each other in love and compassion and forgiveness . . .'

Suddenly Tom starts to hyperventilate.

Phoebe looks at him. She's never seen her husband like this.

'Are you okay?' she asks.

The priest explains that when we get anxious, our breathing becomes irregular as a result, and gets Tom a glass of water. He sips it slowly and his breathing returns to normal.

Eventually Tom is able to get the words out.

'I'm sorry,' he says, 'I don't know what came over me, maybe . . . I haven't prayed in a long time . . . and . . . something's happened with some people we know . . . a . . . model couple. Massively successful. It's all started to unravel . . .'

'Who, Tom?' Phoebe asks.

Tom hesitates, then says, 'Steph and Daniel. It turns out he's been leading this double life, doing stuff on the side. With prostitutes . . . or maybe a mistress.'

Phoebe's eyes grow wide. 'Oh my God. Does Steph know? You heard this from Mitch?'

'That's not the point!' Tom blurts out. 'You're so hung up on sex! What I want to know is whether *you've* been with someone else!'

Phoebe looks stunned, her mouth gaping.

'What? What?'

The colour in Tom's cheeks flares. 'You heard me,' he bites back.

It's not how the priest envisaged ending the session but never mind. Tom has found something he has not allowed himself to broach, let alone touch – his fear and anger. It's good progress. And God will wait; He has infinite patience.

༄

Over the next few sessions with Father Gareth as their guide, Tom and Phoebe explore each other's past. Phoebe is surprised to find that she doesn't know all the details of Tom's family history. She hears for the first time that Tom's paternal grandfather committed suicide when Tom's father was seven. He had come back from World War II service as a GI in the 157th Infantry Regiment, Seventh United States Army, a broken man. He saw unimaginable destruction and took part in the liberation of the Dachau concentration camp. Overcome with rage at the horror he had found, he assisted inmates as they took a deadly revenge on their captured torturers.

Tom's father spent his first seven years the son of a haunted man carrying a world of tragedy on his shoulders, frightened to engage with his two sons lest his own violence spill out. The ex-soldier – Tom's grandfather – needed to hold so much in that he allowed himself barely any emotional movement at all. Unable to bear it any longer, he turned that violence on himself, leaving behind a legacy of fear – fear of hostility, fear of passion, fear of life. Tom's father found meaning in his Catholic faith; as long as he didn't stray from the path, he felt safe and comforted.

When it's Phoebe's turn to talk, Tom hears for the first time that Phoebe would hate her mother after her father fled her outbursts and be worried sick that he wouldn't return, even though – until she was seventeen, at least – he always did, grovelling in his attempt to appease his wife. In the face of her father's humiliation and her mother's maddening triumph, Phoebe, trying to soothe the feeling that her world was falling apart, would roll up on the floor and rock herself.

They've each only known very little about the emotional landscape of their families of origin. Talking about it in the sanctuary of Father Gareth's cosy office makes the differences all the more stark and it deepens their understanding of their own, and the other's, history. They begin to see how the 'rules of engagement' from their earliest years have knotted together to create their sexual and emotional impasse. Tom can now see how, in his family, even slightly heightened expressions of uncomfortable emotion – never mind conflict – were rarely shown. And he begins to appreciate how much this has acted as a powerful filter through which he funnels Phoebe's interactions with him. Because of it, he experiences even muted attempts on her part to engage him as overwhelmingly aggressive and engulfing. Father Gareth points out to Tom that he may be carrying the emotional wounds of the men who came before him and, like them, he is immobilised by a fear of doing harm. It's as if a small fragment of his grandfather's trauma, passed on to him by his father, has lodged within him. The priest suggests that maybe he's hiding parts of himself. He seems too shut down sexually to be acting out. Rather, he's acting *in*, struggling privately with his demons.

Phoebe is surprised when she realises in their seventh session that they've *both* come from families that just couldn't handle conflict. Her fights with her mother, and her pride in her feminism and Africanism, left her believing that she wasn't afraid to handle confrontation, and so it must be all Tom's fault. Now she sees that she's become almost as afraid of conflict as Tom is. Coming together they, like most couples in the face of common anxieties, unconsciously organised their relationship so that they could be protected against this shared anxiety. Phoebe had thought she was taking Tom to see someone for *his* problem; now she sees that she must take responsibility for her part in things – for her unconscious choice of Tom, for her collusion in their passionless union. She understands that she has to examine the whole relationship, including her part in it.

But God help her, she doesn't want to repeat her relationship with her mother. Tom fell in love with Phoebe because she was lively without stretching him too far outside his comfort zone. They were drawn to one another because of the apparent promise of a harmonious, conflict-free relationship. Well, they got it. But at a massive price.

'I'm so frightened of losing you,' Phoebe tells Tom through her tears. 'I'm so scared we'll fight and you'll either collapse or leave me. I don't want to be like my mother!'

'You're nothing like your mother,' protests Tom, looking to the priest for confirmation.

'Or if I push you for intimacy. If we *know* we'll never have sex again, we won't be able to go on, will we? How will we have children? I don't want to never make love again. I'm a sexual being, Tom. Other men find me sexy. I don't want to be rejected by my own husband because you don't want me anymore.'

'It's not that. I don't want anyone else. If only I could get my health right . . .'

'Tom! Stop making that old excuse!' Phoebe's head is in her hands, muffling her angry sobs.

'It's not –'

'Jesus,' interrupts Phoebe, turning to Father Gareth, her voice tremulous with frustration. 'Do you know what it's like never having sex?'

Tom and the priest are stricken speechless.

Phoebe looks up into their awkward silence. 'I . . . I, Father, I'm . . .'

But the priest chuckles, and Phoebe smiles. And then Tom is laughing, and then Phoebe can't stop the giggles bubbling up from deep inside her.

∾

Humour – a natural third position – brings some relief, and Tom and Phoebe leave the session feeling lighter.

That night Phoebe walks naked from the bathroom into the bedroom. Tom is already in bed, reading. She snuggles up to him, her breasts against his T-shirt. He switches off the light, and turns towards her. She helps him out of his T-shirt and shorts.

'No pressure,' she whispers. 'Let's just cuddle for a bit.'

Her thigh rests against his genitals as she strokes his chest. She traces her fingertips from his forehead, over his nose, resting on his lips, and then down, hovering, stroking, playing at the base of his stomach, avoiding touching his penis, which lies soft against her thigh.

'I'm sorry,' he says after a while. The rest of his body is as rigid as his penis is limp. He takes her hand away from his belly. 'I just can't do it . . . it . . . it feels wrong, like we're brother and sister or something.'

Sex, aggression and shame

The mood is sombre at the next session. On their own, they haven't spoken about their latest failed attempt at physical intimacy.

Phoebe dives right in. 'I want to ask Tom something.'

Father Gareth looks enquiringly at Tom.

'Okay,' says Tom, a little nervously.

'I've been thinking about what you said. You see,' she turns to the priest to explain, 'after our last session I snuggled up to Tom and he said he couldn't because it felt wrong, as if we were siblings. And, well, I was reading something about how a bad experience as a child can make you feel shame and guilt, and that can make you impotent, and it made me think of an ex-lover of mine who was sexually abused as a child. So, I was wondering whether, maybe, Tom, you've had something like that happen to you?'

Tom is horrified. 'What? You're saying someone in my family?'

'No, I'm not accusing anyone in your family. I'm just wondering whether you've had some sort of bad experience that's left you feeling so bad about having sex. I just can't understand how anyone can feel so traumatised by what, to me, seems like the most natural thing in the world.'

Tom shakes his head and looks at Phoebe oddly, feeling further and further away from her.

∽

It's understandable. Phoebe's grasping for an explanation. If Tom had been sexually abused in the past, she'd be right in drawing a connection with impotence or other sexual problems as an adult. Critical phases for attachments occur very early in life, and sexuality is one part. When children discover their genitalia and gender differences, they fondle, masturbate and experience early unformed sensations of excitement. Little boys and girls play 'doctor, doctor' and other games that license nascent exploration and discovery. They're curious about how babies are made and what their parents get up to behind closed doors and all this is healthy and normal. But children's psychosexual development is acutely vulnerable and malleable. One of the reasons abuse is so shattering is that it can utterly warp a child's later sexual attachments, leaving a legacy of guilt, shame and anger that might be acted out sexually, or result in repressed sexuality. Children often take responsibility – at an unconscious level – for things they couldn't possibly control, as if they had somehow invited the attention. Most victims of childhood sexual abuse end up with a complex, often contradictory set of post-traumatic feelings and symptoms to resolve, including feeling helpless and enraged about having been violated, as well as crippling feelings of worthlessness. The brain maps for sexuality shaped by our early environment may be changeable but the more searing the trauma the more difficult it is to heal.

In a family as phobic of 'messy' emotions as Tom's, sexuality would already have been an area fraught with latent guilt, even without the potential horrendous intervention of a paedophile. Of course, we can understand Phoebe's need to grasp a dramatic explanation for the fact that Tom doesn't get turned on by her anymore. But she is wrong. Tom was never abused. The complex weave of his childhood development, family dynamics, and possible biogenetic influences, combined with the dynamics Phoebe brings into the relationship, explains his impotence.

17.
Re-enactments

IT'S BEEN SAID THAT IF we put a dollar in a jar for every time we have sex in the first year of marriage, it would take the rest of our lives to empty the jar if we removed a coin every time we have sex thereafter. But keeping books of account in the bedroom can bankrupt romance, especially since quantity is usually offset by quality as we get better at making love to the same person over time. Nevertheless, in those early years, there's a fair bit of bonking going on, and we gorge on it like an all-you-can-eat buffet. But that shag-a-thon isn't sustainable in the long term due to exhaustion, children, cable television and other distractions. All-you-can-eat becomes à la carte nouvelle cuisine. Sometimes, in a bad month, the best we can hope for is a glimpse at the menu.

This is normal. Shifts in relationships are inevitable. Part of our ongoing work to keep intimacy alive is to accept these fluctuations without feeling threatened that she no longer finds us attractive or he's bored.

When we talk of 'settling down' and 'finding our feet' in a relationship, what we often mean is 'we're having less sex'. As romance fades and emotional attachment sets in, a far more complicated process of subtle sexual and emotional shifts occurs.

∞

Erin and Mitch are back from their honeymoon and, two months into their life together, have started to sense subtle changes in the bedroom. They're still having plenty of sex, but not as often. It's not always raw and urgent, sometimes it's soft and slow. She doesn't always have an orgasm, and is happy to just go to sleep. Occasionally she doesn't feel like giving him a blow job, so she makes him come quickly with her hand. Inside these new dimensions, there have been a few precious moments when their lovemaking has crossed a new threshold into a scary place of closeness which neither of them has experienced before, when he's deep inside her and she feels him, and it's not just physical. Neither of them has mentioned 'that night' again. But whenever Erin thinks of it, she smiles quietly to herself. On their honeymoon in Tanzania, when they were making love on the four-poster bed in the lodge's elevated guest hut, with only a mosquito net between them and the Serengeti night around them, they came together and Mitch collapsed on top of her, his face pressed into her, his tears wetting her breasts, with no way of explaining where they were from or why he was crying.

The fear of intensity

The journey of intimacy has a way of unravelling even the most committed of travellers. Sometimes when we touch this place of shared pleasure and joy with another person, and feel something so exquisite we have no language for it, things can fall apart. Out there in Africa, Mitch experienced something he'd craved since he was a baby and has longed for in adulthood: a deep connection with a loving woman. And it frightened the shit out of him. By dinnertime the next day, he'd already found something to be grumpy about: Erin was taking her time getting ready to go out. Muttering under his breath, he went out onto the balcony, cross, anxious and withdrawn. The mix of infantile craving and adult desire evoked by their gorgeous, generous lovemaking felt unbearable. The only response he's ever known to his neediness has been a harassed, depressed albeit well-meaning mother who withdrew from him in his moment of need. To survive back then, he learned to back away from needing too much, to be satisfied with less, splitting off from his own desires. Now, as a grown man, with the promise of this kind of closeness on offer, Mitch's unconscious terror runs riot, making him feel panicked, as if he might disintegrate.

In that moment of connection with Erin, Mitch touched an exquisite void – it may have been the most illuminating moment of his adult life – but it shattered him to feel how precarious a thing joy and intimacy are to find, and how easy they are to lose. He connected not only with the woman he loves, but with something inside himself he's never had access to: to be deeply known, and to know another deeply. And with that came a lifetime's worth of how much he's missed and lost, of the impoverishment of his past relationships with family, friends and lovers. And then his terror – now that he's known it, he could lose it. He could lose Erin. It's all too much to bear, and he has to stand back from the frontline of intimacy.

So, back from their honeymoon and in the real world, he's lapsed into his usual default self: the solid, silent fireman. He tries not to think about what happened in Tanzania. Maybe he had a virus. Maybe he ate something funny. You know, the usual bullshit we try out on ourselves when we're in protection mode. But he knows something real happened there and he knows Erin knows. It's the crack in his armour and it has raised the stakes between them. As he backs away from Erin to preserve his sense of previous intactness, a re-enactment from his past is about to be triggered that will shake things up between him and Erin, causing bits of their past that have so far been relatively well managed to come tumbling out.

Erin and Mitch fall down a dark, familial hole

'Don't forget we're all taking my mother out for her birthday tomorrow night,' Erin says.

'Are we?' Mitch asks, looking bewildered. 'Who's taking her out?' He honestly doesn't remember her telling him.

'I told you last week. All of us – Rob and Tariq, Steph and Daniel, Aunt Jenny and Uncle Gabe and us.'

'Steph and–?' He stops himself from saying Daniel's name. He hasn't told Erin yet about what he saw in the park the other night. He was just waiting for the right time to bring it up.

Erin's smile is strained. 'I've booked a table at that great new restaurant down the road from my mother.'

'Oh, jeez, the football season kicks off tomorrow. I'm sure I would have told you if you'd mentioned dinner.' He feels momentarily relieved that he's got an excuse to get out of having to make small talk with that prick Daniel.

'I did tell you, Mitch.'

'Bean, I can't get out of this match . . . my team counts on me. It's too late for them to find another keeper.'

'It's just one match, Mitch! This is my mother's birthday. Please don't let me down. It's not like you're playing for Manchester United.'

'It's the *first* division.' He feels his jaw clench. Okay, it's the local league but it's still the first division.

'Oh, shit, Mitch. Is this going to be like last season? You running off to play football all the time?'

'I train once a week and I have a game once a week – that's hardly "all the time".'

'It's always when I need you. It's like you have to get away.'

'It's the one thing I do for myself. The one thing in my week that I actually look forward to.'

Erin looks crestfallen. 'You don't look forward to spending time with me?'

'No, I didn't mean it like that.' Mitch's throat tightens.

'Then just exactly how did you mean it? You've been so distant since we came back from our honeymoon. It feels like you're running away.' Erin feels tears pricking her eyes. She knows she's being petty and childish and unfair, but she feels just the way she did when she found out Gus was sleeping around. She looks away, trying to control her words. They spill out anyway. 'Are you sorry we got married?'

'C'mon Erin, don't be ridiculous. Of course I'm not sorry. But you're being so clingy.'

Mitch fumbles internally, trying to find words to attach to the emotional free radicals coursing through his body. She's being petty, pathetic, needy. He can't articulate it, but unconsciously she reminds him of when he was responsible for a desperate and tearful mother. He should make it better. But right now, he doesn't want to. He wants to go to football. And he doesn't care if he hurts Erin. He wonders for a moment if that means he doesn't love her. He just wants to run away.

'You horrible selfish bastard,' says Erin, wanting to throw something at him. Her, clingy? What crap! 'I'm not the one who's being ridiculous. I *told* you about the dinner. My mother will freak if you go and kick a ball with your mates instead of being there. She'll never forgive you. Or me. It'll mean years of snide comments from her. And in any case, if my cousin's husband can be there, how can her son-in-law not?'

'Daniel!' he splutters. 'That paragon of virtue! I wouldn't be comparing me to *him*!' He hadn't meant to bring Daniel into it. Fuck it. This isn't the way to break the news to Erin about her cousin's precious husband. He tries to switch tack. 'And I'm not being selfish! It's not my fault your mother's bitter and lonely. She's the one who couldn't keep your father. It's no surprise he walked away given how she carries on.'

This is below the belt stuff. Mitch puffs out his cheeks. How'd he end up here? Erin's beautiful eyes are cold, as if he's a stranger to her. He feels sick in his guts.

She studies him, her frown deepening, 'I thought you liked Daniel.'

Mitch shakes his head. A night with Trish queening about the place, getting drunk while Daniel plays God's gift to the family. And all that instead of a football match. Football is the only place where he's really free, and no-one's life depends on him. He turns away from Erin. He needs to get outside, to breathe.

'Don't walk away from me!' Erin pleads. 'We're not finished talking about this.'

Mitch knows he's heading the wrong way as he opens the door and goes stoop-shouldered into the crisp air of the night.

༄

They're not really fighting about Erin's mother's birthday dinner, or about football. They're not even fighting about Daniel and Stephanie. These are just *triggers*.

This fight is an understandable blow-up, in a relationship of emerging complexity, as the excitement and idealisation of the honeymoon period is wearing off, like an anaesthetic. Suddenly they start to notice things in each other that they don't like – selfishness, pettiness, untidiness, small-mindedness, arrogance, meanness, self-pity, neurosis. Was this all there before? They didn't see it because lust and romance had laced their senses. What they have to do now is manage everything they've projected onto each other so that they can learn to know each other, and themselves, better.

The boy in his room: Mitch's haven

As a baby, Mitch retreated into a safe space in his own mind to protect himself from his absent parents. He learned to subdue and repress his emotions and desires because to express them only led to disappointment. No-one ever came to his rescue. And so on the Serengeti, when those castaway emotions came drifting back, Mitch did the only thing he knew how to do – he pulled back, even though Erin is not an 'unavailable woman' like his mother was. Erin, in fact, refuses to let him retreat to a faraway place. She comes to collect him and hauls him out in a way his depressed mother and distant father never did. He both desperately needs her to do this and he sometimes hates her for it, because he doesn't know who he is or could be if he allowed his emotions to be felt. In the early months of their relationship, he adored this quality in her. As time goes by, he's become more wary, frightened to remain attached in the alive way he'd managed when they first met, the shadow of the past not so far-reaching, when there was less at stake.

Part of why Mitch is so drawn to Erin is because she is so *not* like his mother. She fights him with energy (not depression) and opposes him stridently. She's strong enough to understand his vulnerabilities, and not shame him for them. He can bump up against her because she offers this durable resistance, which frees him up to show his anger towards her – something he learned not to do with his mother but could do towards his sister, Kayla.

So during their fight, it's safe for Mitch to unleash the full throttle of his anger against Erin as he explodes about her mum, Trish. But really, he wouldn't have cause for such strong feelings about his mother-in-law, whom on all other occasions he tolerates with good humour and mild indifference. The strength of his outburst is a clue – this is a massive projection of his unresolved feelings towards his own mother. What he really means when he spits out, 'She's the one who couldn't keep your father,' is that his own mother couldn't 'keep' Mitch.

Mitch doesn't really want Erin to withdraw because that's what his depressed mother did. If Erin actually does become depressed, and withdraws, Mitch would be left where he started, feeling abandoned. What Erin has done for Mitch in this moment is help him to retrieve this loss and disappointment, which Mitch as a grown man is now ready to grieve and face again, and hopefully resolve when it is mirrored back to him by the woman he loves and trusts – and who won't abandon him.

A note on solitude and connection

We can't sustain the connection of intimacy unless we're grounded in who we are, and we get there by being skilled at being on our own. Downtime, daydreaming, or just 'leave-me-alone' time, allows us to restore our sense of balance for when we come together as a couple. Children naturally create this space when they invent solitary games and imaginary friends. As adults we go into transitional spaces, and these act as pauses or bridges between closeness and independence.

But what happens when we're too attached to these spaces, when they are not so much *transitional* ones but more *permanent* structures within the personality, a refuge from relationships? Far from the separateness allowing us to re-enter our relationship more connected, we return as defensive as ever, or even further away from the person so that the physical 'return' may actually evoke deeper feelings of abandonment or disconnection. We can get stuck here, cut off from meaningful contact with our partners like Mrs Brown in Michael Cunningham's Pulitzer prizewinning book *The Hours*, who books herself into a hotel for the day so she can read her book uninterrupted. There she is unburdened by the demands of being a wife and mother, roles she experiences as annihilating. Some of us join gangs, religious groups, poker clubs, meditation groups, book clubs or yoga schools. Artists and writers go off to paint, sculpt and write. Sometimes people retreat into addictions (drugs or gambling); even work ('but honey, it's for you and the kids') or sport ('it's healthy, it's an outlet, I'll see you Tuesday next week'). We pick retreats that contain our anxieties.

The only way to tell whether Mitch's retreat is healthy or destructive is to assess whether he's able to transition from his retreat back into his life with Erin with a renewed sense of personal or internal composure. If he returns with the desire to connect strengthened, his retreat is working for him. But if he re-emerges into the relationship with a sinking feeling, counting the days until he can 'escape' again, he may need to look at why escape is more attractive than intimacy.

The girl in her castle: Erin's dependency

Erin's always thought of herself as an independent woman. She was never going to fall into the trap her mother was in, that of the bitter woman, making her bed in a big pile of grievances. When she caught Gus cheating, she didn't hesitate in giving him the flick. As a kid, Erin watched how her dad both disappointed and excited her mother. But around the age of six Erin became 'daddy's girl'; he showered her with love and attention, and gifts. Following the divorce, in her teenage years, her relationship with him shifted again. There were too many girlfriends to compete with, and she dropped to forgotten status in his hierarchy of affections. She hated him, lashed out and didn't see him for months on end.

The psyche is slippery, and tries to match us up with our wounds. Despite her best intentions, Erin still found herself attracted to guys just like her father – ambitious, powerful, charming men. This is a common re-enactment – we choose people to love who remind us of the people who have hurt us, so we can re-enact a happier ending. Erin, in looking for her father's love, became hooked on the thrill of attention from narcissistic men.

But Mitch was nothing like this. That's why she married him. She came back from their honeymoon high on love. But the two months since then have flattened her mood. She's frustrated and even worried at times. When Mitch doesn't come home at the expected time, she's anxious – has something happened to him? – and then angry that he's late, or hasn't let her know. Is Mitch falling out of love with her? Has she done something wrong? Why's he withdrawing from her? Is he doing to her what her father did to her mother? If Mitch is a different kind of man to her father and Gus, how come she's feeling the same way – let down by a self-absorbed, absent man? Is Trish going to get the opportunity to say, 'See, all men are the same'?

It's natural to compress the mysterious peaks and valleys of our partner's personalities and to be quick to assume we've got them all worked out. In Erin's case, what she knows of a man who's distant is that his attentions are going elsewhere and it ends badly, with a deserted woman in pain. And so she projects this 'knowledge' onto Mitch, assuming his withdrawn mood means that he loves something or someone more than he loves her (the threatening 'third'). She can't conceive of him being the imperfect man struggling with *how much* he loves her, with how frightened he is of their intimacy. She is threatened by his withdrawal and is too overwhelmed by her unresolved feelings of abandonment to be able to stand back or stand firm in the face of his unsteadiness. She simply cannot think in a new way about him or their relationship.

So she pleads – 'Please don't let me down' – and then insults him – 'It's not like you're playing for Manchester United'.

Strong, independent Erin strains at the seams, as old disappointment and rage surfaces. She discovers that she also struggles with trust, is terrified of loss, and finds it hard to maintain a steady sense of herself while connecting with Mitch. Both Mitch and Erin, in fact, operate at similar levels of differentiation – they just take up different roles. Erin carries the responsibility to pursue closeness while Mitch regulates distance.

Erin and Mitch's re-enactment
Erin is furious that Mitch would dare to suggest that she's being clingy. She can let a man go with one 'Get out of my life'. Ask Gus. She knows exactly how to stand up for herself, thank you very much. She doesn't 'need' anyone. At the same time, Mitch doesn't know where she gets that he's 'selfish'. Seriously? He's dedicated his *whole life* to the service of others. Such bullshit. Erin's just being dramatic and needy.

So what's really going on behind the scenes of this slinging match? When someone tells us something about ourselves that doesn't fit our self-image, either they've got it wrong or we've got it wrong. It's called cognitive and emotional dissonance. And don't we all bloody hate it when feedback doesn't line up nicely with self-perception? We usually reject responses we don't like. Both Erin and Mitch have spent a lot of energy defining themselves as independent and unselfish. But in their relationship, each one conscripts the other to take part in their internal narratives, through *projective identification.* Mitch has disowned his own needy, clingy bits by projecting them into Erin. It's a double-whammy because not only does Erin get to act out Mitch's clinginess, but she has her own dependency needs, which latch onto what he's put into her.

Simultaneously, Erin, in her fury, insults Mitch, disowning the parts of herself that are identified with her mother by using exactly the same techniques Trish uses (humiliation and shaming). Mitch has this feeling projected into him, where it happily links up with his own store of shame. And *voila!* – they've just co-created re-enactments of their earlier dramas.

This is a place Erin and Mitch will visit often as they slip into these re-enactments over the course of their relationship. Typically, what happens over time for a couple with powerful, unresolved re-enactments is that they'll be drawn more and more into this space until there's little left over of what was different and good about their earlier relationship. Couples who end up in acrimonious separations have almost always walked this path. They start out loving each other, and end up hating each other. They began their relationships in the hope of a different experience, and get pulled inexorably by the meshing of their internal dynamics towards the same experience, and despair.

Is this, in Erin and Mitch's case, the beginning of them falling out of love? It could get to that, but in these early encounters it's what's happening in the face of their deepening intimacy. If they can rise to the challenge by addressing and processing their fight, it may well be the charter that leads them to fall more deeply in love. Ultimately, intimacy is measured in the way in which we handle conflict. We have choices. We can manage it creatively, destructively, humorously, punishingly or not at all. Couples who team up to resolve and move through trauma and pain, by holding together the vision of a committed relationship, invariably find a way there.

The beautiful crisis

Mitch doesn't get far. Just to the street. He stops, flooded with images of the Erin he loves, upstairs, distressed and in pain. His anger has melted away, lying in puddles on the pavement. He can't bear the thought of losing her. He is struck by his stupid, over-the-top reaction. He knows she doesn't deserve this response. He feels sick inside, tearful, and remembers the last time he cried, on their honeymoon. Something inside him opens up. He just wants to hold her and be held by her. He runs back inside.

'I'm sorry,' he says, shaking his head. 'I don't know what's been going on with me since we got back from Tanzania. I've been acting like an idiot. I've never known anyone like you. I don't know these feelings. You know, the love thing . . . Sometimes I just don't know how to handle it. Erin, I love you. I love being married to you. I'll come to the dinner, anything, I just want us back.'

He holds her hands. She resists for a moment but his vulnerability softens her. She doesn't want to fight either. She folds into his arms. 'Don't do that again, run out like that,' Erin admonishes. 'It reminds me of my father.' She draws back a little so he can see her smile. 'And I'll try not to be such a nag of a wife.' *Like my mother*, she thinks, but can't quite bear to say that out aloud.

The lovemaking that follows is unlike Erin's parents' serial reconciliations. Erin and Mitch gaze into each other's eyes. They've found a way back to each other that completely changes their view of the relationship; they see and take responsibility for how they've each been acting, they acknowledge the impact its had on the other, and they have a sense of themselves as a couple. The fight they had about dinner was just the elephant's tail. What they have between them is the whole, wonderful elephant of love. They've contained the dynamic where Erin pursues closeness, while Mitch regulates distance. As they face challenges they will bump up against this dynamic; the more they come to recognise it, the more quickly they can restore a healthier intimacy.

☙

It's a mini-crisis. Crises shake us up. We can go into lockdown, or we can open ourselves up to new possibilities. We may need to defend before we can lower our defences. Each of these challenges of intimacy acts as a crossroads; to the right lies a re-enactment of past unresolved conflict; to the left lies the creation of something new. We will find ourselves back at the same crossroads again and again, and at other ones. Couples and families must move through these transitions. Unsuccessful or partially resolved transitions will magnify in the next stage and, without curative experience, in the next after that, until the relationship becomes untenable.

For almost all couples, there's no avoiding the pull towards re-enactment. It's just a fact of life. It's what we do. We are complex beings. It's not a failure to end up re-enacting things, it's purely the material we have to work with. A sculptor sitting down in front of a piece of wood will need to work with what is in front of her, take note of the texture, the grain, the shape, the knotholes. The creative couple sits before their piece of wood – the intercourse of their internal dynamics – and must work with it. What matters is what we do about this pull. It's a wonderful opportunity to grow. Things can change. Re-enactments can be modified. The differences that once attracted us can do so again. And those we can't find attractive we can learn to live with. We all know we're not perfect, so what makes us expect our partner to be?

To resolve our re-enactments we have to recognise, understand, and work with them. We can't do that if we pretend they're not there, sidestep our blind spots or choose to remain in the dark. We can't do that if we think we can just suddenly get rid of them all at once, like stripping a building of the girders that hold it up. It's a slow, patient process of mirroring and reflecting. We need each other to do this. We can make our own shadows more visible. Every conscious re-enactment brings light into these dark places and gives us a chance to drop what is holding us back.

∾

Later, as they lie in each other's arms, Mitch summons the courage to share something else he has been keeping from Erin. 'I need to tell you something about Daniel.'

18.

Gridlock

WHAT HAPPENS WHEN COUPLES REACH gridlock? They may be crazy about each other, but they've locked horns over a problem and nothing's moving: she wants to live in the country and grow vegetables and his job forces city life; he wants their kids baptised, she wants bar mitzvahs; she wants them to put his new bonus towards a deposit for a house, he wants a new car; one believes 'a good smack never hurt a kid', while the other can't even enforce 'time-outs'. Who wins when the needs of two people cancel each other out? Do they arm wrestle? Toss a coin? Or toss each other out?

Modern Family

It's their favourite show, *Modern Family*. Robert and Tariq are snuggled on the couch, sharing a bottle of Merlot. In this episode, the gay couple Mitchell and Cameron's adopted daughter, Lily, has a birthday party where Cameron wants to dress up as a clown and Mitchell is doing his best to dissuade him. Rob laughs hysterically. Tariq is quiet. Rob glances at Tariq – he's got that funny look on his face again. Rob knows what's coming. As the credits roll, Tariq turns to face Rob, his big brown eyes imploring.

'Look, Rob, I know we've spoken about it . . .'

'Forget it, Tariq, you knew when we met, I told you on our first date . . . Don't you remember?'

Tariq nods.

'So, what, did you think you'd change my mind?' Rob sighs. He wishes the Merlot wasn't finished.

'I thought that maybe once we'd been together long enough, and we were confident of our future together, you'd give it fresh thought. That maybe when you saw how important it was to me . . . Don't you want something for the future? To leave something behind?'

'Tariq, I don't want kids. I never have, never will. I spend all day teaching kids and that's my contribution to the future. You knew what you were getting involved with. I haven't changed. You came in with your eyes open, you can't complain now.'

Tariq's eyes prick with tears. 'But I can't imagine my life, growing old, without being a parent. I've always adored kids. I have so much love to give. Don't you want to teach your kid to kick a ball, or take her to the ballet?'

'No, I'd rather go with you to the football or the ballet. And you've got about a hundred nieces and nephews – can't you give them all that extra love? And I could do with some of that too,' Rob says, reaching for his hand.

Tariq doesn't offer his back. 'But it's so much easier for gay people to adopt, or we could look into finding an egg donor, or a surrogate and use your sperm. I wouldn't even have to be the biological father. I just want to have kids. I'd settle for one. Just one. I bet if I was a woman and you were straight, this wouldn't even be an issue. You'd have had kids. It's because we're gay . . .'

Robert inhales deeply, a hot curled fist in his belly. 'Firstly, there's no point in hypothesising. There was never a chance of me being in a heterosexual relationship. Secondly, my mother nearly had a heart attack when I came out. You remember how she behaved when I introduced her to you? Can you imagine if I told her we were going to have a kid?'

'See? It's because we're gay. We can't have a kid because of how your mother will react.' Tariq shakes his head. 'It's pathetic, Rob. What are you, twelve years old? What do you care how your mother reacts? She drives you crazy. You're acting like you care more about her than about me.'

Rob does find his mother impossible. She wouldn't know a boundary if it were an electric fence topped with razor wire. She often arrives at their home, unannounced, bearing inappropriately expensive or useless gifts. Rob invariably feels like she's snooping. Secretly, he knows she's hoping her one and only son, her 'prince', will finally get over his 'little homosexual phase' and settle down with a nice girl. As much as she loves Tariq, she still tests the waters by hinting at someone or other's daughter who's doing medicine or law. Rob's just given up trying to make her understand.

Rob looks over at the man he loves. Tariq's in real pain. But Rob doesn't know how to make this better. He wonders if he'd leave the relationship rather than have kids. The thought gives him an ache in his chest. He puts his hand on Tariq's.

'I don't feel like talking about this now; can we talk about it some other time?'

'When, Rob? We don't have forever. I'm in my thirties. If we wanted to start the process, we should start it now.'

'Would you leave me if I don't change my mind?' Rob asks.

'I don't know. I'd hate to have to choose.'

'You know, there's no guarantee we could have kids.'

'And there's no guarantee we'll stay together either,' Tariq says angrily.

'It would change everything between us, our whole life, our life-style. You can't even be sure you'll have a healthy kid. Kids come with problems, disabilities, they cost so much . . .'

'I'm tired, Rob. I'm going to bed,' Tariq says, gathering up the wine glasses and heading for the kitchen, leaving Rob alone on the couch.

When are differences irreconcilable?

There's an old story about Zhuang Zi who was walking along one day with his friend Hui Zi beside a stream. Zhuang Zi, looking into the water, said, 'Look how happy the fish are.' To which Hui Zi replied, 'You are not a fish, so how do you know the fish are happy?'

'And how do you know that I don't know the fish are happy? You are not me,' Zhuang Zi replied.

There will always be times when two people see things differently. We'll clash over and be in constant negotiation over value systems, how to load the dishwasher, gender roles, who we should vote for, how much sex we should be having, who – if anyone – we should pray to. Conflicts over how we spend our money, whose job it is to clean up after dinner, or how much contact to have with each of our parents, are circumstantial and with a bit of a win-win mentality, can be figured out – though some couples do get divorced over such issues. Here's where any of the similarities that brought us together help give us a common language and ground on which to reach agreement.

But what about deal-breakers – problems that stubbornly resist resolution and compromise? The type of 'irreconcilable differences' that provide grounds for divorce in many jurisdictions? No matter how many ladders we climb together, the snake we keep landing on brings us sliding down. Each time the issue returns for another cycle of futile rehashing, we feel more and more alone and misunderstood. We don't budge from our position and neither does our partner, even though we're right and they're wrong. We lose our sense of humour as well as any tenderness or kindness, and grow an exoskeleton of prickly criticism and blame. Over time, our positions become more and more polarised until we don't care at all about what our partner thinks or feels about the issue – or about anything else, for that matter. When we have conflict, we have to work out:

- Is this problem solvable or is it a deal-breaker?
- If it's solvable, can we work out a win-win situation?
- If not, what does it mean for the relationship?

We can't force anyone to share our views of the world, or feel as we do about everything, though some of us give it a good go. Maintaining our own emotional and cognitive balance by insisting on agreement from our partner is a prescription for catastrophe. Intimacy isn't the art of partner-sculpting, where we get to shape or contort someone so that they fit into our way of doing it. Nor can we expect someone to give up on their dreams because they clash with our own. So what are we to do? How do we sort it out and stay together?

Rob and Tariq's conflict certainly looks like a deal-breaker. But is it? Is there a way to deal with their differences that can provide a way forward? When we're in gridlock, we get fixated on the issue that's come between us, and we lose sight of what the issue represents as well as how we deal with it. *How* we fight (rather than *what* we fight about) tells us more about our relationship than our apparent difference. Obstinate couples who display contempt for one another and blame each other for problems invariably get stuck – even over the trivial stuff.

Right now Tariq and Robert can't get beyond the statement of their desires: 'I want a child' versus 'I don't'. Rob's afraid of losing Tariq if he doesn't agree and Tariq can't hide his grief and disappointment at the thought of never being a parent, which will be Rob's fault. This is the overt expression of the conflict, but what lies beneath? Why doesn't Rob want kids? Why does Tariq want kids? Does Rob's objection have to do with his jealousy? If he couldn't handle Steven coming for dinner with the two of them, how's he going to manage the omnipresence of a child? Is he afraid he'll lose out in a new threesome? Similarly, has Tariq really explored what having a child will mean for his relationship with Rob? Is he prepared for the changes a child will bring?

Sometimes, what looks like an entrenched, diametrically opposed view has more to do with the way we organise ourselves in defence against change or intrusion. It seems as if Tariq is absolutely clear on what he wants, but it's easy for him because of Rob's intransigence. What if Rob turned around one day and said, 'Okay, let's find a surrogate and make a baby.' Would Tariq have second thoughts if it suddenly became a reality? He might find himself hesitating, or at least thinking in a more realistic way about what it means. Couples often take up oppositional viewpoints, sometimes almost arbitrarily, in order to avoid change. Or one of us may be designated the party-pooper, the other the gung-ho one.

With understanding, Rob might see that his resistance to children isn't about nappies and sleepless nights as much as it is about his fear of sharing or losing Tariq. If he could own this fear and pull back the projection of loss, he could think in a new way about what it might mean to him to become a father. And if Tariq understood Rob's fear, he wouldn't take Rob's struggle personally, might soften with compassion and help Rob think through the challenges and potential rewards for their relationship of becoming parents.

⁊

Rob walks into the bedroom. Tariq is kneeling on the ground in front of a little wooden statue of Ganesha, the Hindu god of wisdom. Rob remembers how last year when he and Tariq visited Tariq's parents in India, they watched locals in Mumbai approach the large statue of Ganesha, break coconuts and prostrate themselves before the deity's great elephant head. Rob couldn't believe that in the age of the internet, people still worshipped idols with sacrifices. Tariq had swatted him with their travel guide, and told him not to be so quick to judge with his Western assumptions. 'Ganesha is the god that removes obstacles. The coconut is broken to symbolise the breaking of the ego and human pride — you should try it sometime,' Tariq had joked. Rob looked again, this time with new eyes. He wasn't one for ritual himself, but could sense the surrender in the ceremony. As a gesture of making amends, Rob had secretly gone off and bought a little wooden Ganesha statue for Tariq which he presented to him on the last night of their trip.

Now, Tariq looks up and sees Rob watching him.

'What does Ganesha say?' Rob asks softly.

'Not much,' Tariq says.

Rob sits down on the end of the bed. Tariq has been crying alone while Rob's been tidying up.

'Look, T, I don't know how to make this better. But we've worked through lots of difficult things. We'll figure this one out.'

Tariq nods.

Rob picks up the statue and holds it to his ear. He nods as if he's listening. 'Uh-uh, right, gotcha,' he says.

Tariq smiles weakly. He knows Rob's trying to diffuse the tension with humour but right now it's difficult to find anything comical about the impossible gulf between them.

'What'd he say?' Tariq asks.

'He said you and I make a great couple. And he's never seen such beautiful brown eyes as yours – not on any living creature . . . except maybe on a gorgeous cow he once knew.'

'You know,' Tariq says, laying his head on Rob's knee, 'there aren't many people I think would make as fantastic a father as you.'

Choosing another path

Our words manifest our thoughts and lead to consequences, despite what we chant about sticks and stones. What and how we speak are choices we make. So many words pass between people without consideration for the impact they will have on those we love. We blurt, we blab, we gossip, we lash out. We make a lot of noise. In Buddhism, one of the tenets of the eight-fold path towards enlightenment is *right speech*, a reminder to ask ourselves before we talk, 'Is it true, is it kind and is it necessary?' Honesty may be one of the virtues of communication – but kindness is another. Brutal honesty, which hurts, may not be the compassionate response, nor is it the way to overcome gridlock. How we communicate with the people we love determines the quality of our intimacy.

Rob goes to find Tariq in the bedroom and together they are able to shift the mood between them. Tariq performs a ritual from his spiritual tradition, a natural third position that gently acknowledges a higher force, beyond logic and human ego, and which embraces the imperfection, the wabi-sabi of his human relationship. Instead of maintaining their defensive positions (Rob's avoidance and delaying tactics, Tariq's anger and passive-aggressive withdrawal), they begin to face and be fully present in their situation. Sadness, vulnerability, love and perhaps even a little hope enters the room. It doesn't matter that they're not conscious of it – they're reaching for the third position, and perhaps nowhere else is this more important than when it comes to resolving apparently irreconcilable differences. If we are to grow our capacities to be authentically intimate, we need to learn to hold our loved one's desires and wishes on a par with our own.

Egos will always clash, sometimes sparking healthy friction. Certainly conflict helps us differentiate ourselves and hold onto a good solid sense of who we are. Even gridlock can be overcome, if we can drop our egos and look more deeply at what we're holding onto so tightly. Even if we can't resolve the problem so we both get what we originally wanted, we can always work through the loss inherent in changing our position. It's not *what* we decide in gridlock but *how*, and in what ways we sew each other's dreams into the fabric of our intimacy. We have to surrender the 'winner and loser' mentality, and lock out pride and the need to be right. Intimacy doesn't thrive on domination and manipulation; it prefers humility. In any form of the third position, we want what's best for the two of us, not just what's best for either one of us. We know that if one person loses, the relationship loses.

If even one of us in a relationship can hold this space, and reach for an understanding of our partner's pain, shifts can happen. We might change our minds if we realise we could lose the person we love over this, or be prepared to compromise because we recognise our own position isn't as tied to our sense of life's purpose as our partner's is. We can contain the contaminations of the past when we acknowledge our contribution to the gang of family relationships that crowd the bed. Rob, for instance, has to separate out his mother's desires from his own (or, at least, his projections onto her).

It starts with Rob owning his feelings of exclusion. If he also recognises that not being a father doesn't matter to him as much as being a father matters to Tariq, he may be prepared to walk that path with Tariq. Rob may realise that having a child is imperative to Tariq's happiness, and hold Tariq's happiness as part of his – Rob's – vision for their relationship.

Rob and Tariq can work it out. They can talk to a mutual friend, a parent, a therapist who can help them listen and see which bit of the elephant they're each holding onto as well as the whole creature – everything they have together as a couple, everything they've worked towards.

Phoebe and Tom have shown us that it's right to fight when there's something to fight about and that to chafe against each other isn't necessarily catastrophic. But, as we've seen with Daniel and Steph, if badly handled, it can lay waste to the relationship. Each relationship has its own Queensberry rules, the principles of conflict engagement. Some fights might scare the neighbours into calling the cops, others freeze silently into the sulk or passive-aggressive routine. Some are choreographed with door slams and arm-waving while others thrash it out over glasses of chardonnay in a restaurant. Whatever grievance-airing works for us as a couple.

No matter what we fight about, we can strive to fight fair. Even in disagreement, we can use our words and communicate respect. It's not only ugly names and R-rated expletives that hurt the good fight. Subtle sabotage includes the timing chosen to raise an issue, being focused only on our own pain while ignoring our partner's, or refusing to take responsibility for our own part in the conflict. A fair fight means we own our own wounds and do our best to see how we're contributing to the problem. A winning formula is to say, 'I want to work this out with you' and 'I'm willing to do the inner work to help us get there.' We have a choice: to blame the other person for screwing up our lives, or to find our partner's foibles or idiosyncrasies funny or cute instead. We can opt to work around them, see them as part of the whole package, mellow about what drives us crazy about them, to see who they are as complex and interesting even if it's frustrating. We can elect to accept them for who they are and forgive them for their wounds, their worries and their struggles. That's what commitment asks of us. A healthy part-nership should support two different people to be who they are and to become who they want to be.

∾

Will Tariq and Rob resolve the child issue? A lot depends on the choices they make.

In relationships we're often called on to extend ourselves in uncomfortable ways for the sake of the ones we love. It's a barter of kindness: we exchange generosities; we stretch ourselves to hold our partner's dreams together with our own. These are the terms of intimacy. We honour and do our best to help the person we love to live the fullest life possible. But if doing so means dishonouring the vision we have for our own lives, we've reached stalemate. We can't sacrifice ourselves out of existence in order to fulfil someone else's dream. There are parts of ourselves we may be willing to renounce, but we can't sacrifice our essence. To do this, we need to know who we are, what dreams lie at the core of our beings, so we know what we can and cannot surrender.

19.

Breaking (Up and Open)

ERIN IS STRUGGLING TO FOCUS on her breath. The class is crowded today. She keeps having intrusive thoughts. Images of Daniel getting a blow job in the park. Ugh. Focus, she reminds herself. She tries to breathe below her diaphragm, the way she's been taught, but it's as if her breath won't let her go too deep. Shit, she can't meditate, not with all this drama going on inside her.

She touches her belly and smiles. She'll never forget the expression on Mitch's face when she told him about her missed period, and then when the pregnancy was confirmed and his eyes had teared up . . . and now he can't get that silly grin off his face. She wonders whether Daniel reacted the same way when Steph told him about their first pregnancy. Daniel! Bugger it, why does he have to be spoiling things now?

The voice of her meditation teacher reminds her that she is here, now, that all the thoughts running riot through her head are just that – thoughts. That she should notice them, without judgement or criticism. Yes, well, thanks very much. Not so easy to be neutral about her cousin's husband's extra-marital activities. She just hasn't been able to get any clarity. Should she tell Steph and hurt her? Or keep it from her and hurt her, just in a different way? If it were her, she'd want to know. And of course Tara would have no trouble bounding in with 'terrible news' if ever Mitch took to blow jobs from other women. Tara takes some measure of joy in other people's love

176

problems. Erin wonders what the Buddha would do. He was big on right thought, right speech and right action. Sounds so simple, she mutters internally, squeaking an eyelid open to see if anyone else is struggling to just 'be with the breath' like she is. But around her, all is calm. No-one else looks as if their serenity is being spammed with pornographic pop-ups.

∽

'You can't tell Steph.' That was Mitch's view. But Mitch puts out fires. He doesn't like conflict. He'd do anything to keep the peace.

'What if it was your sister's husband doing the dirty on her?' Erin had asked.

Mitch had shrugged. 'You couldn't pay me enough to face Kayla with that kind of news. I'd take that secret to the grave.'

A few days after that conversation, with Erin still trying to figure out what to do, they had discovered she was pregnant, and that had eclipsed everything for a while.

∽

And now Erin still isn't sure. She wants Steph to know, but she doesn't want to be the one to break it to her. Maybe an anonymous note left in her post box? Bloody cowardly. As she sits on the cushion, the teacher says they'll end their practice with a *loving-kindness* meditation.

'Think of someone you love,' the teacher says. Erin's heart opens and Steph is there. Poor, lovely, worn-down Steph.

'And now silently say to this person, "May you be well, may you be happy, may you be free from danger, and may you be at peace."' Erin sends these loving thoughts to Steph.

'Now, think of someone you're having difficulty with,' the teacher says. 'No trouble with that,' Erin mutters to herself. Daniel. The prick. 'Now, silently say to this person, "May you be well, may you be happy, may you be free from danger, and may you be at peace."'

Erin feels something in her constrict. It's resistance. She breathes into it. She feels something in her softening. And she sends these loving thoughts to Daniel, the bastard.

At the end of her meditation, Erin knows what she has to do.

∽

Most of us confront obstacles in our lives as we would a hostile stranger – with antipathy, adrenaline and resistance, ready to fight, freeze or flee. The spiritual teacher Stephen Levine suggests we try to meet pain (physical or emotional) with a 'soft belly'. Instead of tightening against it, he urges us to open to it, welcome it right in, and be fully present with it. Sure, it's entirely counter-intuitive, like inviting the person who stabbed you in the back for a nice cup of tea. But not if we hold the truth close to us, that all things – even pain and difficulty – are impermanent, imperfect and incomplete. They will pass. We have a choice about how to encounter them. We can lock them out and get an AVO against them like we would against a psychotic stalker.

Or we can, through loving-kindness, do the opposite. We can send love to people who have hurt us. It is the anticlockwise move, the antidote to our narcissism, which wants to know 'What's in it for me?' or 'Why should I?' or 'I don't feel like it'. Loving-kindness steers us towards understanding the incomprehensible, and loving the unlovable. It takes us into an internal third position, where we (even momentarily) hold the whole picture in our consciousness, including the fragile humanity of someone we rationally despise. In opening our hearts this way, we allow for the possibility that we cannot know all there is to know, that we cannot judge on partial understanding, and so we choose to do the one thing that that can do no harm, the one practice that holds all other practices – we can love people in their brokenness and in their imperfection.

One of the major obstacles to this generosity in intimate relation-ships is a fear that if we don't oppose our partners' demands, they'll swamp us. If we relinquish our complaints and demands against them, that freed-up territory will be taken over by them. We're afraid they'll greedily fill the space we have just vacated, and that the relationship will become imbalanced with us doing all the hard work. 'That's not fair!' we protest. But this isn't a license for our partners to become the sole recipients of nurture. We shouldn't give up our rights; we should still be firm in our boundary setting. Loving compassionately is not a compromising move. If the narcissist in all of us could only see: there's plenty 'in it for me'. When we hang out with compassion and extend it to others, there's a spillover as we soften inwards to our own faults and mistakes. Every time we do not judge others, we restrain our inner critic who, given any airtime, spews bile not only about others but about us too. Just as we cannot hurt others without hurting ourselves, so we cannot love others without also loving ourselves. Love is automatically super-sized. You buy one, you get one for free.

We don't know the power of prayer, or loving-kindness meditation, in the quantum physical universe. There are those who claim that the energy of these love-filled vibrations does have a causal effect, in the same way that hatred translates into violence. By sending loving-kindness to others, we embrace paradox, we enlarge our sense of what we are connected to and are responsible for. We take our place in the family of all living, loving, imperfect creatures.

∾

'Erin, what a surprise!' Steph smiles, though her expression is strained. *She looks tired*, Erin thinks. 'My favourite cousin,' Steph says. 'Come on in and have some of the carrot cake I made last night.'

Erin walks into the expansive living room, which leads into the fabulous kitchen Steph and Daniel built only a few years ago; until a short while ago, Erin saw all this as part of Steph and Daniel's perfect life.

'Coffee?' Steph asks.

Erin shakes her head. 'Water will be good,' she says.

'Are you okay?' Steph asks. 'You look like something big is happening. You're not pregnant? Oh my God, are you pregnant?' Steph looks at her excitedly.

Erin can't believe Steph has picked it up and can't hide her smile. But it's detracting from her mission. This wasn't how things were supposed to go.

'Erin, this is so exciting!' Steph cuddles Erin's tummy. 'You must let me organise your baby shower. When's the baby due?'

Erin lets Steph natter on a while about the baby; she waits for a pause.

'Look, Steph, I actually came over to talk about something else . . .' Erin bites her lip. She remembers to breathe into her belly. She wants to be skilful, helpful, and not cause damage or pain. 'How are things going between you and Daniel?' she asks.

Steph raises her eyebrows. 'Oh, you know, the same.' She gives a silvery laugh.

'But, honestly?' Erin asks. 'How are things *really* going between you?'

Steph looks at her quizzically. 'They're, well, I guess they're so-so. We must be going through the seventeen-year-itch or something like that. Why are you asking?'

Erin puts her hand on Steph's. 'I don't want to be the bearer of this news, and God knows I've been agonising over whether to tell you . . . I don't want to hurt you or to cause any trouble between you and Daniel –'

'He's having an affair, isn't he?' Steph suddenly says. She exhales. 'I fucking knew it!'

'No, not that, well, I don't know about that,' Erin says, 'but Mitch saw him in the park the other night and . . . '

Erin goes on to tell Steph what Mitch saw. The words topple out of her, like items stuffed in a closet whose door is suddenly wrenched open.

Erin waits for Steph to explode, to be furious, to cry, to do . . . something, anything. But Steph just listens. She doesn't even question whether Mitch is sure he saw what he saw. Maybe he got it wrong. It was dusk; maybe it was a colleague from work . . . Erin wants her to be angry. To deny it. To tell her Mitch is mistaken. But Steph just takes it.

'I'm so sorry,' Erin says, 'but I felt you had a right to know.'

Steph takes her cake fork and plunges it into the slice on her plate. 'It's okay, Erin. Things between us have been really shit for a long time. I'm not surprised.' Suddenly there's a crack in Steph's voice. 'I guess my marriage is pretty much over. I just feel sad for the kids.'

'Is it over? Does it have to be over?' Erin asks.

'I don't know. I don't know how to save our marriage. I don't know how you come back from something like this.'

'Do you still love him?' Erin asks.

Steph shrugs. 'I'm not sure.'

The unwelcome guest

This is the relationship equivalent of a cancer diagnosis. As terror, fear and confusion flood us all at once we may feel as if we've been exiled from our own lives. As Dante writes in *The Divine Comedy*, 'In the middle of the road of my life / I awoke in the dark wood / where the true way was wholly lost.' The poet Mark Nepo, who himself had cancer as a young man, calls an experience that challenges us – a betrayal, an illness, the loss of someone we love – an 'unwelcome guest'. These moments are initiations, an invitation to stay present in our lives, just at the point when we have no idea what life is asking of us.

Viktor Frankl, in *Man's Search for Meaning*, says it is possible to find meaning in all of life's experiences, including those of untold suffering, because even when our circumstances cannot be changed, we can still choose how to respond to them. A crisis can break us. But what will be broken? Our illusions that our lives, our health, our relationships were perfect? What is really so terrible about being broken? Nepo says crises like these can either break us or break us open, forcing a collision with the truths we've been avoiding for a long time. Everything that has been denied and repressed between Steph and Daniel has now come to a head. Finally the demons have spilled out into the relationship. Because it's so painful, we think this is a terrible thing. But a diagnosis of an illness is also a new beginning. It gives us a chance to heal.

⚭

The light on the front porch is off. That's odd. Steph usually switches it on when night falls, so that when Daniel pulls up in the driveway, the front door is illuminated. Maybe the globe has blown. He climbs the stairs to the front door in the dark, and fumbles to get his key in the keyhole.

Inside, everything is quiet. The lights in the living room are off, and only the light in the kitchen is on.

'Steph?' he calls. 'Justin? Georgia? Where the hell is everyone?' Did he forget something? Is Steph out having dinner at her folks'? He'd remember that.

He drops his briefcase on the sofa and takes off his jacket. He walks into the kitchen. There's no dinner cooking. Nothing on the stove-top, nothing in the oven. It looks as if the surfaces have been wiped down and the dishwasher is on. He opens the fridge to grab a beer – he bought a six-pack of fancy German beers on the weekend and only drank two of them. But there are no beers in the fridge. Steph doesn't drink beer. Who's drunk his beers?

Suddenly he hears her footsteps on the stairwell.

'Well,' he says as she walks in to the kitchen. 'I was just about to dial emergency. What the hell's going on here? It's only 7.30. Where are the kids?'

Steph walks past him, not making any eye contact.

'They're in their rooms,' she says coolly.

'Already? No TV tonight?'

Steph doesn't respond.

'Have you eaten?' Daniel asks.

'I don't have much of an appetite.' Sarcasm hangs like stalactites on her words.

'Well, I'm starving,' Daniel says. 'Is there any dinner? Any leftovers? And what the hell happened to my beers?'

'No, there's no dinner. There's no leftovers.' Steph walks over to the trash. She picks out four empty beer bottles and places them with exaggerated care on the counter. 'I poured them down the drain.'

'What the hell is going on with you?' Daniel says. Those are *imported* beers! Suddenly Daniel's blood is boiling. What has gotten into Steph? Has she lost her mind?

'Oh, I'm sorry, you sleazy prick. I just figured since you've got enough cash to pay a prostitute, you'd have no problem replacing your fucking imported beers!'

'What are you talking about?' Daniel asks, raking his fingers through his hair. 'Prostitute? Are you mad?'

'No, Daniel. I'm not the one who's mad. I'm not the one having sleazy blow jobs in my car in the park.'

Daniel feels himself choking.

'*What?*'

'You heard me. How long has that little joke been going on? I know you've been slobbering over porn, but going to prostitutes . . .' Steph gags.

'She's not a . . .' Daniel stops himself.

'What is she then?' Steph asks. 'Your girlfriend? Your mistress? Ugh, I don't even care what you call her. You're a pervert. I should have known that. You're a sex addict. You need help.'

Daniel struggles to breathe. Adrenalin bolts through him. How did Steph find out? Who could have told her? He feels bile rising up inside him. He's going to be sick. '*I* need help? What about you? You fucking drove me to it, you cold bitch! What do you expect, when I can't get a kiss out of you, a hug – I mean, sex isn't even on your to-do list, not even if you made it out for the next ten years. I've been trying . . .' Daniel tears at his hair. 'It . . . I was desperate . . .'

'Well, no need to be desperate anymore,' Steph says, arms folded across her chest. 'You can pack your bags right now and go to your girlfriend. Just get out of the house, and get out of our lives.'

'What do you mean?' Daniel says, panicking. 'I'm not moving out, I don't want to go anywhere, I'm . . . I'm . . . what about the kids?'

'What do you care about the kids? They're better off without you in their lives. What sort of a person . . .? What sort of a father . . .?' Steph feels her throat tightening, tears threatening.

'Steph, please,' Daniel implores, approaching her. 'I'm sorry.'

Steph backs off. 'Don't come near me. Don't touch me with your filthy hands. Get away from me you bastard.'

Daniel stops. He puts his head in his hands. He makes no sound, but his back heaves. Is he crying? Steph glares at him, part of her lapping up this glorious moment, her husband broken in front of her. She feels the power surging inside her, the moral high ground lifting her above him. Watching him squirm makes her feel stronger than she's felt all her married life. And, oddly, more wretched. A thought of Alistair bolts through her mind. No, she dismisses the errant thought, it's not the same thing. Not the same at all. So she's been Facebooking him. Big deal. That's just harmless flirting. Harmless. Alistair lives all the way in

Los Angeles. She hasn't had his dick in her mouth. Though . . . Steph did turn red when that message came through, the one retelling the dream he'd had of the two of them making love.

'I deserve it,' Daniel says, finally looking up, his face streaked. 'Call me any names you want. I'm sorry. I love you. I made a mistake. I'll never do it again. Don't kick me out, please. Don't throw me out of our kids' lives. Give me another chance.'

Steph's fury wrestles with shock at seeing Daniel cry. 'I hate you,' she chokes.

Daniel nods.

'You're a pig.'

'Yes.'

'You betrayed me, you betrayed the kids.'

The tears pour down Daniel's face. He feels his knees buckling under him.

'She meant nothing . . . I was just so . . . so . . . lonely.'

Steph swallows. 'Lonely or horny?'

'Both, maybe. But mostly, lonely. I have been for a long time.' Daniel sinks onto a bar stool, propping himself up on the kitchen counter with an elbow, his features dishevelled. 'I just want . . . something . . . some tenderness from you. But it's like I disgust you.'

'I don't know what you mean,' Steph says icily. 'I want plenty from you. I want someone who cares about me and what I'm going through. Someone who listens to what I say, and who shares the hardships of my day. I know it's not glamorous compared to your big day at the office, but it's still my life.' Steph feels her voice faltering. Over the past few months she's taken to telling Alistair all the details of her day – shit, Alistair knows more about Steph's daily dramas than Daniel does – because he's *interested* in her life.

Daniel says nothing. Steph stands at the far end of the kitchen. Between them on the kitchen table stand the four empty beer bottles. The clock on the kitchen wall ticks loudly. The dishwasher beeps, its cycle complete.

Finally Daniel says, 'Please don't throw me out, Steph. I love you. I have always loved you. I know it's hard for you to believe that, but it's true. My dick just got in the way, but I'm more than my dick. And even if you never wanted to have sex with me again, it would be better than living a life without you. I'd take just waking up in the bed next to you for the rest of my life over sex. Just so I could watch you sleep.'

Steph is repulsed by his words. His pathetic grovelling makes her feel even worse. That's not what she wants – a broken man.

'Erin and Mitch know,' Steph says. 'Mitch saw you! Don't you even have the good sense to do it in secret? You had to do it in public. Do you have any idea how humiliating it is? I've got to live with people knowing my husband was having sleazy sex with strangers. I don't know that I can forgive this.' Steph turns and walks out of the kitchen.

'Steph, please, can I stay?'

Without turning to face him she says, 'You can sleep on the couch. And make sure you're up early so the kids don't ask questions. If it weren't for them, you'd be out on your arse.'

And with that, she climbs the lonely staircase to her empty bed, which has been emptying quietly for years.

The story of Kisa Gotami

Many years ago, in the time of the Buddha, Kisa Gotami, the wife of a wealthy man, lost her only son who died in his sleep. The poor woman was so overcome with grief she went to the Buddha and begged him to bring her son back to life. He agreed, on condition that she bring him back a handful of mustard seeds from a family that had not lost a loved one. She was overjoyed and set off on her quest to find these mustard seeds. She knocked on the door of the first home and told her story, asking for a handful of mustard seeds, which the owner happily gave to her. 'Oh, and just one more thing – no-one has died in your home, have they?' At this, the woman's face fell. 'Yes, just last week, my beloved father died.' Sadly, Kisa Gotami returned the mustard seeds and went to the next house. At each house, she found that someone had lost a person they loved; in every face she found a mirror of the grief in her own. And so she went from home to home, realising that she was not alone in her suffering, and she returned to the Buddha, awake. Through the worst grief that broke her, she was broken open into enlightenment.

∞

It's a crossroads in Steph and Daniel's relationship. Their challenge is to find a way to make meaning from this experience. Only they can do it, by moving beyond the bits of the elephant they're each clutching. The truth between them is not simple; it is a rich tapestry of many silences, betrayals, sadness, and failure to hold on to each other. They're not energetically separate; they are parts of a whole. Even if Daniel has acted out the adulterous energy of their relationship and carries the relationship's shadow self, and Steph embodies the virtuous energy (despite her niggles of conscience about the Facebook flirting with Alistair), they've co-created their situation. Daniel is not only a betrayer, and neither is Steph only faithful. There's a much bigger elephant in their bedroom. They have a chance to reach beyond partial understanding and to use this experience to transform their relationship. Who's to say that their relationship doesn't need to be burnt to the ground, so that the phoenix can rise from the ashes?

Daniel has gone too far. And in doing so, he's unconsciously brought them to the brink. Sometimes we have to stand at the precipice of disaster, to come within an inch of losing everything, before we wake up. *This*, then, is the alarm.

20.

When It's Time to Split

No-one picks monogamy imagining that one day they'll have to pull the plug on it. We pledge ourselves to love, like women give birth – full of hopes and dreams of the happiest of ever-afters. Even in the most successful relationships, there'll be 'what was I thinking?' and 'is this the best I can do?' moments, wishes for the odd free pass to bonk someone else, or to fall in love again. Over a lifetime, we change our lifestyles, eating habits, taste in movies, and our political and religious views as part of inevitable personal growth. Monogamy imposes this unique restriction – that we'll remain forever fixed to one person, despite how much each of us will transform and our relationship may change. Some religions and societies make divorce and separation so impossible, excruciating or at the very least catastrophically shameful, that it's just easier to stay and be miserable. But life is too short to commit to a lifetime of unhappiness. Sometimes, as heartbreaking as it is, it will be time to call it quits.

The wet spot

In Tom and Phoebe's case, the absence of sex is bleeding their relationship dry. But what desiccates a relationship isn't the lack of wet spots per se, it's what clean sheets means to each of us. For some, no sex may be grounds for The End, for others it's no big deal. If two people prefer a shared glass of good wine over a sweaty orgasm, there's no desire discrepancy. What's not so fabulous is if one of us wants a snog while the other would rather take the dog for a walk, watch *CSI*, or clean the car. If sex is in the equivalent vicinity on our priority list (not top on yours and bottom on mine, but at least in the same quarter or third), neither of us will feel particularly short-changed. Where there is a big variance between libidos, as David Schnarch says in *Passionate Marriage,* the partner with the lowest libido controls the frequency of sex (in a relationship that's not abusive) and the other will be a bristling bale of sexual frustration.

What we have to do is accommodate the way we each change individually and keep checking in on each other and the relationship to make sure we're both keeping up and transforming. To keep intimacy growing, we have to keep our hearts and minds open. As we invariably work through patterns of painful re-enactments, some of us will exit the spiral to engage in a deeper, more aware interaction, while others will get stuck, replaying the same pattern, unable to find a way out, like a hamster caught on its wheel. One of us could grow east and the other west. One of us might blossom into self-awareness, while the other prefers the damp dark cave of 'this is who I am, like it or lump it'. Perhaps we both want the same thing, but can't reach it because our relationship has lost its elasticity. Left brittle for too long, now all that's left are fossils.

There are gazillions of reasons people stay in relationships that seem to be going nowhere. Fear of change, financial insecurity, being in a (sometimes not so comfortable) comfort zone, and often co-dependence. Couples become so entangled, re-enacting powerful scripts, that they cannot untie themselves, literally feeling that they won't know who they are beyond the relationship. Even in dangerously toxic relationships such as those involving domestic violence, the abused partner often elects to stay, or forgive – for the umpteenth time – the apparently contrite abuser. From the outside it seems inexplicable, but inside the relationship there are complex forces at play in which both partners are hooked by projective identification to play out their compatible, albeit perverted scripts. We are, of course, not referring to cases in which a woman becomes trapped against her will by a dictatorial societal or religious system, or perhaps may fear for the life of her children or herself. Unhealthy re-enactments lead to unhealthy relationships. If we've had an experience of 'good enough' love we're more likely to end up in relationships that feel 'good enough', and will re-enact healthier patterns.

It's easy to walk away from what we're indifferent to – the mild, ineffectual, boring partnerships that leave us grey and emotionally constipated. Relationships where there's a lot of conflict and drama are *harder* to leave, because there's a lot more attachment – whatever pisses us off, enrages us and hurts us deeply, also has us deeply, unconsciously invested and hooked in, where we are playing our part in this dance, if only to have someone to act as a container for the parts of ourselves we can't stand. Hate is a passionate dynamic. It's often a disguise for a deep and frightening need, and so doesn't provide, on its own, sufficient impetus for a break-up. Or, as with many couples, there are fluctuations in mood, from good to bad, bearable to unbearable, oscillations between hate and love.

Many people attempt to address the question 'is it time to split?' by falling in love with someone else – a particular kind of triangulation of a third party. When there's the option of an alternative bed to hop into that looks far more inviting than our troubled one at home, it's easier to say 'I'm outta here', especially as the new relationship is usually still in the phase of sexual desire and romantic love. But even then, a sense of obligation to children, parents, God (if you've involved Him) as well as financial stressors and a hundred other concerns may stand between us and the door.

Relationship CPR

Some people can do a hit and run. They can drive off without a backwards glance, too afraid of or indifferent to the wreckage they've left behind them. Some of us flee our relationships, even the families we've created, without much visible angst. Perhaps we've spent too long trying to be happy and are completely internally resolved about our decision even if it's come as 'news' to the other. Maybe we've been lying to ourselves. We've always known this isn't the relationship for us but we've only just discovered the internal girders or resolve to walk away. On the other hand, we could just be too far from our own truths to face the reality of what we're doing.

But if we've invested any amount of time, effort, emotion or money in a relationship, we'll probably try to make it work for a time, if only so we can say 'I did all I could', the way we'd try all remedies to resuscitate a loved one whose life is ebbing away. We hang in there, giving all the CPR we can, because losing a relationship makes us feel like a loser. It's an admission of failure, a public announcement of personal love error — one that will become yet another piece of our 'baggage' we'll have to work through before getting into another relationship.

No-one likes a goodbye. Switching off the machines on a flatlining relationship is still an act of termination. Ending a partnership is an energetic abortion. And with it, we'll lose the vitality we invested in it. So, of course Tom and Phoebe will try anything to make things work.

∾

Father Gareth welcomes Tom and Phoebe every week with a cup of tea and some shortbread biscuits. But as the months of their therapy pass by, despair begins to creep in. Father Gareth, having initially felt full of hope for the lovely young couple before him, has begun to wonder. Divorce is not an option, not only because he's a Catholic priest, but he can't understand why the love between them, coupled with prayer, isn't sufficient to see them through. They love each other. That's clear. And they both want it to work. Why can't it?

Father Gareth suggests that maybe Tom would benefit from individual psychotherapy, to run concurrently with the marital therapy. 'Why not Phoebe?' Tom asks defensively.

'I'll go to psychotherapy too – I'll do anything,' Phoebe says. In her naked willingness to give anything a go, Tom sees why Father Gareth has suggested he goes and not Phoebe. He's the one who's stuck. Not her.

Tom agrees. It's helpful, because in these sessions he doesn't feel he has to censor what he says for fear of hurting Phoebe. He becomes a bit looser in his confessions and then to his surprise finds himself weeping when he talks about being a little boy whose mother kept being taken away from him at regular intervals as she became pregnant, and confined to bed for weeks on end to try to prevent the miscarriage she'd come to expect.

190

Over the weeks, Tom starts to understand that his fear of aggression is wrapped up with sex in a deeply unconscious way, dating back to his childhood. He remembers that whenever his mother fell pregnant ('Daddy puts his pee-pee in mummy, and his egg joins with mummy's egg to make a baby', his mother explained) she'd be taken away from him, to lie in her bed – saving herself, not for him, but for the child inside her. He slowly remembers his frustrated outbursts as a toddler and preschooler, yelling at his mother – 'Why won't you play with me? You're with the baby all day! I wish the baby would go away!' And then the miscarriage happened, leaving him with the sense that he'd got his wish, that he'd caused these unborn babies to die.

At one session with Phoebe and Father Gareth, Tom shares this. Phoebe, hearing this for the first time, grows pale.

'Tom,' she says quietly, 'what does that mean for . . .? I mean . . . the termination?' She quells an impulse to look guiltily in the priest's direction. Dammit, she's not sacrificing her feminist principles by feeling guilty about exercising her inalienable right to make decisions about her own body.

Tom's hands flinch instinctively, curling themselves into fists. He stares out the window.

After a pause, Father Gareth says, as gently as he can manage, 'The two of you had a termination?'

Phoebe nods. 'It was a few months into our relationship. We weren't sure whether we'd be together long-term and there was no way I was going to be a single mother. It was early days. And I hadn't planned on children at least until I was in my thirties.'

'And how did *you* feel about it, Tom?' asks Father Gareth.

'He was okay at the time,' says Phoebe, 'weren't you, love?'

'No, I was not!' hisses Tom, still looking out the window. Phoebe cringes at his response. She's so rarely seen this from Tom: anger. And then it pours out: how much agony he'd felt going along with it; that he'd wanted Phoebe not to do it, that he'd tried to talk her out of it, but that she'd been adamant. 'I tried . . .' he stammers, 'I tried . . . to save our baby . . .'

JOANNE FEDLER & GRAEME FRIEDMAN

'It was a seven-week foetus, Tom,' Phoebe says, sternly. 'You know, you could have used birth control. That was in your power, too. I am not wearing this. It was in your power too.'

'A seven-week foetus . . . it was still our baby,' Tom says bitterly. Phoebe looks at Tom as if he is a stranger. Never once did he voice his true feelings to her. She has had no idea that he felt this way. And in this moment, she feels an ocean roar between them.

೧෧

Impotence. No man's dream. Few things are as emasculating, and yet, so common, often being brought on by financial stress, health issues, psychological traumas and any number of other factors. In Tom's case, it's tied up with his feeling powerless to save their unborn baby. The pain and shame evoked by Phoebe's termination lodged in Tom's psyche, wrapped up with the deeply repressed emotions associated with his mother's miscarriages. As soon as Phoebe terminated her pregnancy, in Tom's unconscious, she became twisted up in his mind with his own mother. Though Tom loved his mother, he cannot become sexually aroused by someone who reminds him of her. He can't bear the thought of making Phoebe pregnant, and the best contraceptive is impotence.

೧෧

This is a breakthrough. Tom's beginning to understand his internal world. Over the next few weeks, Phoebe and Tom try to work with these insights. Phoebe is understanding, apologetic. But Tom's anger seems spent, his defences rearranging themselves around the breach in their wall. More weeks go by, and Phoebe's frustration has turned into a nagging, throbbing hum, seldom leaving her. At home – even she wouldn't bring this up in front of a priest – Phoebe suggests they try a threesome. Perhaps they could hire a sex worker, someone Tom is attracted to? Tom looks at her aghast, unable to own up to the excite-ment the idea stirs in him. In his own therapy, he plays with the idea but he can't let it gain traction: if it worked, it'd be because he got it up for the whore, and then he'd feel even more ashamed and distant from Phoebe.

Phoebe meets with Erin for a coffee, and tells her that she wonders if she was ever really sexually attracted to Tom: 'You know, *really* attracted, like I wanted to fuck his brains out.' Maybe what she thought was sexual excitement was her wanting a warm cuddle? She confesses that she's never felt the excitement with Tom that she experiences when she fantasises about Jake and other men. 'What the hell have I been doing? I feel like I've been stranded on a barren island while romance and sex is happening over there on the mainland. I've been doing what I did as a little girl when my parents fought – curl up in my room and rock myself. And now I'm doing the same thing – only I'm an adult woman alone in my room with a frigging vibrator!'

And yet, she loves Tom. 'You know, people say you marry your father. Well, I think I have. This lovely, wonderful man who I can feel safe and warm with.'

She'd settle for a half-decent sexual relationship, she cries in frustration. Erin suggests viagra. Phoebe brings it up with Tom (without, of course, mentioning that it was Erin's idea). Not a chance, says Tom. He's heard about the side effects. Some guys have hard-ons for days and there've been some deaths, and not just of old guys with high blood pressure.

'Maybe Tom's depressed,' suggests Erin. 'What about an anti-depressant?'

'He'd never agree,' says Phoebe. 'And anyway, I think I'm the one who's depressed.' That night at home, she casts her last lifeline: 'Tom, maybe we should try a sex therapist.'

They take a break from their sessions with Father Gareth and consult a sex therapist, who offers to guide them through several weeks of exercises aimed at reducing sexual anxiety and increasing eroticism. After three sessions, Tom and Phoebe return to Father Gareth even more despairing. Failure hangs about them like iron chains.

They sit quietly. There are no words but there is a story being told in the room. Father Gareth, feeling as if he's administering the Last Rites, asks their permission to open with a prayer, to ask for God's guidance in helping His children make a decision that will bring them both peace. They nod their assent. When he's finished, Phoebe reaches out

JOANNE FEDLER & GRAEME FRIEDMAN

to take Tom's hand. Her tears fall before any words can slip between her trembling lips.

Tom's eyes hover, holding Phoebe's gaze for a moment before dropping away to the floor.

'Tom, my darling –' Phoebe's voice cracks, her eyes searching his face. 'You need to let me go.'

Letting go

Doing the work we need to do inside ourselves and together with our partners will usually lead to change. But not necessarily in the direction we imagined. Insight might reveal a new path – one that doesn't lead us back to each other, but away from the relationship. Phoebe and Tom, despite desperately wanting to stay together, have to face the reality that their partnership was born too much from unresolved, immature parts of themselves. Hopefully Tom will continue to work on untangling his aggression/potency conundrum and, once he's made enough movement, there's no reason why he won't resolve what's holding him back and father a child with a woman he loves. But it won't be with Phoebe. Neurons that fire together, wire together. And for Tom, his wiring, when it comes to Phoebe, has become so fused it's impossible to unravel.

Despite their newfound capacity to disagree, there remains no erotic rub, nothing to create that spark. By choosing each other, their needs for safety trumped – and suffocated – passion. Perhaps if they'd addressed these issues earlier there may have been more hope of arresting the loss of sexual attraction, tame as it might have been in the beginning. Sometimes a dynamic becomes so set between two people that the only solution to break it is to separate, and to recognise that the best chance for both to enjoy a more intimate relationship is to take the lessons learned in this one, and move on. Something has become so moulded between them, so set in stone, that it cannot be budged.

Tom could probably have mooched along in the relationship indefinitely, but Phoebe wasn't satisfied with this. She was the spokesperson for the relationship, the speaker of truth.

It's heartbreaking to lose someone we love. But in time, Tom and

Phoebe will come to understand that they were an integral – and perhaps, inevitable – part of each other's growth. Second marriages are so often more successful than first ones: people have learned, matured, understood themselves better, and make better choices second time around.

∽

In southern Myanmar, monkeys are hunted for food. Though they're one of nature's most intelligent creatures, the trap is simple. Hunters carve holes in coconuts the size of a monkey's paw and fill the hollowed out coconuts with peanuts or rice and then tie the coconuts to trees. Monkeys, lured by the smell coming from the coconuts, reach into the coconuts and grab a handful of rice or peanuts. But the opening, now too small for them to remove their fists, stops them. And so they stay, their hands full of peanuts or rice, trapped because they cannot let go.

Sometimes what we're holding on to is what is trapping us. We have to let go in order to be free.

PART V

The Practice of Intimacy

21.

The Intervention

We say, 'A person is a person through other persons.'
I need you in order to be me
and you need me in order to be you.
— Archbishop Desmond Tutu

SO WHAT WILL BECOME OF Steph and Daniel? Is their relationship doomed, like Tom and Phoebe's? Is there a way back to each other after such a fall? And how will their crisis affect their friends and family?

The witness

Erin checks the table one more time. It's covered in platters of food and rose petals.

'It looks perfect,' Mitch says, kissing her on the top of her head, and cupping her pregnant belly in his hands. 'Hey, I think he just scored a goal.'

'Mitch! All of a sudden you know it's a he?'

'Okay, well then *she* scored a goal.'

'I hope I'm not scoring an own goal tonight,' Erin says.

'You're nervous?' asks Mitch.

'I am, a bit,' Erin confesses.

'Don't worry. Rob and Tariq will be here as backup. And don't forget about me, I'm also here.'

'Yeah, speaking of my dear brother, where the hell is he? Steph and Daniel are going to get here before they do, at this rate. You know how she is about being on time.'

∞

It had been Erin's idea. One night as she and Mitch lay entwined in each other's arms, thinking about names for the baby – due in four months – she asked, 'Babe, you wouldn't do anything like this to me, would you? Even if I was old and ugly and we hadn't had sex in a decade, you wouldn't cheat on me, would you?'

Mitch sighed. 'I can't even imagine it, Bean.'

'But you can't say for certain, can you? I mean, what if ten years down the line, we just, like, grew apart? Just stopped loving each other?'

Mitch had swept Erin's hair from her face, tracing each eyebrow with his fingers, the bridge of her nose, the shape of her mouth, the contours of this face he'd come to know so well. Something slow and solid had started growing between them, as if they'd both stopped in the same place, and in stopping, had grown roots that were knotting together. There is no way he could ever imagine doing something to jeopardise their love. How the hell did Daniel get to that point in the park?

He doesn't need to stray in order to know what it would feel like to lose her. It's as if he lives in two universes at the same time. In one he wakes up with Erin and the baby inside her, cuddles them in his big arms until he can't put off the responsibilities of the day any longer, rises, dresses, goes to work, comes home, enjoys dinner with Erin, maybe gets to make love to her (how lucky is he that Erin is one those women who gets horny in her second trimester?) and then goes to sleep. In the other universe he falls into nightmarish places of such loneliness. It makes no sense. He has everything he could ever wish for, and yet whenever he feels it, *really* feels the high of connection and gratitude, he looks over his shoulder and runs, chased by fear. Whenever he allows himself to love her deeply, he feels he's losing her, as if she's died or gone off to love someone else. And then it's the Serengeti all over again: the intense pain-joy of connection followed by his withdrawal and a bewildering sense of emptiness.

With their baby growing inside Erin, it frightens Mitch to feel that there is so much love still to unravel between them. The bottomlessness of it is shattering; it sometimes takes his breath away. He wonders if everyone feels this way, only to discover it's like the life in the ocean, the ozone – fragile and finite.

He tries to hide the grumpiness that comes with his feelings of emptiness, not wanting to trouble Erin with it. It's his private battle, and he is determined to win it. Only once has he managed to confess some mild version of his fear to her. She had taken his hand gently and said, 'Will you do something weird with me?'

'How weird?' he asked.

'It's a hugging meditation,' she'd said. 'Something I read about in one of my books.' Then she explained how they needed to both take a few deep breaths. Then they needed to 'bow' to each other. Mitch had felt ridiculous, but he'd followed her lead. 'Now, we hold each other, and we say silently to ourselves, as we breathe in, "I know you are alive in my arms," and as we breathe out, we say, "I feel so happy," and we do this three times.'

Mitch had found this easy.

'It gets harder,' Erin had warned.

'Well, I can feel something getting harder,' Mitch had teased.

'Naughty, we're *meditating*,' she'd chided. 'Now we hug and say silently, "I see myself already dead, and you, my love, are alive."' Strangely, Mitch hadn't found this too difficult.

But it was the next level where he struggled, when he had to hold Erin in his arms and say, 'You are already dead, and I am still alive.' With his arms around her, he felt something straining in his chest, a sob. Erin had held him. She'd not let him go. She'd been there.

And finally, once again, Erin led him to the last step, to say again, 'I know you are alive in my arms, and I feel so happy.'

Since then, they'd done the hugging meditation a few times, and each time, as he faced the transience of their love, their physical bodies, this moment between them, it always hurt, but he was learning not to be as frightened of it.

രൗ

But that night as they lay there with Erin's 'what-if' question about the future, Mitch squeezed her and then let go, suddenly frightened he might hurt the baby. 'I guess it's like the things I see at work. No-one ever thinks they'll be caught in a fire or trapped in a car. We can't live with that possibility, so we go about our lives thinking it'll never happen to us. But it happens to people all the time. Only I'm sure as hell not going to set the fire. Or not that kind of fire.'

Erin sighed into him, softening like a beanbag against his chest. 'But if it did . . . what would you want your friends to do about it?'

'My friends? Is it any of their business?'

'Why not? When people you care about are in trouble, isn't it your duty to help them? Why wouldn't it be our friends' business?' Erin asked. 'Justin and Georgia look so lost, so confused. Did I tell you Georgia started wetting her bed? At the age of ten!'

'Don't we kinda want people to stay out of our marriages? Privacy and all that? Wouldn't it be interfering?'

'Even when things are falling apart? Isn't that the problem? I feel so helpless sitting by and watching Steph and Daniel struggle. I was a bridesmaid at their wedding. I witnessed their vows. I was there when they promised each other forever, a lifetime, through sickness and health, through good times and bad. This is one of those bad times.' She went quiet for a moment, reflecting. 'They were my role models, you know. You should have seen them then. So happy. And they couldn't keep their hands off each other. They were . . . like us.'

'What are you plotting?'

'I was just thinking about something Phoebe once said, that where she comes from, it takes a village to support a marriage, not only to raise a child. Maybe if she and Tom had had more support?'

'So, instead of us staying out of Daniel and Steph's business . . .'

'. . . why don't we do something for them, to show them we support them?'

'What, like an intervention?' Mitch chuckled. 'Rush in with the jaws-of-life?'

'Babe,' she tugged at a little bundle of his chest hair. 'They're trapped in something and we have to help get them out. Like, by reminding them of everything they've shared together. What if they can't remember how great they were together? Well, I can. I can remind them. And you know how things are now. Daniel's totally the bad guy and Steph's so high up on the moral high ground, it's a wonder she can breathe at all. But is it ever just that simple? I always thought my dad was the villain and my mum the poor cheated-on wife but now I know it's more complicated than that. What if we showed Steph and Daniel we weren't judging either of them, or taking sides, just that we were here for them? For their relationship?'

Mitch had smiled. 'We don't even know if they want to be a couple anymore. Steph will never buy it.'

It had been over three months since the incident in the park. Daniel had moved out. Steph had hired a full-time housekeeper who doubled as a babysitter so she could go out at night. And she was doing it with a vengeance, by all accounts. Erin was seeing a different side to her cousin, Steph opening up in a way she'd never done before. Steph's initial anger seemed to have marginally subsided and she and Daniel had gone to a few sessions of couple therapy.

Nonetheless, Erin had plucked up the courage and called Steph.

'Would you and Daniel come over for a special dinner in your honour at our place?' Erin asked.

'God, why would you want to do that?' Steph asked. 'In our *honour*? You should be holding a funeral for us. Don't you get it? Whose side are you on?'

Erin swallowed. 'The side of your relationship.'

Steph went silent. 'I'm still furious with him, you know. But I'll think about it.'

Two days later she texted Erin saying, 'Go on then, invite the prick.'

෧෧

We tend to think of love as a private territory between two people, but each island of intimacy belongs to the landscape of our communities. Though intimacy is a secret and mysterious microcosm between two people, it's cradled in the macrocosm of family, community, society. Indigenous cultures honour the role of community more readily than Western ones, understanding that communities hold people, just as plasma carries cells through the body, or the air carries light.

In Africa, the term 'ubuntu' – the name taken by that restaurant Phoebe and Tom didn't manage to eat at – literally means 'people are people through other people'. The Shona people of Zimbabwe greet each other like this:

'*Makadii?*' (How are you?)

'*Ndiripo Makadiwo.*' (I am here if you are here.)

'*Ndiripo.*' (I am here.)

Without the other, there is no 'I'. Jung's notion of the collective unconscious threads us psychically to the past, to all people everywhere, as if we were all part of the same 'stories' being played out. Notions of privacy are mostly Western, born from our history of learning to honour individuality, and enshrined in human rights documents with the aim of preventing the repetition of historical atrocities. The internet is more than just a virtual space of information. Our unique individuality sits inside the notion that we are all one, all connected energetically and psychically as one of those paradoxes we cannot escape.

When a relationship is born we often 'welcome' it with a communal ritual we call a 'marriage' or a commitment ceremony. While the historical incarnations of a public ceremony are rooted in the need for the state to 'control' and 'sanction' marriage, there are other more enlarging ways to understand it. The presence of others when we make a vow anchors us to community and grounds our commitment within a larger context. Witnesses become the 'third' in our relationship, offering stability and containment. As a witness, we become a container for other people's togetherness, and share the responsibility of their success with them. Witnessing other people's relationships also offers each of us a chance to reflect on our own, acting as a 'third position' in our own partnerships.

∞

The night she confronted Daniel was a sleepless one for Steph. At 3.47 am she threw some of his clothes in a bag. At 5.14 am she went downstairs to find him snoring on the couch. She dumped the bag next to him, shook him roughly by the shoulder and ordered him to leave the house. When he protested, then begged, she hissed, 'If you want there to be any chance of working this out, you'll leave now. I'm so angry I could kill you. You need to get out of my sight.' She told the kids that 'Dad had to go away on business for a few weeks' and at first forbade Daniel to see them. Justin shrugged and seemed to get on with his life with a few teenage grunts, but as the days went by Georgia began to have nightmares and within a week started wetting her bed. Every time she changed her sheets, Steph swore. Daniel should be changing the bloody sheets.

Steph got onto a divorce lawyer who congratulated her on getting Daniel out of the house – 'it weakens his position' – and filled her in about her legal rights. Daniel phoned two or three times a day to speak to the kids and plead with Steph to take him back. Eventually Jenny, her mother, managed to persuade Steph that the kids needed their father: 'He cheated on you, not them', that Daniel had a right to see them, and so began the discordant dance of the separated spouses – arguing over arrangements for the kids, tension at handovers, recriminations about bits of homework that weren't done or school notices that weren't passed on.

One night, Erin invited Steph to come with her to meditation while Mitch played Wii with the kids.

'I'd rather go to the movies,' Steph complained, though she tagged along, happy to have a night out. Steph fidgeted as they arrived at the meditation hall. 'I have no idea what to do.'

Erin put her arm around her cousin and said, 'All you have to do is be here.'

For the first half hour while she sat on the meditation mat, all Steph could think about was how uncomfortable she was, how sore her back was and how painful her knees were. At some point, she tuned into the voice of the meditation teacher, who was asking everyone to check in with their bodies and to release any feelings of anger, blame, stress or fear. Steph scanned her body and realised that her neck was really sore. There was also pain in her stomach, almost like cramps. 'Now instead of fighting any pain in your body, and constricting against it, turn towards it, with softness and tenderness,' the teacher said. Steph didn't have a clue what he meant but something about his gentle instruction brought tears to her eyes. And for the hour of meditation, she couldn't stop crying. Memories of her and Daniel in happier times kept coming back to her. She remembered how, a while back, he surprised her by booking a weekend away for the two of them in a five-star hotel along-side a rainforest, and how she refused to go because the kids had too many arrangements. 'Can't you just let go and be spontaneous for once in your over-scheduled life?' Daniel had shouted. But see, he'd sprung it on her and not given her a chance to plan ahead. Now, for the first time, she sees how ungenerous it was to throw it back at him. They'd spent the weekend in cold silence as they passed each other taking the kids to their sporting fixtures and friends.

Steph wonders if it's true. That she somehow 'pushed' Daniel to look outside the marriage. She thinks about her contact with Alistair on Skype and Facebook. She does get that fluttery sensation when she sees a message from him, and talking to him, even for five minutes, is usually the highlight of her day. It's not the same though. They haven't had sex. Fuck it, they haven't even kissed.

'Where are you present in your life, and where are you not present?' the soft voice of the teacher wafts into Steph's unkempt thoughts.

Steph wonders when she stopped being present in her marriage. When she checked out emotionally. She thinks about that woman with her husband's penis in her mouth and inside her something burns like a furnace. *How dare she?* That's *her* husband, her penis to touch. The one Daniel said would be hers exclusively. Not that she's given it much attention in the past few months, or even years . . . and suddenly Steph wants Daniel. She *really* wants him. She wants his arms around her and she wants to feel him inside her. She shudders involuntarily, the moment passing as quickly and unfathomably as it came, only to be replaced by an overwhelming sense of revulsion, and her conviction that he'll never touch her again.

'No matter what emotions or sensations arise in you,' the teacher's voice continues, 'can you meet each one without judgement? With compassion? With forgiveness?'

Forgiveness . . . can she ever forgive Daniel? The words swirl inside her like lottery balls.

When a fist becomes an open hand

It's easy to love people who don't hurt us. There's no challenge in loving what does not irritate, challenge or push us to our limits. Love gets real, it gets grown-up, when we've loved through and in times of hardship, when we want to run but we choose to stay; when we want to lash out but we open our arms instead; when invective curls on the tip of our tongues and we keep it in our mouths until we figure out a skilful way to respond.

∽

In a Buddhist monastery, there were once two monks who, despite their many years of meditation and Buddhist practice, couldn't get on with each other. In fact, such animosity grew between them that once, in an altercation, one said to the other, 'Let's take this outside.' The two of them stormed outdoors, ready to punch each other. One monk made a fist, when suddenly, his hands came together in prayer, and he dropped to the ground and bowed before the other monk. In the instant of righteous anger, beholding his nemesis, the monk shifted into the third position and awoke to see the whole elephant in front of him, including his fellow monk's humanity, vulnerability, frailty and imperfection. And, dropping to his knees in reverence, he not only bowed down to the monk's humanity, but to his own.

Runners preparing for marathons talk about 'running ugly'. They train in extremes of heat and rain so that on the day of the race, no matter the weather conditions, they have a body memory of pushing through pain before, and they find the strength again. We train for love by loving ugly too. Affairs, addictions, betrayals and other painful chapters teach us how to love someone when we don't feel very loving towards them. We learn to offer compassion when it is hard for us to find it in ourselves and we're literally scraping the bottom of the barrel. When we want to punch them, but instead choose to fall to our knees and honour them.

∽

Rob and Tariq arrive at the front door and Erin greets them with relief. Tariq is carrying a platter full of beautifully sliced fruits, and Rob has a bottle of champagne. 'It's the Save A Marriage Brigade, ma'am,' Rob says.

'Now, now, Rob,' Tariq says, and puts the platter down on the table. He looks admiringly at Erin's pregnant tummy.

'May I?' he asks, his palms open to Erin's belly, waiting for permission to touch her.

'Sure,' she smiles, taking his hands and placing them on the melon of her stomach.

He feels the warmth of her body beneath the thin cotton of her blouse and then there is a movement, like a slow wave, as the baby turns inside her. 'Wow,' he says, and lets his hands fall to his sides.

Erin kisses him on the cheek and then turns to hug her brother. 'You've got to give this man a child,' she whispers in Rob's ear. 'In fact, I've just had a great idea for my next intervention.'

Rob sighs. 'You too, sis?'

'You'd make a great dad,' Erin says, no longer whispering.

'You mean unlike ours?'

'Oh, he was a good dad – in some ways.'

'Till he dropped us,' Rob says wryly.

'Would you have hung around with Trish?' Erin asks pointedly.

'With enough alcohol, anything's possible,' Rob laughs. 'But I take your point.'

'Yes, and you and Tariq have a different relationship to Mum and Dad.'

'That is a good point,' says Rob, finding a response which isn't laced with his trademark sarcasm. 'But let's concentrate on tonight's mission, shall we? When is the happy couple expected?'

'Be nice, Rob,' says Erin. 'You understand the purpose of tonight.'

'Yeah, we're going to rally around them, tell them it will all be okay, as long as Daniel keeps his cock for marital use only.'

'Unhelpful, Rob,' Erin says.

'I'm just kidding. But seriously, this is just what Dad did, just in a more sleazy way.'

Erin stops. She hasn't thought about it like that. 'We're here to offer them support, Rob.'

'Yeah, yeah, I know. Tariq insisted on buying them vouchers for a Tantric massage. He thinks that will solve all their problems. Come to think of it, Steph probably needs a good fuck. She's so bloody uptight it's amazing they have kids.'

Erin puts her hands on her hips. 'Now that you've got all that off your chest . . .'

'Don't worry about me, I'll behave,' Rob says, with the cheeky boy smile he's used to charm his way out of countless troubles in the past.

'I'm counting on you.'

∽

Steph is the next to arrive. She looks wan and nervous at the front door. She walks in and the first thing she says is, 'This is stupid. I don't know what I was thinking. Daniel probably won't even show up.'

Erin leads her to the dining room table, which is resplendent. Steph swallows. There's her favourite haloumi and beetroot salad, and sashimi that Daniel could polish off on his own, given the chance.

'Jeez, you've gone to a lot of trouble.'

'Hey, guys,' says Mitch as he comes into the room, giving Steph a bear hug, followed by one each for Rob and Tariq. 'So, what does everyone want to drink?'

'A stiff whisky, I think,' Steph says, trailing after Erin into the kitchen.

The doorbell rings. Everyone freezes. 'I'll get it,' Mitch smiles.

Steph emerges from the kitchen. And there in front of her is Daniel – dressed in a tuxedo. It looks tight and uncomfortable on him. *OMG. It's his wedding tuxedo*, she realises. But he's about ten kilos heavier since they got married. That top button on the pants must be gaping open underneath the olive cummerbund. In his left hand, he holds a bunch of pink roses. His right hand is behind his back. He looks bashful and self-conscious.

'These are for you,' he says to Erin, handing her the pink roses.

'And this,' he says carefully, bringing his right hand forward, 'is for you.' He hands over a single flower – its white petticoat of petals overlaid with lavender quills radiating from a deep purple heart, from which protrudes, like an organic sculpture, a luminous star of a stamen.

Steph inhales sharply. A passion flower. How did Daniel know?

∽

How does the evening go?

It's awkward at first. Erin has placed Steph and Daniel alongside each other at the round dining table, with Mitch to the left of Daniel and herself to the right of Steph. No-one knows what's up for conversation and what's taboo. Steph and Daniel haven't been a 'couple' for a while and he's totally overdressed in that undersized tuxedo, like it's a fancy-dress party. They're like frightened children. It's Tariq who starts talking about a building he's working on in the inner city and the crazy millionaire he's working with who's got more money than brains and isn't that always the case? Rob jumps in with his usual outrageous commentary and soon everyone is giggling. The food is fabulous. The six of them sit around the table, another invisible occupant of the room – the elephant – hovering quietly in the corner. Until Erin invites it into the circle.

She raises her wine glass filled with mineral water. 'Steph and Daniel, we know you guys have been through a difficult time lately and you're probably cringing, wondering what I'm going to say. I'm not going to say much, just that I was a bridesmaid at your wedding. And I remember that tuxedo, Daniel. I thought you looked so handsome –'

'Yeah, Daniel, you were hot, back then,' Rob cuts in.

'It's all gone to the dogs now,' Mitch chimes.

Daniel laughs. Even Steph wrings out a smile.

'And Steph . . . you were the most magnificent bride. Not that I'd seen many brides by then, but I watched you walk down the beach, remember, with all those lanterns and white stones and yellow rose petals . . . and I knew I should keep looking at you, but I didn't. I turned to look at Daniel. And he had a look on his face I can't describe. But I remember thinking, I want my husband to look at me like that some day . . .'

'Oh, Tariq looks at me like that all the time,' Rob says.

'Shh, you're interrupting,' Tariq chides. 'This is a poignant moment, Robert.'

'Yeah, put a cork in it for a moment, bro,' Erin says. 'Look, maybe love doesn't stay the same, and we just have to move with the changes, but I just wanted to remember that moment together with you again. Because sometimes we forget why we love each other. So this is a toast to remembering.'

And as one, they raise their glasses and drink to remembering.

22.

Awoken

SIDDHARTHA, BEFORE HE BECAME THE Buddha, had been a pretty damn fine-looking prince. One day, soon after he became enlightened, he was walking along, a completely blissed-out smile on his face, swathed in golden robes, probably contemplating impermanence without attachment or some such insight. Everyone stopped and stared, like we do at celebrities these days. 'Who *is* this guy?' folk thought. 'What's got him so happy?'

People asked, 'Are you an angel?'

The Buddha shook his head.

'Are you a god?'

'No,' the Buddha smiled.

'A wizard? A magician?'

'Nope.'

'Are you a man, then? What are you?'

All the Buddha said was, 'I am awake.'

☙

Unlike Sleeping Beauty, who probably also uttered 'I am awake' after being smooched after a hundred years, the Buddha meant more than 'I'm not sleeping'. The modesty of these three words doesn't reveal the years which the Buddha spent trying to understand the nature of human suffering, taking him from extremes of asceticism to his meditation under the Bodhi tree, from which he vowed he'd not move until he got what this whole human gig was about. To be 'awake' means to be fully present in the moment. In Jewish mysticism, the word 'hineni', a Hebrew word from the Bible, means 'here I am', in response to a call from God. To be awake, or to be here, means simply to understand who we are. The reason we might bother with spending time inside ourselves, making friends with our pain and our past, is so that we might 'awaken' from our pretentions, unhealthy attachments, memories, impulses and desires. We've walked some internal avenues, been into the dungeon, released our psychic prisoners, and looked deeply at ourselves with kindness and compassion. In other words, we've got a grip on reality. We're not deluded.

Part of the problem is that we don't know in what ways we're asleep, or blind to what's in front of us. It took the shock of seeing old, sick and dying people for the first time beyond the palace walls for Siddhartha to begin his journey of waking up. And once we do 'see', it's an ongoing process of wiping away the grit and dust from our perception, or of remembering. There are countless paths towards 'awakening' – the psychological, the spiritual, the religious, the mystical, the self-help – we just have to pick one. See, it makes no difference how we choose to wake up – many paths lead to the same destination, just like Abraham's tent, in the Bible, which had four entrances, facing each direction, so guests would always arrive at the front door, no matter whether they approached from the north, the south, the east or the west.

The only obstacle is that we may not want to wake up and give up the safety of our comfort zones. For some of us, the prospect of change or understanding ourselves may just be way too confronting and frightening. It may all seem too hard. But the truth is – it doesn't have to be. We can start anywhere, anytime. Alone or in a relationship, because whether we like it or not, if what we're doing no longer works for us, a crisis or ongoing unhappiness will, at some point in our lives, kick our butts out of complacency and into internal investigation.

One way to 'wake up' is through a relationship. Intimacy offers all the conditions for inner work by providing conflict, opportunities for projective identification, triggers for our wounds and internal harassment. But for some of us, there'll be long periods in our lives when we won't be in a relationship with someone else. We'll be on our own. But this is not a drama – it's simply another fantastic opportunity to wake up and do the work we need to do on ourselves. Unlike massage, we can practise intimacy on ourselves. Single, we can learn to become intimate with who *we* are. We can offer love and compassion towards the parts of ourselves we've disowned. We can work at being inwardly patient and generous. We can practise being awake and healing whatever is wounded inside ourselves.

Being single is not a crime. It is not a failing. It is not an error of our personality. For some, it is a conscious choice. For others, it's the booby prize. The terror of becoming a spinster, or left on the shelf, or missing the boat, means we inhabit our aloneness with a sense of dread, waiting for the relationship that will save us from loneliness to come along, instead of using it as the chance to come alive inside ourselves in a new way and to take responsibility for who we are.

What happens to Tara?

Tara stays in therapy for a while. She gets that something inside her has to change. She makes a decision not to date anyone for at least six months while she figures out how her past relationships are sabotaging her search for love. There are many nights when she cries herself to sleep. She's terrified that she's getting too old – one of those women guys just won't touch. At the end of the six months, she contacts Ben again and asks if she can take him out for coffee. His tone is clipped. It's clear she hurt him.

'I'm seeing someone,' he tells her.

'That's great,' she says. 'I hope she's lovely, and that you're happy. I'm not asking you out on a date. I just . . . this is embarrassing, and I'm not sure how to say it, but I'd just like to explain to you what was going on for me during that time. I'm sure you don't need to hear it but I'd kind of like to say it.'

Ben agrees to meet with her.

Over coffee, Tara explains to Ben that she's been in therapy, and that she's had a long journey inside herself to try to understand why she always rejects 'nice guys'.

JOANNE FEDLER & GRAEME FRIEDMAN

Ben smiles. It's a backhanded compliment, but at least she recognises he's a nice guy.

'I know this is probably too much information,' she begins, 'but . . .' and she goes on to explain her family dynamics and why she's ended up where she is. Alone and unhappy. As she speaks, she starts to cry.

Ben puts his hand on hers on the table. 'You shouldn't be so hard on yourself, Tara. You're a great woman. And any guy would be lucky to be with you. I don't understand the attraction girls have to guys who treat them like shit, but . . .' he shrugs, 'hopefully you'll get over that, because long-term, you want a guy who makes you breakfast.'

'Thanks so much for meeting with me,' Tara says, paying for the coffees.

'You're welcome,' Ben says, giving her a hug.

'I wish I'd met you now,' Tara says.

∽

So does Tara find love?

Well, she's doing the hard work. She's taken responsibility for her life and her happiness. She probably still has a way to go, but she's waking up. Now when she finds herself attracted to bullies and bad guys, she recognises that these are her habitual patterns, that she's managed the wounds of her childhood by chasing after 'glamour' – the hot guy with the high-status job and the arrogant attitude. She understands how she has zeroed unerringly towards exactly the 'right' fit for her unresolved dynamics – the guy who'd tantalise her and then reject her.

Just as importantly, she sees how both sides of this dynamic reside within herself, how she has taken up the opposing role – the hot girl with the arrogant attitude – with guys who wanted to fall in love with her. She now owns the fact that she's been both victim and perpetrator in this sad dead-end approach to intimacy.

Will she be able to go the next step: recognise and hold onto the love a 'nice' guy might offer her? Someone who is not defending against his own vulnerability by being a prat? Hell yes, we're hoping she will. And why shouldn't she? She's bringing her stories into therapy where she is learning to sit with her vulnerability, sadness, feelings of abandonment and shame with kindness and compassion. And there's a damn good chance she'll soon be able to sit with a man who owns some of these feelings himself. Way to go, Tara.

What happens to Antonio?

As long as he's having fun Antonio will go on for a long time doing what he's doing.

But the party will have to end sometime. Maybe it happens when, in his late forties, he's diagnosed with a melanoma on his back – the one Tara noticed that night when they hooked up. After leaving the doctor's office, Antonio goes home to his empty house, and drinks an entire bottle of whisky on his own, with his dogs at his feet.

He wonders who he can call to tell. He phones Sam.

Sam's phone goes to voicemail. 'Hey, my friend,' Antonio slurs. 'Got some shitty news this afternoon. Seems like I've got a melanoma on my back.' He laughs. 'Not sure what the prognosis is. Not feeling so shit-hot about it. Give us a call if you're around, or you feel like having a beer.'

Antonio falls into a drunken sleep on his couch, Vixen and Nixon arranged on the carpet alongside him. He's woken at 6.35 am by the ring of his mobile phone's loud refrain and a wet sensation lathering his face. It's Nixon's tongue. Vixen's arthritis makes her waking ritual lumbered, unable to muster enthusiasm for a good morning lick. Clapton's 'Layla' is playing on high volume. Jesus, why the fuck does he have *that* song as his ringtone? Foggily he sorts the slobbering tongue from the love song, and the slowly forming shape of knowledge – *you have cancer* – that strides steadily towards him from the fog of his alcohol bender. His hand rests on Nixon's beautiful head. Of the three of them in the house, Nixon is the only healthy one. And who's going to look after him?

Antonio wouldn't ordinarily answer anyone calling this early. But he grasps for the phone. It's Sam, who's 'really sorry to hear the news'. They agree to meet for a drink later on in the day. As Antonio ends the call, he realises he hardly knows Sam. He scrolls through his phone, but there's no-one he can really call. *Christ!* – the insight hits him with a jolt – he's had 'Layla' as his ringtone for what, seven, eight years? Ever since . . . ever since things went sour with Claudette.

Every time his phone rings, he hears a song about longing and unre-quited love. *Fu-u-u-ck!*

He remembers that chick, what was her name — Tina? — who said a couple of years ago, 'What's that on your back?' He should've followed up, gone to the doctor then. He should call her and tell her. But there's no Tina in his phone. He scrolls to the top of the listings for 'T': Talia, Tamika, Tammy . . . there must be forty women's names beginning with T in his contacts. What was the point of keeping all these numbers if he was never going to call them back? But in a flash of clarity he picks out her name: Tara. The photograph of the little girl with blonde curls and a butterfly painted on her face. Tara with the resigned eyes. He calls. Her phone goes to voicemail.

'Hey Tara, it's Antonio. Not sure you remember me. We hooked up . . . a while back . . . just found out I've got a malignant melanoma on my back. I remember you saw it. So, bit crazy, but I've only just had it checked out, it started to bleed in the shower, so anyway . . . just thought I'd let you know. I . . . uh . . . yeah, I hope you're well . . . um . . . yeah, anyway . . . cheers.' He hangs up. He feels like a complete idiot. Why would she give a shit?

Tara gets the message. And a day later, she texts back: 'So sorry to hear that. I wish you well. Best of luck. Tara.'

And for no reason he can understand, as he reads her words, Antonio breaks down and cries.

৩৩

Does Antonio die? Does he go into remission? Does this encounter with his mortality 'wake him up'? There's nothing like a health crisis to force us out of our complacency and into a deeper contemplation of who we are, and how we'd like to live the rest of our lives. Will Antonio use this as an opportunity to re-evaluate his life and his choices? Who knows? It could go either way. Maybe, realising he won't live forever, he'll decide he'd like to share whatever time he has left with someone — if it's not too late. Maybe he'll do a complete flip and go into all the alternative therapies to heal — Reiki, Chinese herbal medicine, meditation, visuali-sation — which might open his mind to new ways of thinking and give him a doorway into looking at how he's become the man he is.

But it could get tragic. He might do the macho thing and harden into denial, retreating further from any inner work. He may decide he's going to go out with a bang and bonk as many young babes as he can before the cancer chews up so much of him he can't get it up anymore.

In one version of his story, the melanoma is advanced, and his time is limited, so he puts his dogs down and dies alone. In another, he survives the melanoma and either spends the rest of his life in his empty mansion, or decides it's time to do the hard work and find some real intimacy. Irrespective of his prognosis, it's up to Antonio. He can choose to 'wake up' or stay the way he is. You know which one we're hoping for.

Non-attachment and the pursuit of happiness

We all chase happiness as if it were a commodity we could capture and keep. Being in a relationship has somehow become synonymous with happiness, even though the reality is that all relationships are difficult and stressful. Viktor Frankl, in *Man's Search for Meaning*, suggests that beyond chasing pleasure and avoiding pain, we should focus on finding meaning in our lives. Our job is to retain a 'tragic optimism' – to say 'yes' to all that life has to offer, despite the realities of pain, suffering and ultimately death. One of the ways we can find meaning in our lives, Frankl's logotherapy suggests, is through 'someone' or 'something'. He says that happiness, like success, can't be pursued – it's the unintended side effect of committing oneself to a cause or a person other than oneself. In loving someone, we find meaning, and in finding meaning, happiness ensues.

When we let go of our pursuit of happiness and of the ideal relationship, it becomes easier to be fully present with whatever is real in our lives. We stop leading with our egos and move from our hearts. We stop judging ourselves and others. We learn to be inwardly trustworthy, committed, loving, passionate and dependable. We drop the fear-based behaviour and start looking after ourselves, giving ourselves the time we need to rest, be nourished, creative and active. We take responsibility for our thoughts, our speech and our actions. We become faithful and loving to ourselves.

23.
Forgiveness and Beyond

Out beyond notions of right and wrong is a field.
Meet me there.

— Rumi

CAN WE EVER REALLY FORGIVE someone who's betrayed us? And even if we do, what hope is there for a relationship scarred by a history of failed trust?

The Passion Flower

Outside Erin and Mitch's apartment, Daniel and Steph stand under the glow of a street lamp. Steph holds the passion flower Daniel brought for her, touching its waxy petals with her fingers.

'It's so lovely . . . my favourite flower,' she says.

'I know. Carnations were a mistake. God, I could kick myself for those carnations.'

For their last anniversary, Daniel had arrived home with a bunch of pink carnations – carnations! It was an 'I-haven't-been-paying-attention-to-a-thing-you've-been-saying-for-the-past-fifteen-years' purchase. She threw them in the bin, seething. It must have been more than a year ago, when she did that watercolour painting course for bored housewives every Tuesday morning. She picked a passion flower from a photograph in *National Geographic*, a thing of sculptural beauty.

218

Daniel hadn't ever commented on the painting that lay unframed in her study for weeks before she filed it away with her other dreams.

'I'm still angry,' Steph says.

Daniel grimaces. 'You have every right to be. And I'm sorry. You have no idea how sorry I am . . .' These words feel so unfit for what he really feels. But language was never his strong point. He wants to tell her that last week he found himself in a synagogue. She wouldn't believe it. He can hardly believe it, much less explain it. He was driving home from work and passed a synagogue he'd never even noticed before. People were walking in singly and in little family groups. He remembered that it was the evening of Yom Kippur, the Jewish Day of Atonement, only because his business associate Adam had left a meeting early to get home for the traditional last meal before twenty-four hours of fasting. When he was a child his father would take him to a small synagogue for this, the holiest day of the Jewish calendar. Daniel had always found it excruciating.

Without thinking, Daniel had pulled over and gone in. The place was full of men draped in white shawls, praying. It was sort of bizarre but oddly comforting. He had walked into the Kol Nidre service, the introduction to this day of atoning for one's sins. Daniel had no *kippah*, the traditional head covering for men, and so he'd folded his handkerchief as best he could and put it on his head, sitting down near the back. A man tapped him on the shoulder, pointed to his head and reached into his pocket, producing a *kippah* which he handed to Daniel. Daniel had thanked him. He waited, hoping to hear the rabbi blow the *shofar*, the ram's horn. The last time he'd heard the *shofar*'s cry, the sound so primal and eerie, he'd been a boy; for some reason, he really needed to hear it tonight. Daniel vaguely remembered it had to do with Abraham sacrificing a ram, instead of his son Isaac, whom God had saved just in time. Daniel had wondered if he'd sacrificed his family with his stupidity and if God would save him. But he didn't believe in God, and if he did, God probably wouldn't have time for a detribalised self-hating Jew like him. Nonetheless, as he sat there, surrounded by other Jews, he found himself talking inside himself, there in the synagogue, asking to be forgiven. Maybe prayer was just self-confession. Turning inward to face what you don't want to see. And then the service was over and everyone was leaving, but the *shofar* hadn't been blown. When he returned the skullcap to its owner, he asked him about it. 'That's only at the end of the fast, tomorrow night. Come back if you want to hear it,' he smiled. And Daniel did, this time with a baseball cap to cover his head, the sound cutting through him like a laser.

Steph sees a whole story play out on Daniel's face and is about to say something snide, but she stops. Last week, alone in their bedroom, she'd watched a documentary on Nelson Mandela. 'Resentment is like drinking poison,' he'd said, 'and then hoping it will kill your enemies.' She *was* resentful. It wasn't just the betrayal. It was the years of her life that had seeped away in housework and unhappiness and now *this* was all she had to show for it. He was the one who suggested couple therapy while she was looking for a good divorce lawyer. She only agreed because she wanted a chance to hear what else he'd acknowledge he'd done wrong over the years. She was sure he'd own up to one or two other affairs, giving the usual 'they meant nothing, it's you I love' excuse. But he didn't. What he did own up to was not listening to her, trying to fill the space between them with his wishes and desires, and not figuring out why hers didn't match his. But then there was Shantelle. Steph had wanted to know everything. How often they'd made love. 'It was only sex,' he'd said. 'I never made love with her. I had chatroom sex twice. Actual sex once. And that blow job Mitch saw me getting in the park. Jesus, I'm so sorry.' Not sorry enough, thought Steph, to have avoided doing it in the first place. Beneath the humiliation, the shame and the pain of it, Steph just felt stupid. Duped, like those idiots who fall for internet scams. Maybe it would have been better not to know.

In their third session with the couple therapist, Daniel, responding to Steph's angry resolve, once again begged for her forgiveness. 'I'll forgive you when hell freezes over,' she'd spat at him, and announced that she wasn't ready to carry on with marital counselling. Not yet. Maybe not ever.

For the next few weeks, she honed in on the kids and their routines even more than usual, obsessing about their homework, their extra-curricular activities, Georgia's weight, Justin's writing exercises. By night, she was reckless. She left the babysitter, a young Japanese woman called Ayumi, at home to deal with the kids while she went out clubbing with her friend Sandy, crawling home in the wee hours of the morning, as if drinking margaritas and dancing with strangers half her age would make her feel better. It never did. Sandy told her that the only way to get even was to go out and 'screw as many guys as you can'. Steph wondered how that might feel. Maybe if Alistair was in the same city as her . . . She emailed him to let him know that her marriage was on the rocks and that she was thinking of leaving Daniel. Instead of his usual quick response, it took him a few days to get back to her. He was sorry, he hoped they could work it out, all marriages go through shit, et cetera. Why wasn't he urging her to leave Daniel?

Then, one morning in the haze of a hangover, it struck her: Alistair is married. Not to 'whatever her name is', but to a woman called Cassandra (it's there on Facebook for everyone to see), who is probably a really nice woman. *What a crap idea, Steph*, said a little voice in her head. And later on that same day she'd had a deeper insight. *I've been looking for something from Alistair. Daniel was looking for something from Shantelle. We both wanted to feel wanted. Except they had sex.* And then that little voice piped up again. *And if Alistair had been around and willing? Then what?*

Later that day she'd sat in front of her computer for a long, long time. Alistair had only been flirting with her, or at most all he'd wanted was a little fling. But obviously her availability had scared him off. He just wasn't that into her. That hurt. But what had she really expected? What had she really wanted from him? Bored and depressed, feeling disappointed and distant from Daniel, she'd needed someone to acknowledge her as a desirable, worthy woman. She'd turned to Alastair for that. Finally she began to type: *Hi Al, you're right, all marriages go through shit. And I need to sort out what I'm going to do with mine, without looking for distractions. So, thanks for your support but I guess it's best if we say goodbye. Fondest, Steph.* She clicked on the send button, shuddered involuntarily, and began to cry with a sadness that seemed, for the moment, bleached of anger and recrimination.

Daniel knew nothing of this. And now, standing with him under the street lamp outside Erin and Mitch's place, Steph softens. Daniel

221

may have wandered from their marriage sexually, but she'd wandered emotionally. Maybe it's the same thing, maybe it's even worse.

'I've been offered a job at the Art Museum, coordinating a kids' program,' Steph says.

'Wow, that's fantastic.'

'It means I won't be home all day. I've got someone to help with the kids. There's some overseas travel involved too. Exhibitions and stuff.'

She is sparkling. Alive in the way he remembers her when they first met. He nods, smiling. 'I could help with the kids,' he says. 'I mean, I'd like to.'

Daniel is genuinely happy for her. Steph realises that she's been longing to share this news with someone who would be as thrilled for her as she is about it. In this moment, something inside her flares. He isn't trying to keep her static, he wants change for her as much as she wants it for herself.

'Maybe . . .' Steph says.

'Anyway, it's awesome. I am stoked for you,' he shuffles uncomfortably. 'These pants are so frigging tight. I need to lose a few . . . I know, I look ridiculous.'

'You do, like a man in a boy's outfit.'

Daniel undoes the cummerbund. The top button of his trousers is gaping. She can see his underwear. 'That is not a good look, Dan.'

Daniel holds his hands over his gaping trouser top.

'I know it's a big ask, and I'll understand if you say no and want to get on with your life without me, but . . .' he trails off, remembering his visits to the synagogue, seeing the choices he's made – from focusing on his career, to trawling chatrooms, Shantelle, to disowning his own history – his own shame, regret and desperation standing like a criminal line-up in front of him. If only he could go back and make things right.

He looks imploringly into Steph's eyes. 'Do you believe in second chances?'

Steph shakes her head. 'I don't know. The kids will be grown-up in a few years, they'll leave home, and then it would be you and me again. And we haven't been happy for so long. What will we have together once the kids aren't there anymore? I don't want to keep being miserable. Or keep you miserable.'

'Maybe we could meet again one Sunday night at the fruit and veg section in the supermarket. I'll pre-bruise some bananas and make a couple of really terrible banana jokes.'

At this, Steph laughs. She really laughs.

Something warm courses through Daniel's veins. He hasn't seen her laugh like that, in . . . in years. He gets tears in his eyes.

'I thought I'd lost the ability to . . . I love your laugh.'

Steph wipes her eyes. 'You're still funny.'

Daniel sighs, flooded by a new feeling that had been happening of late, of not being able to trust himself to speak.

They stand there together for a while, neither of them speaking.

Finally Daniel says, 'Do you think you could ever forgive me?'

Steph shrugs. 'I don't know, Dan. I don't know.'

Daniel's eyes fall.

'But I'd like to try,' Steph says. 'And God knows I probably need a little forgiving too. Let's talk later in the week.'

And she offers him her cheek to kiss, her hand instinctively moving forward, her fingers coming to rest on his forearm.

Revenge versus forgiveness

Why is it so hard to forgive? We all know we *should* forgive. But then again, the Bible tells us, an eye for an eye and a tooth for a tooth. How about a shag for a shag?

It was Gandhi who proclaimed that an eye for an eye makes everyone blind. There's no way we can ever see the whole elephant with less vision than we already have. But we're only human, not Jesus on the cross who forgave those who persecuted him, declaring, 'Forgive them, Father, for they know not what they do.' Pain contracts us. When we're feeling hurt and small, we just want to make the pain go away – or to pass it on to someone else.

Part of the problem with forgiveness is that we're attached to our wounds in deeply unconscious ways. We hang onto our hatred, resentment and anger as if they are trophies, a testimony to our honour. We fantasise about ways of exacting revenge and punishment.

To make them feel what we felt, teach them a lesson. We get high blood pressure. Ulcers. Depression. And that's not all! We have someone to blame when things go wrong in our lives. We get to be a victim, with status. We get so good at it that we create our identities around our wound, which becomes the trellis for the vines of our personality. We can't detach ourselves, even when we know that what we're holding onto is keeping us stuck, like monkeys with our hands in a coconut.

Inflicting or experiencing pain creates a powerful, invisible energetic bond between people. When we give that pain any thought or emotion, we shrink whatever energy we have for the present moment. We can think of it mathematically, as a subtraction from our lives. Holding onto past hurt is one way we distract ourselves from being in the present. As long as we're a 'victim', we're not fully available in the moment. We're still on a 'Poor Me' tour, wandering energetically through our history. Commitment to any relationship – whether with someone else or ourselves – means we have to get closure. The only way to sever ties with the pain of the past is through forgiveness.

For Steph, being the 'wronged' spouse comes with all sorts of perks, including rights to the moral high ground and a victim-passport she can use for the rest of her life. She gets to keep her feelings of being 'hard done by' as well as being seen by the law as the one with 'clean hands' – she could even use it as leverage in a divorce settlement, to gain custody, a better financial deal, or in getting friends to pick her over Daniel. Or, rather than playing the divorce card, she might let him back into the house, on *her* terms, 'for the sake of the kids'. And this may work for as long as it takes Daniel to feel he has paid his penance. But because it's a highly conditional comeback riddled with malignant tendencies, it's not taking their relationship anywhere. If she chooses to forgive Daniel and give him a second chance by going back into marital therapy, accepting his apology and acknowledging that he knows he's done her wrong, she may let the past go. And she'll get a chance to explain what she meant when she said to him under the street lamp: 'And God knows I probably need a little forgiving too.' If their relationship stands a chance, it's got to go through forgiveness.

To rescue a relationship, we have to make healthy choices. Forgiveness feels counter-intuitive because there's no logic to it. It may even offend our sense of 'justice' or 'what's right', especially when someone's done the dirty on us. But here's the error of our thoughts: we don't forgive people because they deserve it. Forgiveness has nothing to do with the other person. It's about us. Forgiveness is a choice we make. We *choose* to let go of our pain. And in the process, we get ourselves back energetically.

Beyond forgiveness

Authentic forgiveness lies in third position territory. It's about reaching a deep understanding of a relationship. Let's break it down:

Phase 1: Daniel has sex with another woman. Steph's sense of betrayal is felt at the very core of her being. The pain of the present is multiplied by that of the past, but attributed only to the present. The triangle of her, Daniel and Shantelle thrusts her back – unconsciously – to the original triangle that caused her terrible shame: her mother, her father and herself. It was there that her parents' unresolved marital conflict left her in the unwelcome position of a surrogate wife for her father. It's not a good place for anyone to be, and so to defend against her own shame at the implications of supplanting her mother, Steph became rigid and hypervigilant.

Phase 2: Perhaps triggered by Alistair popping her bubble of excitement about him, Steph has to wonder whether what she's been doing with Alistair has been some sort of emotional affair. This is another source of shame, against which she's defended by 'splitting': Daniel's affair was sexual, therefore he is the immoral one. By making him totally bad, she can be the victimised good person.

Phase 3: There is another, crucial source of shame, and that has to do with the way in which both have mishandled their relationship. Steph's challenge is to understand how she has been the co-writer of the extramarital sex scene in Daniel's script, and vice versa. This is where the third position comes into it. They will need to recognise their patterns of defensiveness and resentment, that for years they have been competing with each other, jealously guarding their own right to say 'look at me' while ignoring the same plea from the other. Not being heard also triggers old layers of shame from a time when they felt excluded and abandoned as children. Then shame becomes a hot potato they chuck at each other, hoping it'll land and stay in the other's lap.

If they're able to untangle this web of shame, they might recognise that Daniel's sexual affair and Steph's reaching out to Alistair are purely the sound of a fire alarm going off and that, paradoxically, forgiveness lies in each of them owning their own shame, in forgiving their own selves. Forgiving each other, then, becomes almost a redundant act.

Steph's connection with Alistair may be helpful in giving her perspective. When we feel betrayed and as if we've done nothing wrong, it's more difficult for us to locate the problem in the relationship, especially if we have a fragile sense of self. Of course, there may well be times when the problem belongs more with one person than the other – remember Erin's ex-boyfriend Gus? – in which case, the issue becomes one of 'when it's time to split'. But that's not the territory in which Steph and Daniel find themselves.

Getting close to an ex-boyfriend is only one way of seeking involvement with a 'third' in order to create distance. There are other forms of destructive attachments, such as alcohol or drug abuse, and over-involvement with work/a hobby/Facebook. All of these can provide a disguise for disengagement and some may provide the added cover of self-righteousness – 'I'm working for us' or 'it's healthy to have a hobby'. If Steph stays invested in being 'right' and is not interested in looking at her role in the dynamic between her and Daniel, she'll fast-track their eventual separation. And if Daniel is only going through the motions and saying the right things, like 'I accept responsibility for my behaviour' (out of fear of losing her and the kids) but really believes Steph 'drove him to it', then he too is damning their future together. But if he does the inner work to understand why he acted out like this, and can commit (internally) to staying present in his marriage with Steph, and working on ways of reaching her, there's hope.

❦

Forgiving someone who has betrayed us takes a wise, generous heart, but is it enough? Surely it must be, it's so damn hard to do.

Forgiveness is the first step. But it only takes us so far. There is still further to go.

When we forgive someone, it's from our place on the victim podium. Forgiveness still relies on dualistic notions of victims and wrongdoers, right and wrong. While its effects are promising and positive, they still keep us grounded in the model of judgement and blame. There is a field beyond these notions, as Rumi says. And it's full of elephants.

Steph may choose to embrace her power by letting go of her need to be 'right' or to be the martyr in the relationship. She has made empowering decisions and acted on them: she's got a job and she's ended her communication with Alistair. Steph and Daniel can go back into couple therapy, where they can explore how their marriage got to this point.

It's going to take time. Both their egos need to be stabilised to repair the damage. It's going to take each of them doing some inner work, alone and with the support of a third person (therapist, healer, spiritual teacher or friend), to help them process the trauma. In marital therapy, a therapist can help them transition into the third position so that they can see their whole relationship. They can accept that there are things they cannot change – that Daniel did have extra-marital sex; that their relationship is not perfect. They can let go of the sense of entitlement relationships give us (*How dare you do this to me?*) and focus instead on renewing their investment in one another. They can let go of the illusion of a perfect marriage and simply embrace the reality of the marriage they have. With generosity, compassion and humility, they can both stop holding onto the bit of the elephant they've become fixated on ('You never have sex with me' / 'You betrayed me'), and they can try to see that their relationship is a process, and bigger than any one incident.

Despite all indications to the contrary, Steph and Daniel have a magnificent opportunity in front of them. Erin's dinner party was a reminder to think of themselves as caretakers, guardians of their relationship. Together, they are the caretakers of tenderness. Relationships give us a chance to wake up, to open up to what is in front of us, to be present fully in each moment.

What are we waiting for?
Once there was a flood that destroyed a village. A man climbed to the top of his house and waited there. Some people came past in a rowboat

and said 'Hop in', but the man shook his head and said 'God will save me', so the people rowed on. Later a helicopter came past and sent down a rope for him, but the man would not take the rope and said, 'I have faith, God will save me.' The flood rose and rose while the man waited for God to save him, but eventually he drowned. In heaven when he came in front of the Almighty, he asked God, 'I was a man of such strong faith all my life, why didn't you save me in my time of need?' And God said, 'I don't understand. I sent you a rowboat and a helicopter.'

∽

What are we waiting for? What do we imagine love is going to look like? We're so distracted looking out for it that our illusions of its grandeur keep us blinded to what has been sent. What if love's greatest teaching comes in the form of betrayal? How deep might love take us if we found our way back to each other from a wound called 'Shantelle'? Spiritual wisdom brings us right back to where we are now. It's the pain, the confusion, the elation, the devastation, the aversion, the resistance and the illumination, all mixed up. We can't get away from it. All we can do is meet what's there. These are the ordinary tortures of everyday existence we can transform by our embracing of them. Whatever we're looking for is already in front of us. Just because we can't see the whole elephant doesn't mean it's not there.

24.
Giving Yourself to One Thing

So how do we hang on to each other through the freak-outs and storms that lie ahead? Can we marry our fantasies of 'romance' with the daily grind of human interaction? Can the profound work of intimacy become a thing of joy?

A hundred and one meanings of a kiss

'So, that wasn't too freaky, was it?' Erin asks, clearing away some of the plates, her pregnant belly resting on the table.

'A few two-left-feet moments,' Rob says, grinning, 'but you did good tonight, sis, even if it doesn't go anywhere.'

'Hey,' Mitch says, coming up behind Erin to relieve her of a heavy dessert plate. 'You sit down. We'll clear up.'

'Erin, it really was a very generous thing to do,' Tariq says. 'I think it could turn things around.'

Erin smiles tiredly as she lowers herself into a seat. 'Thanks, guys.' As she takes the weight off her feet, something else frees itself inside her.

'I was pretty sceptical, I have to say,' Mitch says. 'But who knows? Daniel couldn't stop thanking us enough.'

Rob chuckles. 'He's just chuffed we've given him a hand out of his dogbox. Trouble is, Steph's not giving him much of a hand. I reckon she'll take him back the day they start serving ice sorbet in hell. Our dear cousin's too damn uptight. Always has been. Pride cometh before passion and all that.'

Tariq taps him playfully with a fist. 'Thanks for the pessimism update, Rob. Stephanie just needs a bit of time. At some point she's going to think twice about splitting up the family over something like this. And he really looks like he's sorry. He's not just turning on that boyish charm of his.'

'Yeah,' Mitch says, 'but if I were in her shoes, I'd want to know how I could trust him not to do it again.'

Erin sighs. 'You're all missing the point. Daniel's affair is just a symptom of something much deeper. I don't know if Steph's going to get stuck on his bad behaviour, but it's not really about that, as shitty and stupid as it is. It's about what's been going on for years between them.'

'Or what's not been going on,' grins Rob. 'I mean, if the bloke was on a starvation diet who can blame him for getting a little take-out?'

'Oh, come on, Rob,' Tariq butts in. 'You freak out if I so much as look at another man.'

'Yeah, but you're eating gourmet at home.'

Mitch coughs. 'A little too much information, boys.'

'Anyway, point is,' Rob says, 'what if Steph doesn't love Daniel anymore? You can't work *that* out.'

'I don't know if it's as simple as that,' says Erin. 'Maybe she doesn't love him the way she loved him in the beginning. But love's got to evolve, right, if a relationship is going to survive and grow deeper?' She smiles at Mitch. 'And Daniel's not such a bad guy – he's got some great qualities.'

Rob laughs. 'That awful tuxedo is not one of them.' He's at the window, shifting a blind aside to peer down to the street below. 'I might have to take that all back . . . if body language is anything to go by. Fu-uck, look at that, she's laughing!'

'Rob!' says Erin. 'Are you *watching* them?'

'Well, don't you want to know if your intervention was worth all the money and effort you spent on it?'

Erin doesn't know whether to give him crap for spying or join him at the window. 'You know, my folks had an arranged marriage,' Tariq says, 'and they've been happy all their lives. I once asked my mum what it was like not being able to choose her life partner and she said, "You choose to love someone. And I chose to love your father."'

Rob lets the curtains fall and turns away from the window. 'And then they had you, which makes me forever in their debt. But what if she'd wanted kids and he didn't?'

Tariq shrugs, but there's no resignation in his gesture. 'A mountain is only as impossible to climb as its laziest climber.'

'Are you calling me lazy?'

'All I'm saying is that you'd outsource your emotions if you could,' Tariq says.

'Well, what's the point of civilisation if you can't pay someone to do your dirty work for you?'

'You end up like Daniel and Steph,' Mitch says. 'With years of shit piled up outside your bedroom door.'

'And your friends Tom and Phoebe, or Mum and Dad, or . . .' Rob's peeping out the window again. 'Oooh, I think, yes, ladies and gentlemen, he's leaning in to give her a kiss – on the cheek, mind you, but it's a kiss!'

'Rob!' Erin chides. 'Come away from the window.'

Mitch is laughing. 'Rob's the only one who's got the guts to actually have a squiz.'

'Exactly. Thanks, Mitch. And, just to let you all know, as from now, I'm in training to climb mountains. Got a Himalaya to cross, with a cute Indian fella on my back,' he says, winking at Tariq.

Erin and Mitch don't get it but Tariq says quietly, 'You're going to make a beautiful dad.'

'Hey, I only said I'm in training. Don't go rounding up the Sherpas yet.' But Rob leaves his lookout position at the window and goes over and kisses Tariq. 'Just can't imagine my life without you . . .' He trails off, for once not outsourcing his emotions.

And Mitch puts his arms around Erin, the bulge of her belly keeping their faces apart. He leans his big chest in and kisses her on her forehead, his heart strangely full.

Choosing love

And there it is. We choose to love. Even when it's hard. We choose to commit to one person, to make a vow we don't know we can keep. We choose to stay when things go wrong.

Commitment isn't what happens when we live together. Or get married. Or stay together for the sake of the kids. Commitment isn't a choice we make only once, a cold iron gate that clicks shut behind us. It's a choice we make over and over and over again, the way a musician comes to practise a phrasing or replay a song, or a meditator will return to the breath. Some days we'll love it, and some days we'll hate it. It'll bore us at times and awe us at others. But every time we choose to look again, to listen more deeply, to return, we commit afresh. We humble ourselves to what we do not yet know. Think about this: Pablo Neruda wrote one hundred love poems to his beloved. The Japanese artist Hokusai painted Mount Fuji from a hundred different views to try and capture its essence. The marvellous Spanish cellist Pablo Casals, when asked at the age of ninety-three why he still practised several hours a day, replied, 'I'm beginning to notice some improve-ment.' Jack Kornfield, the Buddhist teacher, says that if you want to know happiness, 'choose one thing and give yourself to it – really give yourself to it.' By picking one relationship, one person, and returning over and over again to that same place, we deepen what we bring. We get better at it.

And listen, you don't have to be a saint. Ordinary people like Mitch and Erin, each hurt by their histories, scarred and wounded, will have to work hard at making choices that bring them nearer to who they are, and closer to each other. It takes some curiosity, patience, vulner-ability and mindfulness, but it's within the reach of every one of us. They'll have to learn to hold ambivalent feelings for each other without needing to resolve them: 'This is how it is for me,' and 'This is how it is for you,' and 'This is how it is for us.' And in this way their relationship itself becomes an unanswerable koan, one that helps awaken and trans-form them. It also becomes a third position for everyone who knows them. Like Erin and Mitch, we can be gatekeepers not only of our own intimacy, but of the intimacy of others, by the way we love each other and the ways we witness and support others who are struggling.

Even for those whose relationship has gone off the rails – perhaps especially for those – every day brings an opportunity for renewal. Steph and Daniel stand outside Erin and Mitch's place, laughing together. Something has come alive for them. This is the first truly joyful moment they have shared as a couple in a long, long time. They have revisited a place they have been before, only it is no longer that same place. It has taken a crisis to bring them here, and this moment now carries the pain, and the potential, of their crisis. Not for many years has their intimacy been more authentic. They are waking up. What they do from this point will be up to them.

We ask our lovers to help us with our emotional worlds by holding, containing, making sense of that which we cannot understand on our own, not unlike our parents did for us when we were children. Sharing makes things more bearable, and more joyous. If he remains open to it, Daniel has things to learn from Steph about the way in which he seeks intimacy, and what he does in the face of its absence. If he continues to let his dick do the thinking for him, he won't find the intimacy he seeks. He needs to learn to keep Steph in his consciousness in a different way. Having triggered the possible dissolution of the relationship, he has been immersed in suffering its imminent loss. But this pain brings with it an opportunity to rethink the way in which he holds his relationships in mind.

Stephanie too has much to learn from Daniel, both from observing his stupid behaviour and from listening to his desires, especially when they're expressed in ways that she doesn't get (like a crotch-grind). Seeing his pain, maybe she'll start to wonder about the way she's held herself so tightly against chaos and loss, and how this rigidity has formed an impermeable skin around her, shutting Daniel out. Why has she caged the wide-eyed girl who'd been awoken by Daniel's spirit, and how can she find that girl again? Perhaps in her laugh outside Erin and Mitch's apartment, she's caught a glimpse of that missing girl. But finding the girl won't be enough. She'll have to find the woman who can take up the third position from which she can view the impact of her hard exoskeleton on Daniel, and the combination of comfort and curiosity that will keep passion alive. Together they'll have to work out the right balance.

We can all choose our own path towards the third position that works for us through structural practices, like psychotherapy or meditation, or spiritual ones like ritual or prayer. Others occur without us being fully conscious of them. We continuously act as one another's containers and observers, fulfilling the role of the third. Erin jokes with her brother Rob that his resistance to raising a child with Tariq is going to be the target of her next intervention. But it seems, without anyone putting their conscious mind to it, that both interventions have happened at the same time.

During the course of the evening something dislodges inside Rob and he gives Tariq the first hint that he is open to considering a child. 'I'm in training to climb mountains,' he announces. It isn't something he's thought about beforehand. The moment just seems to take him. Perhaps it's the sense of camaraderie, the closeness of the four of them bound in their mission to restore love from the place it's gone missing, together with the sense – taken from the laughter and kiss in the street below – that they may well have succeeded. Steph and Daniel send a message to Rob that he is wrong, that you *can* come back from loss; and if they can do it, why can't Rob? Still, it's not easy for Rob. When Tariq embraces Rob's gesture, Rob falls back onto his trademark defence of humour: 'Don't go rounding up the Sherpas yet,' he cautions. But then he breaks away from watching Daniel and Steph, goes over to give Tariq a kiss of his own, and tells him that he can't imagine life without him.

Brushing up this close to grief puts us in touch with the enormity of what we have. It helps us feel grateful. And when we feel grateful, we feel generous. Rob's in touch with the possibility of losing Tariq whichever decision he makes – to the affections of a child, or if he refuses to raise that child. But being in touch with loss, and feeling that it can be contained, may trigger liberation of exhilarating proportions. It can free us up to make decisions in hope, rather than balk at them out of fear.

And let's not forget the tiniest witness at that little dinner party – the baby growing inside Erin. The smallest occupant of the room may well have contributed the biggest sense of awe, and of hope – that if giving life is possible, then so is everything else.

The spider and the sage
There's time for one last story. In ancient days there was an old man who went each day to pray in the Ganges. One morning he saw a spider

struggling in the water. Unbeknown to him, the spider was poisonous, but he picked it up gently and as he brought it to the shore, it bit him. Because he was a holy man, the spider's poison didn't kill him. The next morning, he was back at the Ganges, doing his prayers, when he saw the same spider struggling in the water. Once again, he picked it up and carried it to the shore, and again, the spider bit him. On the third morning, he was in the water once again, praying, when the same spider was treading water, and for the third time, he lifted it up to bring it to safety and as he did so, the spider said, 'Don't you understand? I will bite you every time, because that is what I do.' And the sage replied, 'Yes, but don't you understand? I will lift you every time, because that is what *I* do.'

What do YOU do?

Sometimes in our relationships we are the sage and sometimes the spider. Some days we do the biting and some days the lifting. Every moment offers us a choice: between gratitude and entitlement, acceptance and judgement, forgiveness and resentment, service and control, empathy and anger, vulnerability and cynicism. Each choice we make is an act of creative power.

Intimacy offers us all the conditions of self-knowledge and spiritual practice – frustration, disappointment, elation, belonging, passion, empathy . . . Through relationships we come to know ourselves in a way we could never accomplish in isolation. We also come to understand that we can never know everything about ourselves or our loved ones. Our relationships are always unfolding, taking us ever-deeper. Boring? We don't think so.

Only hookers can deliver a happy ending – for the rest of us, intimacy is an ongoing tussle between loneliness and connection, reaching and withdrawing, holding each other and letting go as we move from blindness to seeing what's in front of us.

Sweet honey from old failures

Antonio Machado, the Spanish poet, tragically lost his wife Leonor to tuberculosis when she was very young. Utterly devastated, he didn't know if he'd be able to go on. But in his poetry, he reminds us that we can come alive again, even after we imagine all has been lost. In 'Last night, as I was sleeping', he writes, *'Last night, as I was sleeping / I dreamt — marvellous error! — / that I had a beehive / here inside my heart. And the golden bees / were making white combs / and sweet honey / from my old failures.'*

Intimacy is the practice of making sweet honey from our old failures through the choices that we make. It's up to us — we can choose to be the sage, not the spider; to be the open hand, not the fist; to own our own failures instead of focusing on others'; to open our hearts instead of closing our minds; to be humble not arrogant; to forgive instead of to blame; to be generous instead of withholding.

If we can embrace the fertility inherent in old failures, then meaning is all around us, in the everyday rhythm of life. There are many paths, endless stories, hundreds of ways of encountering intimacy. With every choice we make, we create meaning. We write the next chapter in our love story.

Epilogue

How we found our elephant

It was a risky business.

People warned us that our spouses would get jealous. We'd fall in love. We'd end up despising each other. Mixing business with pleasure always ends badly. One of us would do more than the other. You can't write a book as a team – writing is a solo venture. Someone's voice would have to dominate. We'd see each other's messy bits – the bits that friends make conscious, civilised choices to keep hidden. One of us would feel short-changed, compromised, exploited or overlooked. The friendship would be well and truly fucked by the end of it.

We ignored the advice and signed the contract. We then spent weeks floundering, tossing ideas like confetti at our keyboards and each other. Clutching anxiously at our own voices, we experimented with written 'conversations' between us. 'I don't want to be spoken for or consumed by someone else's ideas,' was Jo's take, while Graeme quietly scanned for too many spiritual or, God forbid, God references. It was flat, dull and lifeless. And both of us knew it.

Our friends and spouses kept asking us how it was going. In one sense it was going like hellfire – chapters backwards and forwards by email, brightly tracked changes with every draft. Finally, in a fit of irritation, one of us suggested, 'Let's drop the tracked changes.' Maybe this doesn't sound very dramatic, but trust us, it *was* a big deal.

It meant that the changes made by the other wouldn't be flagged for our approval. They'd just be there, in the manuscript. We'd each have to let go, and trust each other and the process. We'd have to leave our egos in quarantine, swallow pride and just go with the flow of having our words rewritten, changed, deleted or questioned. And what's more, thoughts that didn't 'belong' to us would be written in one voice, as if they did. There was no way to disown what was uncomfortable. We jettisoned the 'he said, she said' approach, never quite believing we'd find a unified voice. Then somewhere in it all, we remembered: we met in a writers' group — we're *both* story-lovers, writers of fiction. Inventing characters and writing their stories brought us together. And slowly, quietly, the book almost shook itself free of us, to become a third thing — a thing manifested by our writing relationship.

Trepidation gently turned into appreciation as we watched the narrative take shape. The writing process began to reflect the very things we were writing about. Such a cliché but how do you escape what's true?

A story happens when a character changes — it's called the 'character arc'. Part of what we wanted to show in this book is how, through the story of our relationships, we transform. But what we didn't count on was how *we* might change in writing those stories. Doing something this risky means we risk more than just having our words changed.

What happened to Jo during the writing of this book

I've been doing insight meditation for more than twenty years. There aren't many self-help books on the market I haven't read. I've kept a journal since I was fourteen in which I've analysed my 'issues' through the chakras, the Akashic Records, energetic medicine, visualisation, prayer, body work, tapping and breathing. So it niggled me like crazy when Graeme challenged me about my resistance to therapy. I'd tried therapy a few times in my twenties and holy crap, it was tedious. My therapists didn't 'get' me, and all I seemed to be doing was trying to work out how to be a good patient.

Co-writing some of the deeply psychoanalytic chapters made me wonder what it would be like to have someone 'be there' to contain and reflect my pain. Why have I always insisted on doing it all myself? So I decided to give psychotherapy another bash. I wanted to find out what I may have left behind and whether my one-foot-out-the-door approach to relationships has more to do with early wounds than my independent warrior-spirit. I had to literally wrestle with my resistance every single week as my appointment grew near. I kept manufacturing a million excuses for why I'd just do a 'couple' of sessions and wouldn't be staying too long (too expensive, hair appointment, book deadline, a child's swimming carnival – it's my birthday!). What didn't I want to meet?

I wanted therapy to be quick, and not to linger on like some terminal disease, turning me into a snivelling, pathetic wretch. But it soon became clear that my impatience wasn't simply a character trait. I had trouble 'staying' and 'going slowly'. Who, me? Nonsense. I can meditate for *hours*. Every 'ouch' I gathered in therapy, I brought to our book meetings, asking Graeme to reflect back to me what I couldn't see in myself. He was honest, kind and patient. He held things with me that I've never allowed anyone to hold with me. And I didn't run a million miles.

This story of change isn't over yet, but let's just say: I get it now. I'm slowing down.

What happened to Graeme during the writing of this book

Jo introduced me to the story of the four blind men and the elephant, and I fell in love with it. Psychoanalytic ideas have given me a rich framework for my inner exploration and my work as a psychotherapist. For ages, I've realised that the more I know, the more I'm aware of how much I don't know. But even that insight can become a defence against openness; the story of the elephant brought this home to me and I began to read books on relationships from other paradigms.

Then, coincidently (though Jo would say there are no coincidences), my wife booked a holiday in Thailand, and off we went for ten days to soak up the sun, only to discover the resort offered twice-daily yoga classes. Jo's ideas about spirituality and mindfulness had softened up my defences. Phang Nga Bay with its limestone rocks rising like gods from the sea did the rest. There I spent time breathing into my belly, and I could almost hear Jo cheering, because her take on it is that I'm too much 'in the head'.

Back from Thailand, I began reading a book by a Buddhist psychoanalytic therapist. That same week, out of the blue, a patient brought me another book by the very same writer. It's as if serendipity was trying to make a point – to get me to question my cynicism about the ways of the universe. I wanted a rational explanation. I thought back over my sessions with this patient. I knew I hadn't mentioned the writer. Perhaps I'd spoken about mindfulness – I'd started incorporating these ideas into my work since writing this book. Yes, that must be it – I could write off this chance appearance of another Buddhist psychoanalytic text to projective identification – I must have said something in our previous session which my patient had 'acted out' on my behalf. I knew if I told Jo this, she'd just laugh at me, and tell me that not everything can be explained in psychoanalytic terms, that there are some things we can't know – and why am I so uncomfortable with that? The writer in me can accept the mystery and beauty of that possibility, while the therapist in me, under pressure to be helpful, craves certainty. It's a paradox, and I'm being asked to just hold it.

I started this book thinking I'd have to exercise tolerance for Jo's spiritual take on the world. I'd jealously guard the integrity of my ideas, manage our differences, and make sure her views didn't overwhelm mine. I've felt humbled in recognising the defensiveness of that approach. Once again, I've been shown that I must learn my core lessons many times over the course of my life, and will be rewarded by the enrichment of my world of thought and love.

෴

The Zen master Thich Nhat Hanh says, 'Usually when we hear or read something new, we just compare it to our own ideas. If it is the same, we accept it and say that it is correct. If it is not, we say it is incorrect. In either case, we learn nothing.'

Writing this book challenged each of our fundamental beliefs about what it is to be human and what it means to love. Having to really hear 'something new' from each other, only to find echoes within ourselves, we shifted positions. We started out writing a book, but we ended up with so much more – fresh insights, questions, and ways of being.

In front of each of us a new world is taking shape, where the rational perspectives of the West and the spiritual practices of the East are merging into one field of knowledge, and the bits we're each hanging onto don't exclude the bits we cannot see. It's exciting and it's frightening. Because no matter whom each of us is loving, or which path we choose towards intimacy, we're in for surprises that will break us open into learning and seeing new things.

Keep a look out for elephants along the way.

Acknowledgements

IN A BOOK ABOUT LOVE, it's tricky to know where to start thanking all those who have helped us – by loving us, hurting us, romancing us, dumping us, betraying us and committing to us in all the forms in which love and intimacy can be experienced. Thanks to our folks, our families of origin, friends, teachers, colleagues and all those we've kissed, shagged and woken up next to – you've each helped shape our hearts. We can't name you all, but we thank you all.

And then there are those friends, teachers and loved ones who shot bolts of insight, wisdom, encouragement, and better syntax, into the manuscript: Thanissara, Jo's beloved Buddhist teacher and friend, read a draft with such generosity and insight, and offered numerous suggestions and clarifications; Tracey Segel helped fine-tune the tone and content with her careful reading; Belinda Blecher lent her deep understanding of the early learning of love; Michelle Aarons refined the text with her keen eye for detail; Joyce Kornblatt sourced original versions of the Zen story of Ch'ien.

Thanks to the Random House team, especially to: Mark Lewis, our publisher, for helping shape the vision for this book, his belief and enthusiasm along the way and his nifty management of us as co-authors, which included plying us with coffee; and Elena Gomez, our editor, for her hard work in steering the manuscript through the editorial process, and for putting up with two 'can-I-just-make-a-few-more-changes?' writers who seem to think editing – like intimacy – is a never-ending process.

Thanks to Jo's husband Zed and her kids Jesse and Aidan, for letting her practice her intimacy skills with them and for giving her endless cracks at improving her aptitude for loving. They make her want to learn to love more deeply. She just wants to make it clear that she is *not* the elephant in the bedroom, but thanks them for the suggestion nonetheless.

Graeme's gratitude goes to so many people he has worked with in psychotherapy over the years, who have shared their journeys of intimacy with him and who've nurtured his understanding of what it is to be human. His most profound thanks, though, belong at home, with his wife Tracey and children Dave, Matt and Asha, for filling his life with their zany, beautiful selves and being the most generous teachers of love he could wish to find.

What we read, cited and learned from

Arndt, Bettina, *The Sex Diaries: Why Women Go Off Sex and Other Bedroom Battles*, Melbourne University Press, Carlton, Victoria, 2009

Batchelor, Stephen, *Buddhism Without Beliefs: A Contemporary Guide to Awakening*, Bloomsbury, New York, 1997

Behrendt, Greg and Tuccillo, Liz, *He's Just Not That Into You*, HarperElement, London, 2004

Bobes, Tony and Rothman, Barbara, *Doing Couple Therapy: Integrating Theory with Practice*, W. W. Norton & Company, New York, 2002

Bowen, Murray, *Family Therapy in Clinical Practice*, Jason Aronson Inc., Northvale, New Jersey, 1985

Bria, Gina, *The Art of Family: Rituals, Imagination and Everyday Spirituality*, Dell Publishing, New York, 1998

Britton, Ronald, 'The Oedipus Situation and the Depressive Position' in Anderson, Robin (ed.), *Clinical Lectures on Klein and Bion*, Routledge, London, 1992

Britton, Ronald, 'The Missing Link: Parental Sexuality in the Oedipus Complex' in Britton, R., Feldman, M. and O'Shaughnessy, E. (eds.), *The Oedipus Complex Today: Clinical Implications*, Karnac Books, London, 1989

Brizendine, Louann, *The Female Brain*, Morgan Road Books, New York, 2006

Campbell, Joseph with Moyers, Bill, *The Power of Myth*, Anchor Books, New York, 1991

Chopra, Deepak, *Buddha: A Story of Enlightenment*, HarperOne, New York, 2007

Chopra, Deepak, *The Seven Spiritual Laws of Success*, Bantam Press, London, 1996

Claxton, Guy, *The Heart of Buddhism: Practical Wisdom for an Agitated World*, Thorsons, London, 1990

Clulow, Christopher, *Sex, Attachment and Couple Psychotherapy: Psychoanalytic Perspectives*, Karnac, London, 2009

Crastnopol, Margaret, 'The Rub: Sexual Interplay as a Nexus of Lust, Romantic Love, and Emotional Attachment' in *Psychoanalytic Dialogues*, vol. 16, pp. 687–709, 2006

Cunningham, Michael, *The Hours*, Picador, London, 1998

Dalai Lama, His Holiness, *Ancient Wisdom, Modern World: Ethics for a new millennium*, Little Brown & Company, United Kingdom, 1999

De Botton, Alain, *Essays in Love*, Picador, London, 1993

Doidge, Norman, *The Brain That Changes Itself*, Penguin Books, London, 2008

Dowrick, Stephanie, *The Almost-Perfect Marriage: One-minute Relationship Skills*, Allen & Unwin, Crows Nest, Sydney, 2007

Dowrick, Stephanie, *Forgiveness and Other Acts of Love*, Penguin Books, Australia, 1997

Dowrick, Stephanie, *Intimacy and Solitude: Balancing Closeness & Independence*, The Women's Press, London, 1992

Ensler, Eve, *The Vagina Monologues*, Villard, New York, 1998

Epstein, Mark, *Going On Being: Life at the Crossroads of Buddhism and Psychotherapy*, Wisdom Publications, Boston, 2001

Epstein, Mark, *Going To Pieces Without Falling Apart*, Broadway Books, New York, 1999

Fisher, Helen, *Why We Love: The Nature and Chemistry of Romantic Love*, Henry Holt, New York, 2004

Fordham, Frieda, *An Introduction to Jung's Psychology*, Penguin, London, 1953

Frankl, Viktor, *Man's Search for Meaning*, Pocketbooks, New York, 1946

Freud, Sigmund, 'A Case of Hysteria, Three Essays on Sexuality and Other Works' in *The Standard Edition of the Complete Psychological Works of Sigmund Freud*, vol. VII, 1905

Gerhardt, Sue, *Why Love Matters: How Affection Shapes a Baby's Brain*, Routledge, London, 2004

Gilbert, Elizabeth, *Committed*, Bloomsbury, London, 2010

Gottman, John and Silver, Nan, *The Seven Principles for Making Marriage Work*, Orion, London, 2000

Grayson, Henry, *Mindful Loving: 10 Practices for Creating Deeper Connections*, Gotham Books, New York, 2004

Hanh, Thich Nhat, *The Art of Mindful Living: How to Bring Love, Compassion and Peace into your Daily Life*, CD by Sounds True, Unified Buddhist Church, USA, 2000

Hanh, Thich Nhat, *Being Peace*, Rider, USA, 1987

Harvey, Steve, *Act like A Lady, Think like A Man: What Men Really Think About Love, Relationships, Intimacy, and Commitment*, Amistad, USA, 2009

Hite, Shere, *The Hite Reports: Women as Revolutionary Agents of Change*, Bloomsbury, London, 1976

Jong, Erica, *Fear of Flying*, Holt, Rinehart and Winston, New York, 1973

Judith, Anodea, *Eastern Body, Western Mind: Psychology and the Chakra System as a Path to the Self*, Celestial Arts, USA, 1996

Jung, Carl Gustav, *The Portable Jung*, Penguin Books, New York, 1976

Kerner, Ian, *She Comes First: The Thinking Man's Guide to Pleasuring a Woman*, Harper, New York, 2010

Kerner, Ian, *Passionista: The Empowered Woman's Guide to Pleasuring a Man*, Harper, New York, 2008

Khema, Aya, *Being Nobody, Going Nowhere: Meditations on the Buddhist Path*, Wisdom Publications, USA, 1987

Kinsey, Alfred C., *Sexual Behaviour in the Human Male*, W. B. Saunders Company, USA, 1948

Kornfield, Jack, *After the Ecstasy, the Laundry: How the Heart Grows Wise on the Spiritual Path*, Rider, London, 2000

Kornfield, Jack, *A Path With Heart: A Guide Through the Perils and Promises of Spiritual Life*, Rider, New York, 1994

Larkin, Geri, *Stumbling Towards Enlightenment*, Celestial Arts, California, 1997

Lerner, Harriet, *The Dance of Intimacy: A Woman's Guide to Courageous Acts of Change in Key Relationships*, Harper & Row, New York, 1989

Levine, Stephen and Ondrea, *Embracing the Beloved: Relationship as a Path of Awakening*, First Anchor Books, USA, 1996

Lipton, Bruce, *The Biology of Belief*, Hay House, USA, 2005

Machado, Antonio and Lopez, Dolores Romero, *Soledades*, University of Exeter Press, Great Britain, 2006

Mitchell, Stephen, *Can Love Last? The Fate of Romance Over Time*, Norton, New York, 2002

Morgan, Mary, 'Unconscious Beliefs about Being a Couple' in *Fort Da*, vol. 16, pp. 36–55, 2010

Morgan, Mary, 'First Contacts: The Therapist's "Couple State of Mind" as a Factor in the Containment of Couples Seen for Consultations' in Grier, Francis (ed.), *Brief Encounters With Couples: Some Analytical Perspectives*, Karnac, London, 2001

Nepo, Mark, *The Book of Awakening*, Conari Press, San Francisco, 2000

O'Donohue, John, *Eternal Echoes*, Perennial, USA, 1999

O'Donohue, John, *Anam Cara: A Book of Celtic Wisdom*, Harper Perennial, New York, 1997

Perel, Esther, *Mating in Captivity: Unlocking Erotic Intelligence*, Harper, New York, 2007

Richo, David, *How to be an Adult in Relationships: The Five Keys to Mindful Loving*, Shambala, Boston, 2002

Rilke, Rainer Maria, *Letters to a Young Poet*, New World Library, California, 2000

Rinpoche, Patrul, *The Words of My Perfect Teacher*, Shambala, Boston, 1998

Rose, Lorraine, *Learning to Love*, Acer Press, Camberwell, Victoria, 2000

Rumi, *The Essential Rumi*, translated by Coleman Barks with John Moyne, Penguin Books, London, 1995

Schnarch, David, *Passionate Marriage: Keeping Love & Intimacy Alive in Committed Relationships*, Scribe, Melbourne, 2008

Shriver, Lionel, *The Post-Birthday World*, Harper Perennial, USA, 2008

Silverstein, Shel, *The Missing Piece Meets the Big O*, HarperCollins, New York, 1981

Skynner, Robin and Cleese, John, *Families and How to Survive Them*, Methuen, Great Britain, 1983

Solms, Mark and Turnbull, Oliver, *The Brain and the Inner World: An Introduction to the Neuroscience of Subjective Experience*, Other Press, New York, 2002

Somé, Sobunfu, *The Spirit of Intimacy: Ancient African Teachings in the Ways of Relationships*, Harper, New York, 2002

Steiner, John, *Psychic Retreats: Pathological Organizations in Psychotic, Neurotic and Borderline Patients*, Routledge, London, 1994

Swift, Jonathan, *The Poems of Jonathan Swift*, vol. II, Harold Williams (ed.), Oxford University Press, Great Britain, 1937

Szuchman, Paul and Anderson, Jenny, *Spousonomics*, Bantam Press, London, 2011

Tennov, Dorothy, *Love and Limerence: The Experience of Being in Love*, Scarborough House Publishers, USA, 1998

Tisdale, Sally, *Talk Dirty To Me: An Intimate Philosophy of Sex*, Pan Books, New York, 1994

Tutu, Desmond, 'Let South Africa Show the World How to Forgive', *Knowledge of Reality*, issue 19

Walsh, Neal Donald, *Applications for Living from Conversations with God*, Hodder & Stoughton, Great Britain, 1999

Whyte, David, *The Three Marriages: Reimagining Work, Self and Relationship*, Riverhead Books, New York, 2009

Williams, Gianna, *Internal Landscapes and Foreign Bodies: Eating Disorders and Other Pathologies*, Routledge, London, 1998

Winnicott, D. W., 'The Theory of the Parent-Infant Relationship' in *International Journal of Psycho-Analysis*, vol. 41, pp. 585–95, 1960

Yovell, Yoram, 'Is there a drive to love?' *Neuro-Psychoanalysis*, vol. 10, no. 2, pp. 117–44, 2008